Pentecostalism and Christian Unity

Pentecostalism and Christian Unity

Ecumenical Documents and Critical Assessments

EDITED BY

WOLFGANG VONDEY

PICKWICK *Publications* · Eugene, Oregon

PENTECOSTALISM AND CHRISTIAN UNITY
Ecumenical Documents and Critical Assessments

Pickwick Publications
An Imprint of Wipf and Stock Publishers
199 W. 8th Ave., Suite 3
Eugene, OR 97401

www.wipfandstock.com

ISBN 13: 978-1-60899-077-1

Cataloging-in-Publication data:

Pentecostalism and Christian unity : ecumenical documents and critical assessments / edited by Wolfgang Vondey.

xxvi + 278 p.; 23 cm. Includes indexes.

ISBN 13: 978-1-60899-077-1

1. Pentecostalism. 2. Ecumenical movement. I. Vondey, Wolfgang. II. Title.

BX8763 P 2010

Manufactured in the U.S.A.

To Michael A. Fahey, SJ,

and Cecil M. Robeck Jr.,

mentors and pioneers in ecumenical faith

Contents

Preface

THIS VOLUME OF ECUMENICAL documents and critical essays is the first collection of its kind exclusively dedicated to Pentecostalism and its contributions to Christian unity. With few exceptions, these essays were first presented during the first decade of the twenty-first century as part of the interest group in ecumenical studies of the Society for Pentecostal Studies. I was privileged to organize that group in 2001with overwhelming support of the members of the Society and to serve as its chair until 2005. Since its formation, the interest group has encouraged worldwide Pentecostal participation in ecumenical concerns, sponsored Roman Catholic–Pentecostal conversations at the annual meetings of the Society, invited international scholarly debates, engaged in a study process on ecumenical consensus statements, and attended to the younger generation of ecumenical scholars. The selection of essays included in this collection is representative of more than fifty scholarly presentations and panel discussions sponsored by the ecumenical studies group, during the first decade of its existence. In its current form, the group represents the only organized ecumenical think-tank among Pentecostals in North America.

Beyond the particular focus of the interest group in ecumenical studies, this collection also bears witness to the maturing of Pentecostal scholarship and the dedicated scholars, pastors, and theologians who attend the meetings of the Society for Pentecostal Studies. Many of the presentations of the Society eventually find their way to publication, but there are numerous gems and undiscovered ideas in many papers that were never published and are not readily accessible. The contributors to this collection are theologians, historians, philosophers, ethicists, missionaries, and ministers who represent well the rich resources of the Society. *Pentecostalism and Christian Unity* is intended as a motivation to other groups in the Society to share the work of Pentecostal scholarship with those who have never attended a meeting or are still unaware of the existence of the Society. In many ways, all of the different interest groups are ecumenical in character and exist as an invitation to extend the boundaries of Pentecostal thought and praxis into various disciplines and communities.

The book is dedicated to two pioneers in ecumenical faith, who are also mentors of my own work in ecclesiology and ecumenical dialogue. I was privileged to study under the guidance of Michael A. Fahey, SJ, during my graduate work at Marquette University and completed my doctoral thesis under his direction. Michael served as the Emmet Doerr Professor in Catholic Systematic Theology at Marquette, where his expertise as Co-Secretary of the North American Orthodox–Catholic Theological Consultation and as editor of the journal, *Theological Studies*, was widely reflected in his teaching on ecclesiology and ecumenism. In 2006, he received an honorary doctorate from the University of Toronto, St. Michael's College, in recognition of outstanding contributions to the field of theology, and he now teaches as Jesuit Professor of Theology and Ecumenical Studies at Boston College. Michael is unsurpassed in his detailed knowledge of ecumenical history and theology. He opened my heart to the churches and my eyes to the ecumenical movement.

Similarly, my ecumenical experience and scholarship has been shaped by the pioneering work and mentorship of Cecil M. Robeck Jr., who was among the first to embrace my ecumenical efforts at the Society for Pentecostal Studies. Mel is Professor of Church History and Ecumenics at Fuller Theological Seminary and has authored some two hundred articles published in a range of historical, theological, and ecumenical journals, periodicals, and denominational magazines. His seminal historical work on the Azusa Street Mission and Revival continues to shape the self-understanding of Pentecostals in North America. Mel is a dominant voice on ecclesiological and ecumenical issues among Pentecostals, an influence that has left its particular mark on Pentecostal scholarship during his nine years as editor of *Pneuma: The Journal of the Society for Pentecostal Studies*. For nearly 30 years, he has served as the Pentecostal representative on ecumenical dialogue with the World Council of Churches, the Vatican, the World Alliance of Reformed Churches, and numerous other groups. Mel's writings and assessments through the years have sharpened my vision of the particular challenges of Pentecostal participation in ecumenical dialogue. My privilege to put together the essays in this collection is a small reflection of the mentorship I received and wish to pass on to the broader ecumenical community.

Introduction

ECUMENICAL TEXTS STILL DEMAND an introduction. Despite the centenary celebration of the World Missionary Conference that marked the beginning of the modern ecumenical movement in 1910, the idea of ecumenism is not widely understood or appreciated at the beginning of the twenty-first century. General introductions to theology and doctrine are void of references to ecumenism, books on the doctrine of the church often touch only marginally on ecumenical questions, while ecumenical texts often take for granted that the idea of ecumenism is understood in general and defined in similar terms.[1] The effects of this neglect are exacerbated when it comes to the churches, assemblies, and communities of the global Pentecostal movement, which is often associated with anti-ecumenical sentiments. The present collection of ecumenical documents and assessments shows that this evaluation is incorrect. Even so, the joint venture of Pentecostal and ecumenical sensibilities asks for an explanation.

In general, the term "ecumenism" refers to any attempt that seeks to establish and preserve the visible unity among Christians.[2] The word derives from a family of Greek terms that refer to the inhabited world (*oikoumene*), or more basically, the house (*oikos*). These two realms mark the frontiers of all ecumenical endeavors.[3] Historically, an ecumenical

1. See Michael A. Fahey, ed., *Ecumenism: A Bibliographical Overview* (Westport, CT: Greenwood, 1992).

2. See G. R. Evans, *Method in Ecumenical Theology: The Lessons So Far* (Cambridge: Cambridge University Press, 1996) 19–39; Mary R. Sawyer, *Black Ecumenism: Implementing the Demands of Justice* (Valley Forge, PA: Trinity Press International, 1994); Geoffrey Wainwright, "Ecumenical Spirituality," in *The Study of Spirituality*, eds. Cheslyn Jones, Geoffrey Wainwright, Edward Yarnold (New York: Oxford University Press, 1986) 540–48; W. A. Visser t'Hooft, *The Meaning of Ecumenical* (London: SCM, 1954).

3. See Wolfgang Vondey, *People of Bread: Rediscovering Ecclesiology* (New York: Paulist, 2008) 196–212; Michael Kinnamon and Brian E. Cope, eds., *The Ecumenical Movement: An Anthology of Key Texts and Voices* (Grand Rapids: Eerdmans, 1997) 9–78.

praxis emerged from the houses of the faithful that formed the place of meeting for the primitive Christian communities until Christianity became more firmly established and buildings could be designated as the official place of worship. Theologically, the goal of all ecumenical endeavors is the establishment of visible unity among all Christians on a global scale. Ecumenism is therefore determined by both individual and private endeavors as well as by communal, local, national, and international practices that seek the reconciliation, renewal, and unity of the visibly divided churches.

As an image for unity, the notion of the "house" is frequently taken beyond its roots in the actual home and enlarged to communicate a broader ecumenical idea.[4] The New Testament writers speak of the church as a house or building with the particular emphasis that the structure is formed by the faithful themselves. The focus of the image of the "house" is not on the actual building or residence but on the community that imbues the structure with meaning. Hence, Peter speaks of the "family of believers" (1 Pet 2:17) who constitute a "spiritual house" (2:5) and "household of God" (4:17). Likewise, Paul speaks of the Church as "God's building" (1 Cor 3:9) and a "dwelling place for God" (Eph 2:21). In its ecumenical significance, the image of the house takes on a universal dimension.

The universal dimension of any ecumenical endeavor acknowledges that the principle and vision of all efforts is the full communion of all Christians in the inhabited world.[5] The idea of global unity therefore highlights that ecumenism requires the efforts of all Christians not only in the home but also on an organizational level among the churches. In this sense, the emphasis on "visible" unity suggests that an invisible bond already exists among all those who confess their faith in Jesus Christ.[6]

4. See Eva Marie Synek, "'Oikos-Ecclesiology' and 'Church Order' in Eastern Christianity," in *Household, Women, and Christianities in Late Antiquity and the Middle Ages*, eds. Anneke B. Mulder-Bakker and Jocelyn Wogan-Browne (Turnhout: Brepols, 2005) 37–70; Gennaro Lomiento, "Oikos, oikodome, oikonomia: La lingua della comunione nel Commento a Giovanni di Origene," in *Origene e l'alessandrinismo cappadoce (III–IV secolo)* (Bari: Edipuglia, 2002) 29–44; John E. Alsup and Hans Bald, "Die Kirche als Oikos entdecken," in *Kirche und Volk Gottes: Festschrift für Jürgen Roloff zum 70. Geburtstag* (Neukirchen-Vluyn: Neukirchener Verlag, 2000) 110–31.

5. See Kinnamon and Cope, *The Ecumenical Movement*, 79–127.

6. Ola Tjørhom, *Visible Church, Visible Unity: Ecumenical Ecclesiology and "The Great Tradition of the Church"* (Collegeville, MN: Liturgical, 2004); Thomas F. Best, *Living Today towards Visible Unity: The Fifth International Consultation of United and*

The ecumenical task to express this unity in visible forms is essentially a response to the mandate of Christ that "all may be one" (John 17:21) and an endeavor to preserve the gifts the churches have already received from God despite their separation, as they move toward a more visible manifestation of "the unity of the Spirit" (Eph. 4:3).

THE HISTORY OF THE ECUMENICAL MOVEMENT

The praxis of ecumenism is often associated more closely with the so-called ecumenical movement that emerged with the World Missionary Conference in Edinburgh in 1910 and gained momentum with the founding of the World Council of Churches (WCC) in 1948.[7] However, a broader understanding of the ecumenical agenda must also consider the attempts to reconcile the doctrinal divisions that led to the Jerusalem Council in the first century (see Acts 15:1–29), the ecumenical councils beginning with the Council of Nicea (AD 325), the Christological and Trinitarian debates of the first centuries, the rupture between East and West (AD 1054) and the ensuing dialogue between the Greek East and the western Latin Church, the major divisions in the West since the Protestant Reformation, the emergence of churches in North America, the Pentecostal and charismatic renewal movements as well as the diversity of modern theological positions.

The history of ecumenism shows four major divisions among the Christian traditions:[8] (1) Eastern Orthodoxy, which includes the Eastern Orthodox churches, the Oriental Orthodox Churches and the Assyrian Church of the East; (2) Roman Catholicism, which includes the Roman Catholic Church and the Old Catholic churches; (3) Reformation churches, which include the Lutheran churches, Presbyterian churches, Anglican

Uniting Churches (Geneva: WCC, 1988); Jeffrey Gros, *The Search for Visible Unity: Baptism, Eucharist, and Ministry* (New York: Pilgrim, 1984); Max Thurian, *Visible Unity and Tradition* (Baltimore: Helicon, 1962).

7. Jeffrey Gros, Eamon McManus, Ann Riggs, *Introduction to Ecumenism* (New York: Paulist, 1998) 9–34; Thomas E. FitzGerald, *The Ecumenical Movement: An Introductory History* (Westport, CT: Praeger, 2004); Ruth Rouse, Stephen Neill, and Harold E. Fey, eds., *The Ecumenical Advance: A History of the Ecumenical Movement, 1948-1968*, 3rd ed. (Geneva: WCC, 1986).

8. See Roger Haight, *Christian Community in History*, vol. 1, *Historical Ecclesiology* (New York: Continuum, 2004); Ronald G. Robertson, *The Eastern Christian Churches: A Brief Survey* (Rome: University Press of the Pontifical Oriental Institute, 1995); John Meyendorff, *Imperial Unity and Christian Divisions: The Church, 450–680 AD* (Crestwood, NY: St. Vladimir's Seminary Press, 1989).

Communion, Congregationalist churches and Union churches; and (4) Evangelical churches, such as the United Methodist Church, and a large number of communities that adhere to the Free Church tradition, such as the Holiness churches and Classical Pentecostal churches in North America.

A major shortcoming of such a purely historical approach to ecumenism is that it tends to emphasize the already existing divisions of the doctrinal families with little reference to their theological origin and continuing relationship.[9] This can give the impression that ecumenism is defined primarily by the past divisions of Christianity rather than the unity of the churches in the future. The churches are presented as they exist in contradistinction to one another but not as originating from or developing out of the struggle with other existing Christian confessions. A purely descriptive or typological approach to ecumenism has been widely criticized in the twentieth century, which has shown a widespread engagement in ecumenical dialogues and the emergence of a more cohesive landscape of ecumenical theologies that consider not only the present state of visible separation among the churches but also the origin of particular traditions and the continuing interdependence among the Christian doctrinal families.

The history of the ecumenical movement in the twentieth century is marked by a number of transitions.[10] The World Missionary Conference in Edinburgh in 1910 began a foundational era of the modern ecumenical movement that culminated in the formation of the WCC in 1948. Marked by two World Wars, the central motif of this period is seen as a rediscovery of the church and its fundamental position as an essential constituent of the gospel. A second period runs from the inaugural meeting of the WCC in Amsterdam to the assembly in Uppsala in 1968. Characterized by the cold war and the end of colonialism, this period

9. Cf. chapter 5 of Wolfgang Vondey, *Beyond Pentecostalism: The Crisis of Global Christianity and the Renewal of the Theological Agenda* (Grand Rapids: Eerdmans, 2010), forthcoming.

10. See John Briggs, Mercy Amba Oduyoye, Georges Tsetsis, eds., *A History of the Ecumenical Movement*, vol. 3, *1968–2000* (London: SPCK, 2004); Ernest W. Lefever, *Nairobi to Vancouver: The World Council of Churches and the World, 1975–87* (Washington, DC: Ethics and Public Policy Center, 1987); Rouse, Neill, and Fey, *A History of the Ecumenical Movement*; Ernest W. Lefever, *Amsterdam to Nairobi: The World Council of Churches and the Third World* (Washington, DC: Ethics and Public Policy Center, 1979).

saw the convening of Vatican II (1962–65) and the resulting ecumenical involvement of the Roman Catholic Church as well as the membership of the Orthodox churches in the WCC. The central motif of these years is seen as a rediscovery of the role of the churches and their position in and for the world. A third period extends from 1968 to the present and is marked by the experience of pluralism and the effects of a rapid globalization and growing inequality among socially, ethnically or economically defined people groups. The central motif of this period is the role of the church in the creative and redemptive work of God throughout the world.

The contemporary situation of the ecumenical movement can also be seen as a new period characterized by the rise of the Pentecostal and charismatic movements and their involvement in ecumenical dialogue. An emerging motif is the rediscovery of the work of the Holy Spirit in the life of the churches.[11] These movements pose particular challenges to ecumenical theology since these communities are often perceived as distinct from the established mainline churches or as an element of the Evangelical or Free Church traditions.[12] Pentecostals, on the other hand, see themselves as distinct from other churches only insofar as they emerged from a revival and renewal emphasis that originated in those traditions.[13] The present ecumenical movement finds itself therefore in a time of major transition that encompasses the theological perception of the ecumenical agenda and the methodological choices that determine the ecumenical praxis of the churches in the twenty-first century.

One of the most significant emblems of the churches' efforts to attain visible unity since the twentieth century has been the founding of the WCC. The Council affirmed and consolidated three vibrant streams

11. See William R. Barr and Rena M. Yocom, eds., *The Church in the Movement of the Spirit* (Grand Rapids: Eerdmans, 1996); World Council of Churches, ed., *The First Six Years 1948–1954* (Geneva: WCC Publications, 1954).

12. See Roger Haight, *Christian Community in History*, vol. 2, *Comparative Ecclesiology* (New York: Continuum, 2005) 452–77.

13. Cf. Jay Riley Case, "And Ever the Twain Shall Meet: The Holiness Missionary Movement and the Birth of World Pentecostalism, 1870–1920," *Religion and American Culture* 16.2 (2006) 125–59; Edith Blumhofer, "Restoration as Revival: Early American Pentecostalism," in *Modern Christian Revivals*, ed. Edith L. Blumhofer and Randall A. Balmer (Urbana: University of Illinois Press, 1993) 145–61; Grant Wacker, "Playing for Keeps: The Primitivist Impulse in Early Pentecostalism," in *The American Quest for the Primitive Church*, ed. Richard T. Hughes (Urbana: University of Illinois Press, 1988) 196–219.

of the ecumenical life: the mission movement, the Faith and Order movement, and the Life and Work movement.[14] Today, the WCC joins together more than 340 churches, denominations, and fellowships in over 100 countries, including most of the Orthodox churches, Reformation and Union churches, and Evangelical denominations, as well as various communities from the Free Church traditions.[15] In the first fifty years of its history, the center of membership shifted from the founding nations in Europe and North America to the African, Asian, and Latin American continents as well as to the Middle East, the Caribbean, and the Pacific. Representatives of these churches meet approximately every seven years in an assembly that addresses matters of division and unity and casts a vision for the ecumenical future of the Christian churches.

The scope and diversity of the WCC reflects not only the common efforts toward unity but also the tensions still present among the member churches, including the continuing threats of denominationalism, institutionalism, nationalism, and syncretism. The unity of the Council has been preserved largely by a shared emphasis on the centrality of Christ. A shift in emphasis to the cultural context of the Christian life during the 1980s and a rediscovery of the work of the Holy Spirit beginning with 1990s has significantly widened the scope of the ecumenical agenda.[16] The ninth assembly of the WCC in 2006 approved a substantial change in the Council's priorities, structures and relationships, and gave renewed attention to ecumenical formation, spirituality, global justice, and prophetic witness as part of the ecumenical dialogue and work toward Christian unity.

THE PRAXIS OF ECUMENICAL DIALOGUE

The widespread practice of ecumenical dialogue among churches, ecclesial communities, and other religious bodies is a phenomenon of the modern world.[17] The official nature of many of these dialogues has given a new image to ecumenism in the twentieth century and fueled the hope

14. See W. A. Visser't Hooft, *The Genesis and Formation of the World Council of Churches* (Geneva: WCC Publications, 1982).

15. See Huibert Van Beek, *Handbook of Churches and Councils: Profiles of Ecumenical Relationships* (Geneva: WCC, 2006).

16. Cf. Konrad Raiser, *Ecumenism in Transition: A Paradigm Shift in the Ecumenical Movement?* (Geneva: WCC, 1991) 31–53.

17. Angelo Maffeis, *Ecumenical Dialogue*, trans. Lorelei F. Fuchs (Collegeville, MN: Liturgical Press, 2005); Gros, McManus, Riggs, *Introduction to Ecumenism*, 114–32.

of full reconciliation despite the remaining disagreements among the churches in theological and non-theological, theoretical, and practical areas of the Christian life.

Ecumenical dialogues follow a number of unwritten rules of engagement.[18] While the established ecumenical traditions operate largely along these guidelines, new dialogue partners tend to be unaware of their existence, and much of the initial phase of establishing ecumenical relationships is spent identifying such rules.[19] Despite the fact that many actively seek dialogue with Pentecostals, there exists little clarity about the ecumenical presuppositions for such dialogue. Five dominant principles can be distinguished: First, the dialogue partners should be able to clearly define the principles that form the basis for their respective engagement in ecumenical relationships. Second, all participants should contribute to the development, definition, and clarification of realistic goals for the dialogue. Third, the dialogue partners should make explicit their own self-understanding and should exhibit an awareness of their understanding of the dialogue partner. Fourth, each group should define, form, and support the responsibilities and roles of all participants involved in the dialogue. Fifth, the dialogue partners should be able to specify how the results of the dialogue can be implemented in the life of the churches.

1. *The Principles of Engagement*

Ecumenical dialogues differ in method and goal, depending on the nature of relationships and the degree of communion already established between particular churches. It is therefore of primary importance to clarify what kind of dialogue should be expected before the actual discussion of a particular ecumenical agenda takes place. There exists at this time no single ecumenical approach that would allow all churches to

18. See Wolfgang Vondey, "Presuppositions for Pentecostal Engagement in Ecumenical Dialogue," *Exchange: Journal for Missiological and Ecumenical Research* 30.4 (2001) 344–58; John Cogley, "Ten Commandments for the Ecumenical Age," in *Steps to Unity*, ed. John O'Brien (New York: Doubleday, 1964) 244–64; Robert McAfee Brown, "Rules for the Dialogue," *Christian Century* 77 (February 17, 1960) 183–85; also *Study Encounter* 1.3 (1965) 133–34.

19. See "The Church as Communion in Christ," *Mid-Stream* 41.4 (2002) 96–114; "Agreement between Reformation Churches in Europe: The Leuenberg Agreement (Konkordie)," *Ecumenical Review* 25.3 (1973) 355–59; Leonard Hodgson, ed., *The Second World Conference on Faith and Order, held at Edinburgh, August 3–18, 1937* (New York: Macmillan, 1938) 250.

conduct ecumenical dialogue with other Christian traditions on all levels according to one definitive and universally applicable pattern. A fundamental question of ecumenism is what elements of Christian teaching the dialogue partners consider essential.[20] The history of the ecumenical movement since the twentieth century has been clearly characterized by its emphasis on the doctrine of Christ. This Christological focus identified all aspects related to the life, death, and resurrection of Christ as essential to the achievement of visible unity among the churches. At the end of the century, other doctrines have also been emphasized, and dialogues have covered a much broader basis, such as the work of the Holy Spirit in the world, the role of the Church in the history of salvation, or the significance of the sacraments and liturgical celebrations. The answer to the question of essential doctrines determines not only the basis of ecumenism in general but, more specifically, a direction for dialogue with a particular partner. For many churches, identifying the essential elements of their teaching is, above all, a matter of finding their ecclesial and ecumenical identity. In order to ensure that all participants fully embrace the outcome of a particular dialogue, the churches must first present the basis for that dialogue on which all will then also be able to interpret the results.

2. *A Common Definition of Goals*

A second principle of ecumenical relationships is a joint definition of the goals for a particular dialogue. Not all ecumenical dialogues intend full, visible unity from the outset. In some cases, the framework for dialogue has to be established before actual discussion can take place. In other dialogues, only minor distinctions of liturgical practice separate the communities. Whereas some churches possess a network of ecumenical offices, other churches do not have an ecumenical institution.[21] From the outset, it is therefore important that all participants are informed about what the dialogue is trying to achieve. These goals can follow at least three interrelated principles. First, the group emphasizes what

20. Cf. "The Church as Communion in Christ," *Mid-Stream* 33 (April 1994) 219–39; H. N. Bate, ed., *Faith and Order: Proceedings of the World Conference, Lausanne, August 3–21, 1927* (London: SCM, 1927) 21.

21. Cf. Wolfgang Vondey, "Appeal for a Pentecostal Council for Ecumenical Dialogue," *Mid-Stream* 40.3 (2001) 45–56.

is important as well as what is not important.[22] This distinction helps sharpen the focus on a particular theme and produce relevant results. Second, the group expresses a common vision as well as a realistic goal.[23] This concretization helps produce a challenging, yet realizable task. Third, the dialogue partners state clearly, what can be expected. This articulation helps prevent any unrealistic expectations for a particular ecumenical relationship. The central question is what kind of "visible unity"[24] is envisioned by the dialogue partners. Whether it be *koinonia*[25] or *communio*,[26] partial or comprehensive union, corporate or organic union, conciliar fellowship, union in reconciled diversity,[27] or a form of common witness,[28] the expressed goal presents a basis on which all will then be able to also interpret the results.

3. *A Shared Understanding of Ecumenical Identity*

A third area of concern is the truthful understanding of the doctrinal families that are involved in a particular dialogue. It is essential for all dialogue partners to know the traditions and individuals who participate. This endeavor involves two equally important aspects: On one hand, each group possesses a consistent and shared self-understanding of themselves as they enter the conversation. On the other hand, each

22. Cf. "Joint Declaration on the Doctrine of Justification between the Lutheran World Federation and the Catholic Church," *Information Service* 98 (1998) 81–90; Joint Lutheran/Roman Catholic Study Commission on the Gospel and the Church, ed., *Church and Justification: Understanding the Church in Light of the Doctrine of Justification* (Geneva: Lutheran World Federation, 1994) 173–242.

23. Cf. "Towards a Common Understanding of the Church," in *Deepening Communion: International Ecumenical Documents with Roman Catholic Participation*, eds. William Rusch and Jeffrey Gros (Washington, DC: United States Catholic Conference, 1998) 179–229.

24. Cf. David E. Paton, ed., *Breaking Barriers, Nairobi 1975: Official Report, Fifth Assembly, World Council of Churches* (Geneva: WCC Publications, 1976) 59.

25. Cf. "Perspectives on *Koinonia*: Final Report of the Dialogue between the Pontifical Council for Promoting Christian Unity and Some Classical Pentecostal Churches and Leaders 1985–1989," *Pneuma* 12.2 (1990) 77–183.

26. Cf. Joint Working Group between the Roman Catholic Church and the World Council of Churches, eds., *The Church: Local and Universal* (Geneva: WCC Publications, 1998) 25–47.

27. See "Facing Unity: Models, Forms, and Phases of Catholic-Lutheran Church Fellowship," *Ecumenical Trends* 15.4 (1986) 53–67.

28. Joint Lutheran/Roman Catholic Study Commission, *Church and Justification*, sections 3.4.1 and 4.1.3.

group is also challenged by how it views and understands the other. This does not mean that ecumenical dialogue proceeds without prejudice and preconceived notions. As much as these should be avoided in the first place, an awareness of one's own attitude and expectations with regard to the dialogue partner becomes a fundamental presupposition for discussion, understanding, forgiveness, and reconciliation. For this reason, many dialogues consist of opportunities for those involved to share and establish a common understanding of their identity in addition to any formal dialogue sessions.[29] A theological and non-theological understanding of the faith and praxis of another church has become a fundamental part of ecumenical interaction and establishes a basis for all participants to fully engage in dialogue and to interpret the results of that dialogue.[30] This praxis acknowledges that dialogue of any form usually emerges from the context of human relationships, interactions, and mutual exchanges.

4. A Joint Definition of Ecumenical Responsibility

A fourth principle of ecumenical engagement is concerned with the responsibility taken by the participants of the dialogue. Among these is, first of all, the responsibility to uphold the fundamental truths of the Christian faith, as they are expressed in Scripture, in the Apostles' Creed, and in the Creeds of Nicea and Constantinople.[31] Additionally, each dialogue partner as well as the individual participants accepts responsibility in humility and repentance for what their tradition has done, and continues to do, that might encourage and perpetuate the existing divisions among the churches. This fundamental ecumenical attitude addresses the urgent need that each participant will at any given time assume responsibility for his or her involvement in the dialogue as a whole person and not just as a contributor to verbal discourse or doctrinal debate. Finally, ecumenical responsibility also means a proper understanding of one's ecumenical role. In order to prevent that the entire dialogue is set up for disappointment and failure, it is a responsibility of each group to prepare the participating members for the individual dialogue sessions.

29. Cf. Maffeis, *Ecumenical Dialogue*, 49–64.

30. See C. H. Dodd, ed., *Social and Cultural Factors in Church Divisions, Faith and Order Paper 10* (Geneva: WCC, 1952) 26–32; Willard Learoyd Sperry, *The Non-theological Factors in the Making and Unmaking of Church Union* (New York: Harper, 1937).

31. See Karl Rahner and Heinrich Fries, *Unity of the Churches: An Actual Possibility* (Philadelphia: Fortress, 1985) 13–23.

5. *Realization of Ecumenical Implementation*

The goal of every ecumenical dialogue is that the results are implemented in the life of the churches. A formal dialogue therefore has to consider the existence of adequate ecumenical structures and organizations as well as a willingness on all levels to become a messenger of ecumenical relations with other Christian traditions.[32] The goal of ecumenical discourse is not merely to produce an ecumenical document; it is the vision and hope that the churches will hear this document and that through it the faithful will achieve a better understanding of other traditions in the desire to live together as the one body of Christ. The massive amount of literature produced by ecumenical dialogues in the twentieth century has rarely reached the congregations despite the spiritual, theological, and educational value of the documents.[33] In general, the discussion of ecumenical documents is limited; most texts are not received by the faithful and find little public acknowledgment. It remains one of the most challenging tasks of the ecumenical partners to provide the churches with adequate structures that ensure the publication, distribution, and implementation of the lessons learned from the other. The task of appreciating the work of ecumenical dialogues requires the support and initiative of the whole Christian community and remains one of the foremost challenges to the ecumenical agenda.

PENTECOSTALS AND THE ECUMENICAL AGENDA

The principles of engagement outlined in the previous section indicate some of the greater challenges of the ecumenical movement in the twenty-first century. Pentecostalism is still in the process of being shaped by its own participation in this dialogue with other churches, and many of the ecumenical principles among Pentecostals are not yet fully formulated. The essays and documents in this collection bear witness to the particular challenges of worldwide Pentecostalism and model the dedication and commitment among many Pentecostals today who engage the challenges and opportunities of Christian unity. In the first part of the book, a cadre of internationally renowned Pentecostal scholars addresses the

32. Cf. William G. Rusch, *Ecumenical Reception: Its Challenge and Opportunity* (Grand Rapids: Eerdmans, 2007) 89–116; Maffeis, *Ecumenical Dialogue*, 79–93.

33. Cf. Rusch, *Ecumenical Reception*, 54–134; Stewart, Richard L., "Reception: What Do the Churches Do with Ecumenical Agreements?" *Centro Pro Unione Bulletin* no. 25 (Spring 1984) 2–8.

ecumenical heritage and perspectives of the Pentecostal movement. Part two offers a collection of final reports from international dialogues with Pentecostal participation. The final part contains programmatic essays in response to *The Nature and Mission of the Church*, a major study on ecclesiology published by the Faith and Order Commission of the WCC in 2006, and its predecessor, *The Nature and Purpose of the Church*. Together, these essays comprise a snapshot of the ecumenical achievements and anticipations among Pentecostals today.

Douglas Jacobsen traces the ecumenical impulses in early Pentecostal theology in North America and provides insight into the diversity of proponents and opponents of ecumenism among the first generation of classical Pentecostals. He emphasizes the importance of a contextual reading of Pentecostalism and argues that the Pentecostal pioneers generally favored ecumenism over sectarian separation. Harold D. Hunter expands the perspective from North America to the global Pentecostal movement and examines its convergence with the organized ecumenical movement. He contrasts the claim that the Pentecostal movement is inherently ecumenical with the notion that conciliar ecumenism is an inherently exclusive endeavor and calls both sides to devote attention to its ecumenical responsibilities. Carmelo E. Álvarez traces and analyzes the particular context of two Pentecostal churches in Chile, *The Pentecostal Church of Chile* and *The Pentecostal Mission Church of Chile*, which were the first Pentecostal churches to join the WCC. He argues that the story of these Pentecostal pioneers in the ecumenical movement is characterized by active solidarity and growing confidence in international ecumenical participation. Paul van der Laan examines various ecumenical exchanges with Pentecostals in the Netherlands and emphasizes the mutually beneficial nature of the dialogues. His essay offers practical guidelines for dialogue with Pentecostal churches and suggests a possible agenda for the ecumenical future. Raymond R. Pfister examines the past orientations of Pentecostal education with regard to ecumenism and calls for a pedagogy of reconciliation. He suggests that ecumenical theology from a Pentecostal perspective is characterized by an ecumenism of the Spirit that reflects both the development of distinctiveness and sameness for the purpose of unity. Finally, Cecil M. Robeck Jr., speaks from his experience with the international Roman Catholic-Pentecostal dialogue and describes the hard lessons learned during his time as participant and co-chair. Robeck reminds the reader of the not-so-pleasant side of ecumenism and challenges us to confront the issues and problems that still exist not only for the purpose of Christian unity, in general, but for a better understanding of ourselves in communion with others, in particular. This essay serves as a bridge to the second part of the book.

The second part of this collection contains a number of significant documents from international dialogues with Pentecostal participation. Many Pentecostals today are still unaware of the existence of these texts and of the long history of ecumenical relations, particularly with the Roman Catholic Church. These texts tell an important ecumenical story that began in 1972, when South African-born Pentecostal minister, David J. du Plessis, approached the Vatican about the possibility of ecumenical dialogue. The story of this dialogue is told in the first section of each document and is well reflected in the changes apparent in the texts, which transition from short observations, generally presented in the order of discussion, to long and complex statements, often presented in systematic rather than historical order of content. The final reports of the first four rounds of dialogue are for the first time included in a joint collection. The extensive report of the fifth dialogue session has not yet been published. In its place is included the final report of the first dialogue between Pentecostal and Reformed churches, which began in 1996 and is now in its second period. Each of these documents has helped alleviate some of the tensions that exist between Pentecostals and other churches and communities. The document, *Perspectives on Koinonia*, has received particularly wide attention due to a broad focus on the concept in the ecumenical movement, in general. With this text, Pentecostal churches for the first time authorized the participation of officially appointed representatives to ecumenical dialogue. The document is a particularly illuminating example of the great degree of agreement and commitment that characterizes all sides of the dialogue. The dialogues have transitioned from initial discussions and a period of discernment to sophisticated theological conversations. The focus has shifted from a preoccupation with issues that divide to a sweeping interest in areas that unite the churches. In recent years, a number of publications have paid detailed attention to this conversation.[34] The future of these dialogues

34. See Veli-Matti Kärkkäinen, *Spiritus ubi vult spirat: Pneumatology in Roman Catholic-Pentecostal Dialogue (1972–1989)* (Helsinki: Luther-Agricola-Society, 1998); Paul D. Lee, *Pneumatological Ecclesiology in the Roman Catholic–Pentecostal Dialogue: A Catholic Reading of the Third Quinquennium (1985–1989)* (Rome: Pontificiam Universitatem S. Thomae in Urbe, 1994); Terrnece Robert Crowe, *Pentecostal Unity:*

holds great promise for not only significant theological discussion but also a more concrete realization of joint fellowship.

Finally, the essays in the third part of this collection engage the important document, *The Nature and Mission of the Church*, published by the Faith and Order Commission of the World Council of Churches at its ninth general assembly in Porto Alegre, Brazil, in 2006. This document, and its predecessor, *The Nature and Purpose of the Church* (1998), represents the first major ecumenical consensus statement with the promise of containing significant contributions from the Pentecostal community.[35] Although no formal response to the Faith and Order text exists from Pentecostal churches, members of the Society for Pentecostal Studies have produced a series of statements on the ecumenical text. Veli-Matti Kärkkäinen provides a critical analysis of the key themes of the document and raises a number of critical questions. Among the most provocative observations is his suggestion that the ecclesiology of the ecumenical text is written from the perspective of the bygone era of Christendom and ignores the transformations of global Christianity. Frank D. Macchia considers the challenges posed by the text to the Pentecostal community, particularly to the understanding of the movement's own ecclesiality and the visible divisions among Pentecostals. Macchia laments the dominant ecclesiological dualism that distinguishes between the essence of the church and its visible, historical form and calls for a more integrated understanding of the divine and human nature of the church. Finally, my own paper argues that the consensus statement is symptomatic of the larger ecumenical endeavor to form a global ecumenical ecclesiology. I present a summary of Pentecostal perspectives on the church's mission and its relationship to the church's nature and purpose and draw some systematic conclusions regarding the implications of the Pentecostal engagement in the dialogue. The fact that Pentecostalism supports the speaking of "ecclesiologies," in the plural, highlights the dynamic and dialogical dimensions of the ecumenical agenda.

Recurring Frustration and Enduring Hopes (Chicago: Loyola University Press, 1993); Jerry L. Sandidge, *Roman Catholic/Pentecostal Dialogue (1977–1982): A Study in Developing Ecumenism* (Frankfurt: Peter Lang, 1987); Arnold Bittlinger, *Papst und Pfingstler: Der römisch katholisch-pfingstliche Dialog und seine ökumenische Relevanz* (Frankfurt: Lang, 1987).

35. See World Council of Churches, ed., *The Nature and Mission of the Church: A Stage on the Way to a Common Statement*, Faith and Order Paper 198 (Geneva: WCC Publications, 2005); *The Nature and Purpose of the Church: A Stage on the Way to a Common Statement*, Faith and Order Paper 181 (Geneva: WCC Publications, 1998).

All in all, *Pentecostalism and Christian Unity* issues an invitation on at least three interrelated levels to engage, to continue, and to sharpen ecumenical relations. The authors of this collection offer honest, realistic, and deeply personal evaluations of their own experiences in the ecumenical life. Much groundwork remains to be done in initiating conversations with Pentecostals, and we hope that the following essays will motivate both Pentecostals worldwide and the larger ecumenical community to engage each other in mutual dialogue, theological exchange, and shared ministry. In addition, many of the following essays provide fresh insights into existing conversations and offer a unique opportunity to evaluate the current state of affairs. Each essay issues a call to continue existing relations, whether they are still in the early stages or advanced in shared ecumenical experience. From the diverse perspectives of this collection, Pentecostalism calls the world to sharpen and strengthen ecumenical ties for the sake of the unity of the Spirit and the bond of peace.

Part 1

The Ecumenical Heritage and Perspectives of Pentecostalism

1

The Ambivalent Ecumenical Impulse in Early Pentecostal Theology in North America

Douglas Jacobsen

The early leaders of the Pentecostal movement in North America were uncertain what to think about ecumenism, the hope and task of fostering visible Christian unity. This essay examines the views of eight influential first generation Pentecostal leaders, their display of ecumenical attitudes, and their division on the issue of Christian unity, both as a group and in their own individual thinking. Early Pentecostal theology could not agree whether Christian unity was an unmitigated good to be pursued with vigor or a false illusion that should be patently rejected. The main body of opinion was mixed, undecided, and confused. This essay will argue, however, that the long arch of early Pentecostal thinking, understood in historical context, bends toward ecumenism rather than away from it.

FIRST GENERATION VIEWS OF ECUMENISM

The eight first-generation Pentecostal leaders examined in this essay can be loosely grouped into three categories based on their differing ecumenical perspectives. The first group, which includes Richard G. Spurling and David Wesley Myland, was strongly supportive of the goal of Christian unity. A second group of four—Charles Parham, William J. Seymour, Joseph H. King, and Andrew David Urshan—were moderately supportive of ecumenism (at least in comparison with the first group). Finally a third group of early Pentecostal leaders, exemplified by

George F. Taylor and William Durham, were generally anti-ecumenical in attitude. These eight spokespersons do not reflect the total spectrum of opinion that existed within the first generation of the Pentecostal movement in North America, but they are representative of the range of views expressed. They are drawn broadly from the different emergent Pentecostal traditions and indicate that attitudes toward ecumenism were not necessarily directly related to other theological convictions.

STRONG PROPONENTS OF CHRISTIAN UNITY

Richard G. Spurling Jr. (1851–1935)

Perhaps no one in the early Pentecostal movement was as strong a proponent of Christian unity as Richard G. Spurling, a leader in the Church of God (Cleveland, Tennessee). His wonderful little book, *The Lost Link*, lifts up unity and mutual love as the key identifiers of true Christian faith. *The Lost Link* is an analysis of the demise of love in the history of the church and the beginning of its restoration in the Pentecostal revival. Spurling said, the church had begun as a fellowship of equals bound together by love. It lasted in that form for several centuries, but in the early fourth century, the emperor Constantine launched an effort to Christianize the Roman empire. The result was disastrous. As the church gained political power and became more institutionalized, the inter-personal rule of love was slowly replaced by the impersonal rule of creeds. Division within the church was the inevitable result. For Spurling, the composition of the Nicene creed marked the fall of the church from love. From then on, he said, "heretics" (those who could not agree with the creed) were "expelled . . . from their fellowship and communion regardless of their love for God and one another."[1]

In Spurling's judgment, the next thousand years were truly bleak. Christians began to persecute and even to kill each other in the name of pure doctrine. Spurling saw the popes of the Catholic Church as the chief protagonists in this story of persecution and murder, but he knew that Protestantism had also been infected with the disease of hate. This was true of the larger Protestant denominations, and it unfortunately was also true of many local low-church Protestant congregations where "the little preacher in the stand" would often tout his own hobby horse gospel, "branding all others as heretics or devils . . . bring[ing] division

1. Richard G. Spurling, *The Lost Link* (Turtletown, TN: Spurling, 1920) 23.

instead of unity, hatred instead of love."[2] Spurling argued that this kind of negative, church-dividing preaching was the "greatest hindrance to the cause of Christ."[3] In his mind, it had done more harm to the faith than all the attacks of all the world's greatest atheists combined.

Spurling believed that this pattern of Christian intolerance was slowly beginning to falter during his own lifetime. Spirit-filled Christians were slowly beginning "to hew down the walls of prejudice and cut asunder the lines of separation, to shake off the bonds of men-made creeds and laws, to come into the unity of the Spirit in the bonds of peace unto the faith that sweetly works by love."[4] Spurling did not think this great work of restoring the church to love and unity was anywhere close to being completed, but he was glad it was finally underway. He likened it to the return of the Jews to Palestine after their exile in Babylon, and he warned that "as we return from our captivity in Babylon to rebuild the temple of God, to crown it with the chief cornerstone of Christ and His law," the proponents of legalism and Christian intolerance "will persecute us, they will mock and say that we are a band of cranks and are fanatic."[5] Although he believed that "preachers and leaders of the various denominations [would] shake their gray heads and wave their palsied hands and cry heresy and latitudinarianism,"[6] the cause of love and unity was worth the struggle. The slow return of the rule of love to the church was a sign of God's promise ultimately to restore the church to its original character before the end of the age, and Spurling welcomed that restoration with open arms. He ended his book with these lines of verse:

> Oh God, inspire everyone
> Who may read this little book,
> For union now to pray and look,
> And to adopt God's blessed law,
>
> And cease to build with wood and straw;
> Oh, may some wise and noble one
> Complete the work we have begun,
> Oh, may it catch on every pen,

2. Ibid., 36.
3. Ibid., 36–37.
4. Ibid., 29–30.
5. Ibid., 39–40.
6. Ibid., 40.

And trace the isles from end to end,
And turn each foe into a friend,
And into one God's children blend.[7]

David Wesley Myland (1858–1943)

Myland was a free-lance Pentecostal leader of sorts and liked to state his views in his own words. He was also perhaps a bit more creative than other Pentecostals in the rhetoric he used to describe how God intervened in individual lives, assuming that different people often received the experience of Pentecost in slightly different ways. Myland was quite flexible in his evaluation of the evidence that someone had received the Pentecostal blessing. He believed, for example, that speaking in tongues was one indicator that a person had received the baptism of the Holy Spirit (or the "fulness of God"), but there were others signs, as well, and the longing for Christian unity was one of them. Myland declared: "This is the intent of Pentecost, that my heart might be bound with men and women in Africa, in Japan, in the vastnesses of Tibet; that my spirit might be bound with men and women in India and we are made one in working out the purposes of God."[8]

From Myland's perspective, the ultimate goal of Pentecost was "*homo-thumadon*," meaning "one-accordness," and this sense of Christian oneness was rooted in the very character of God. He wrote: "Seeing then that Pentecost results from the absolute oneness of the Godhead what oneness and unity ought it to produce in us who have received! It ought to make us one body, and it will do it. I am one with everybody that is at all one with God. I simply cannot help it. The only thing that can keep me from being one with others is some work either of the flesh or of the devil."[9] He then asked, in Spurling-esque fashion, whether Christians would be willing to "throw away [their] little scruples and colorings and shades of opinion"[10] for the sake of unity. Myland hoped they would. He knew that unity–especially doctrinal unity–was hard to come by. In fact, he said it was "awful hard to get *minds* to think and speak the same

7. Ibid., 52.

8. David Wesley Myland, *The Latter Rain Covenant and Pentecostal Power with Testimony of Healings and Baptism* (Chicago: Evangel, 1910) 106–7.

9. Ibid., 111.

10. Ibid.

thing."[11] But he was also aware that doctrine was not everything. Love, unity, and service to others were also important elements of Pentecostal faith, so much so that he advised that "if we lose the love element out of [our faith] we had better quit preaching and get back to *practice*."[12] Myland believed that those who opposed unity because of their overly rigorous and detailed definitions of doctrine risked putting themselves in the position of opposition to God—a posture in which no good Pentecostal would want to be found.

MODERATE PROPONENTS OF CHRISTIAN UNITY

If Spurling and Myland represent the more radically supportive edge of early Pentecostal ecumenism, a host of other early leaders voiced their support for Christian unity in weaker and more moderate fashion. These individuals clearly believed that some kind of concern for Christian unity ought to be part of Pentecostal faith, but they were not certain how to weigh it in comparison to other Christian concerns.

Charles Fox Parham (1873–1929)

The ecumenical convictions of this Pentecostal pioneer and author were the result of an odd meeting he had with an unexpected visitor who came to his door one day in 1900 or 1901. This person told Parham that God wanted him to be an "apostle of unity" within the Christian community. As Parham related the event, he wrote: "A very pious man came into our office; a man we had never seen or known before . . . [who] declared that God had caused him to leave his team hitched to the plow in the field for his wife to care for; being led of God, had walked thirty miles, finding the way to our door, the Lord having sent him with the express mission to anoint us an apostle of unity."[13]

Parham was impressed by this encounter and thereafter added a concern for Christian unity to his thinking, even though he was never quite sure how such unity was to be achieved, and despite the fact that he continued to call his theological opponents a host of awful, even hateful names. Like many people, Parham knew more about how unity

11. Ibid., 136.

12. David Wesley Myland, *The Revelation of Jesus Christ* (Chicago: Evangel, 1911) 78.

13. Charles Fox Parham, *Kol Kare Bomidbar: A Voice Crying in the Wilderness* (1902; reprinted, Baxter Springs, KS: Robert L. Parham, 1944) 61.

could not be achieved than how it could. He knew, for example, that the solution was not to try to force people into spiritual "concentration camps where unity seems to be established by the minority yielding to the majority in the interpretation of the Scriptures."[14] He knew the flowering of Christian unity had to be a more natural and voluntary process than that, but all he could suggest was that unity was somehow linked to the ability of Christians to consecrate their lives fully to Jesus, including "lay[ing] all our creeds, doctrines and teachings at Jesus' feet."[15] He said: "When you in your home, wherever that may be and I in mine, seek and find the cleansing blood, purifying from all error and false teaching; it will bring us into unity, whether we ever see each other in this world or not."[16] Christian unity would "not be accomplished by [either] organization or non-organization,"[17] instead it was a matter of attitude and mutual submission. But he could never find that balance himself despite his commitment to the cause of unity in the abstract.

William J. Seymour (1870–1922)

Seymour and the Azusa Street Mission, by many considered the origin of classical Pentecostalism, was pledged to encouraging love and respect among all Christians. Nevertheless, Seymour affirmed that some theological fights and divisions were worth having. Seymour knew that some within the Pentecostal movement wanted simply to ignore theological differences and to luxuriate in the nebulous unity of the Spirit. He quoted such persons as saying: "Let us all come together; if we are not one in doctrine, we can [still] be one in spirit."[18] But his response to such sentiments was unequivocally negative, since he was convinced that "we cannot all be one, except through the word of God,"[19] and he reminded his readers that views contrary to Scripture had to be expunged from the community.

Seymour was a realist in ecumenical matters, not prone to gush about Christian unity without counting the cost. While some differences

14. Ibid., 62.

15. Ibid., 65.

16. Ibid., 68.

17. Ibid.

18. William J. Seymour, "Christ's Message to the Churches," *The Apostolic Faith* 1.11 (1908) 3.

19. Ibid.

of doctrine could be a valid cause for division, Seymour and the others leaders of the Azusa Street Mission knew that many issues of difference were to be tolerated and accepted within the bonds of Christian love. Thus the Mission's monthly paper, the *Apostolic Faith*, declared that: "We [have] to recognize every man that honors the Blood. So let us seek peace and not confusion. We that have the truth should handle it very carefully. The moment we feel we have all the truth or more than anyone else, we will drop. We must deal patiently with the Lord's people."[20]

Seymour's practice of tolerance and acceptance was unusual within the Pentecostal movement, even to the point of welcoming non-Pentecostal Christians into his congregation as equal brothers and sisters in Christ. As early as December of 1906, *The Apostolic Faith* had explicitly declared that all Christians were welcomed as equals at the Mission—including those who were not fully baptized in the Spirit. The paper said: "We do not say that we do not need the justified or the sanctified brother simply because he does not speak in tongues or does not prophesy; but we realize that it takes the justified, the sanctified, and the Pentecost brother all to make the body of Christ."[21] Elsewhere the paper stated that "if a man is saved and living according to the word of God, he is our brother, [even] if he has not got the baptism with the Holy Spirit with tongues."[22] The Azusa Street Mission was a place for all Christians. Regardless of their level of spiritual advance, all were welcome, for all had been welcomed by the same Jesus. The *Apostolic Faith* affirmed: "It is Jesus in justification, Jesus in sanctification and Jesus in the baptism with the Holy Ghost."[23]

The strength of Seymour's ecumenical commitments are made clearer when he discusses the baptism of the Holy Spirit and its accompanying signs. While speaking in tongues was an important marker of the Pentecostal experience, Seymour considered love to be a more fundamental trait of the Spirit-filled life. In an editorial comment in *The Apostolic Faith* he explained that "if you get angry, or speak evil, or backbite, I care not how many tongues you may have, you have not the baptism with the Holy Spirit."[24] Similarly, the final edition of the *Apostolic*

20. "The Church Question," *The Apostolic Faith* 1.5 (1907) 2.

21. "The True Pentecost," *The Apostolic Faith* 1.4 (1906) 2.

22. "Questions Answered," *The Apostolic Faith* 1.11 (1908) 2.

23. "The Baptism with the Holy Ghost," *The Apostolic Faith* 1.11 (1908) 4.

24. "To the Baptized Saints," *The Apostolic Faith* 1.9 (1907) 2.

Faith concluded: "If you find people that get a harsh spirit, and even talk in tongues in a harsh spirit, it is not the Holy Ghost talking. His utterances are in power and glory and with blessing and sweetness . . . He is a meek and humble Spirit—not a harsh Spirit."[25] The sign of tongues was seen as a valid sign of the baptism of the Spirit only if recipients showed other evidence of God's loving and redemptive influence in their lives. Love and concern for other Christians is, of course, not by itself the same as ecumenism, but it is clearly the necessary ground and foundation of Christian unity. Seymour may not have been an explicit ecumenist, but his theology was infused with ecumenical sensitivity.

Joseph H. King (1869–1946)

King was an early leader in the Pentecostal Holiness Church well acquainted with theological conflict and division. King could be quite vehement, and he frequently denounced as "heresy" the so-called "Finished Work" theology that was becoming ever more popular in the Pentecostal world. Yet, he also frequently showed understanding of many of the people with whom he disagreed. He saw in human beings a natural desire to cling to their religious values, and that tendency had to be both resisted and respected: "We cling to our tenets of faith with an undying tenacity . . . We are desperately attached to our doctrinal formulas, and theological dogmas. If they should ever be overthrown, the most of us would be thrown into awful confusion. We get very uneasy when we even think that there is a probability of their being overthrown."[26]

King learned this lesson from his own life. At least twice (at the time when he was first introduced to the notion of the baptism of the Holy Ghost and fire, and at the time when he first encountered the teaching that tongues was the necessary sign of true baptism in the Spirit), King had found himself needing dramatically to revise his own thinking in the light of new revelation. He found both experiences painful, and he was, accordingly, sympathetic with those who were in similar straits. He could understand why differences among Christians were so strong and seemed so permanent. And he did not think that Pentecostals had somehow risen above such intractability. In fact, he suggested that "the Pentecostal people of today, with but few exceptions are the strongest in

25. "Character and Work of the Holy Ghost," *The Apostolic Faith* 2.13 (1908) 2.

26. Joseph Hillery King, *From Passover to Pentecost* (Senath, MO: Short, 1914) 112.

prejudice of any people on earth, except Jesuits, bigoted Jews, and fanatical Mohammedans. And any attempt on the part of any to change it is most stubbornly resisted and bitterly denounced."[27] Religious prejudice was simply part of human nature—whether redeemed and Spirit-filled or not—neither "regeneration, sanctification, nor the baptism [of the Spirit] can remove it."[28]

While King believed that virtually all religious views were bent crooked by prejudice, he also believed that even "heathen" people had some ability to know God. Theologically he grounded this view in an expansive understanding of the atonement that to some degree applied to all of humanity.

> [E]veryone is mysteriously touched by the atonement in that aspect of it which is unconditionally applied. There may be those who have the essential Christ that know nothing of the historical Christ. They may have pressed, in heart, up through the mist of heathenism, and prayed to the God that made the heaven and earth, and in this way touched Christ and found peace. We do not know this to be true, but we infer the same from certain statements in the Word . . . this shows, indirectly, the effect of atonement upon heathen hearts, preventing the absolute erasure of every trace of the divine image from their being, and opening a way whereby truth may find its way into their conscience and reason.[29]

King did not apply this vision of the atonement directly to ecumenical concerns, but it seems safe to assume that if he thought it was possible for people caught in the mists of heathenism to find divine truth, surely he would also be willing to show something of the same generosity to Christians from different theological traditions.

Andrew David Urshan (1884–1967)

Urshan was an important leader of Oneness Pentecostalism during the first generation of the movement. Like many of the other early Pentecostals, he was no glassy-eyed optimist. He knew there were theological divisions worth defending, and he was cautious about fellowshipping with those he felt were not fully committed to Christ or fully steeped in the truth. He believed that he was living in an age of apostasy,

27. Ibid., 131.

28. Ibid.

29. Ibid., 78.

and Christians needed to be very careful with whom they associated. The introduction to his book, *The Doctrine of the New Birth,* reads like a primer for anti-ecumenical, fundamentalist faith.

> The need of a book LIKE THIS, on the infallible and unchangeable doctrine of our Lord is most important; especially in these days of world-wide Apostasy. Just as the worldly commercialists and politicians are continually busy making inventions and machinery to make money and satisfy their mad selfish desires, even so are the modern nominal Christians doing, busy inventing new man-made ways of salvation; they are not only revolutionizing the traditions of their mistaken Elders, but are making many new and strange doctrines under pretense of the Name of Christ.[30]

While Urshan believed that sound doctrine was essential, he also tried to keep doctrinal concerns in proper perspective. Disciplined reflection on the faith was not an unmixed boon; doctrine by itself was not the answer. Urshan knew that even the best of "our own understanding, wisdom and education does not always lead us in the right path."[31] Even if one was wholly biblical in one's beliefs and opinions, there were other ways of falling into error. There were ways of living that were doctrinally correct, but attitudinally wrong or spiritually dead. One of the Pentecostal failures that concerned him the most was the lack of basic respect that prevailed among those with differing theological opinions. Urshan understood the problem of ungracious dogmatism from first-hand experience. He had felt it within his own family, and he had sensed it in larger Pentecostal circles, especially as the so-called "new issue" of Oneness Pentecostalism spread tensions across the Pentecostal community. Urshan himself became convinced that pugnacious orthodoxy had been a bane to Christian faith throughout the centuries, and he sought to avoid it in his own ministry.

> To preach doctrine is most essential, because the true Gospel doctrines are to Christianity, what bones are to the human body. Without Bible doctrines, there would be no Christianity. But it is one thing to preach doctrine with a meek spirit, clothed upon with the love of Christ; and quite another to proclaim the truth in the way my cousin tried to force it upon me. Herein lies the

30. Andrew D. Urshan, *Doctrine of the New Birth* (Cochrane, WI: Witness of God, 1921) 1.

31. Andrew D. Urshan, *The Life Story of Andrew bar David Urshan* (Stockton, CA: Apostolic, 1967) 84.

> defeat and success regarding doctrinal matters. There have been terrible calamities in Christendom from the very beginning to this very day, (which have come through stormy discussions over Christian fundamentals being taught in the churches) because of this human zeal and force.[32]

Urshan admitted that he himself had, at times, contributed to this sorry state of theological animosity. He lamented: "We have all been guilty of this in a measure at sometime or another; and have caused many unnecessary grievances, disasters, persecutions and losses of dear friends. Many splits and divisions have come in among God's people because of this." But his prayer was that, some day soon, God would "forgive us and heal all such wounds in the Body of Christ."[33]

OPPONENTS OF ECUMENISM

The views of the strongest opponents of ecumenical faith within the early Pentecostal movement are relatively easy to present. For the most part, persons who held such views saw the times in which they lived as critical turning points in history. The world was in spiritual crisis, and the great need of the hour was to choose the right side in the eschatological battle that was about to commence. Now was not the time to talk of uniting despite difference; now was the time to stand for truth down to the finest detail of difference. Compromise was simply out of the question.

George Floyd Taylor (1881–1934)

Taylor, a church leader and educator in the Pentecostal Holiness Church, exemplified the anti-ecumenical attitude perhaps as clearly as anyone. He remarked: "These are perilous times; these are judgment days. Where do you stand? Which side of the line are you on?"[34] Taylor saw things in general as "coming to a head," and he firmly believed he was seeing "the final judgment set in" as God was "drawing a line among the saints" through the Pentecostal renewal, a line that "demand[ed] that all the house of God either receive it or reject it."[35] Taylor was primed

32. Ibid., 84–85.

33. Andrew D. Urshan, *Timely Messages of Comfort* (n.p.: n.d.) 19.

34. George Floyd Taylor, *The Spirit and the Bride: A Scriptural Presentation of the Operations, Manifestations, Gifts and Fruit of the Holy Spirit in His Relation to the Bride with Special Reference to the "Latter Rain" Revival* (Dunn, NC: Taylor, 1907) 97.

35. Ibid., 98.

for the battle, and he thundered against all who opposed him: "I believe in progressive theology, in aggressive effort, in agitation, in conflict, in conquest, and in crowns. There can be no movement without friction, no battle without issue, no issue without the drawing of lines."[36] Taylor was simply not an ecumenist at all. He knew what he believed. He knew what was true. And all others were simply wrong.

William H. Durham (1873–1912)

For all their theological differences, William Durham, the leader of the so-called Finished Work school of Pentecostalism, had almost exactly the same attitude as Taylor on the issue of Christian unity. Like Taylor, Durham was fueled by a fierce opposition to error. He believed Christian faith as a whole was under severe attack by modern ideas and ways of life. The spiritual lukewarmness and vacuousness of most churches troubled him deeply, and he believed God would not allow such a situation to endure for long. A great crisis loomed on the horizon—a spiritual crisis which God would use to create a clear line of division between the true church and the multitudes of merely nominal Christians around the world.

As early as 1910, Durham had written that "for years it has been clear to me that we are drawing nearer and nearer to a great religious crisis."[37] This crisis was to be centered on the church. For Durham, the church was supposed to be a bastion of truth and purity—redeemed Christians living holy lives unspotted by all the impurities of the world—but when he looked at the great mass of so-called Christians in his own day, he could hardly see any distinction between them and the world at large. He once huffed: "If God could tell the church and the world apart He could do better than I could."[38] That fuzzy state of affairs required lines to be drawn, and Durham believed that God would be the one to inaugurate that process. Durham actually looked forward to the battle that would follow. He was more than ready to begin slaying dragons for Jesus. In fact, he pronounced without qualification that "the Pentecostal movement is the means that God is using to hasten the crisis . . . It is

36. George Floyd Taylor, *The Second Coming of Jesus* (Falcon, NC: Falcon, 1916) 54.

37. "The Great Crisis," reprinted in *Articles Written by Pastor W. H. Durham* (n.p.: n.d.) 2; "The Great Crisis Number Two," *Pentecostal Testimony* 1.5 (n.d.) 3.

38. "The Great Crisis," 2.

drawing a line around the world, so to speak, and every person that comes in contact with it has to get on one side or the other. There is no half way grounds."[39] If Durham had any ecumenical tendencies, he kept them well buried and out of sight. From all we can see he thought of himself as a warrior for God, and he was not about to compromise with even the slightest whiff of error in a misbegotten quest for Christian unity and peace.

MAKING SENSE OF EARLY PENTECOSTALISM'S ECUMENICAL AMBIVALENCE

The eight perspectives just outlined do not define the entire canvas of early Pentecostal opinions regarding Christian unity and ecumenism—many other shades and nuances could surely be colored in—but they provide enough data to see the general pattern of opinion that prevailed in the first generation. Some Pentecostals believed that the longing for Christian unity was near the center of Pentecostal piety; it was an essential element in true Pentecostal faith. Another group of Pentecostal leaders thought that talk of Christian unity was close to heresy. Instead, they saw the genius of the early Pentecostal movement in the clear lines it drew in the shifting theological sand of the day, unambiguously separating truth from error. Through the Pentecostal movement, God was dividing Christians into two distinct camps that had nothing to do with each other: true and faithful followers of Jesus and all the many other varieties of weak, lukewarm, and indecisive Christians that God would soon spew out of his mouth. Yet a third group of first-generation Pentecostal spokespersons, seemingly the largest, located themselves in between the two extremes. This third group was attracted to some aspects of ecumenism, but for one reason or another found it impossible to fully embrace the ideal or the practice of Christian unity. How can we make sense of this situation? Is there a way to make these early Pentecostal leaders speak with a common voice? Can we find within this mish-mash of divergent opinion a useable history to support Pentecostal ecumenical activity today?

First, I do not think that we can collapse the divergent views of these first-generation Pentecostal leaders into any kind of middle-of-the-road consensus. Pentecostals did not then, and they do not now,

39. "The Great Crisis Number Two," 3.

speak with a common voice on either ecumenism or a host of other important theological issues. This is contentious turf.

Having said that, I am not sure it is necessarily a pointless task to try to discern where the center of gravity of the movement might have been on the topic of Christian unity. The center of gravity of an object is the point around which the object would naturally rotate in a weightless environment. It is a mathematically determined point that may not even exist within the contours of the object itself. For example, the center of gravity of a donut is found in the middle of the hole and not anywhere in the material part of the donut itself. In a similar way, when I speak of the center of gravity of the early Pentecostal movement regarding ecumenism, I am not necessarily trying to discover what most people said or even the one person who articulated that center clearly. Instead, I am trying to discern whether the diverse body of opinion that existed in the early years of the movement is weighted in a more or less ecumenical direction.

So, for the sake of argument, let me propose that we throw out the extreme views as canceling each other out. Let us assume that the center of gravity of early Pentecostalism as a whole was neither stridently opposed to ecumenism nor adamantly committed to ecumenism. The issue then is how to evaluate the general orientation of the folks in the middle. I think the tendency has been to assume that when all was said and done, the Pentecostal leadership was ultimately more partisan than ecumenical. Pentecostals may have valued Christian unity as an abstract ideal, but they lived like non-ecumenical believers in the real world. They may have wanted in some deep sense to tear down the walls of separation between Christians, but in the end they were wall-builders intent on maintaining and patrolling the boundaries that divided true Pentecostal believers from all others. Even in their most ecumenical moments, they seemed to think that the only viable road to Christian unity was through their own movement. The way for the church to be united was for all Christians to become Spirit-filled Pentecostal Christians, just like themselves.

Please allow me a slight tangent at this point. A few years ago, I enrolled in an introductory art class on oil painting. At the beginning of that class, we did very little in the way of actually putting paint to canvas. What we did was discuss colors. We looked at colors. We mixed our paints into different colors. We compared colors. And on occasion we even mused poetically about colors. The main thing I learned is that color is complex. Nothing is just red. It is always a special shade of red, a certain intensity of red, a unique blend of red. And then, after you have oh-so-carefully mixed your colors and come up with what you think is just the right hue and tone—it looks perfect on your palette—you apply it to the canvass next to the other colors that are there, and suddenly your red looks all wrong. Because color is always relative, when you put one color next to another, they both change. Color only makes sense in context—and so does ecumenical faith.

This analogy leads to some important questions. What was the context of early Pentecostalism and how might that context help us better see exactly what color of ecumenism or non-ecumenism Pentecostal leaders had on their theological palettes? And if we place those colors in other contexts, how might that help us better understand the hues with which we are dealing? To switch back to the earlier metaphor I employed, how will sensitivity to context help us better discover the center of gravity of the movement in matters of Christian unity? Two contexts deserve special note in the attempt to find answers.

A First Context

Early Pentecostalism was a movement of reform—of prophetic and revolutionary reform—and for the most part that agenda of renewal and reform was vehemently rejected by the mainstream churches. Pentecostals were strident in their critiques of what they often called the dead "churchianity" of America. In their minds and hearts (Pentecostals never thought just with their minds) true Christianity had nothing to do with the bland faith of most of the nation's denominations. Not surprisingly, the churches and church leaders who were being denounced in this way did not look kindly on their Pentecostal critics, and they in turn accused their Pentecostal opponents of being crazy, demon-possessed, or just plain stupid. It was in this cauldron of charge and counter-charge that the ecumenical identity of classical Pentecostalism was first formed.

The fact that Pentecostals could speak of Christian unity at all in this context of heated exchange and boundary marking is nothing less than remarkable. No doubt, their ecumenical statements were somewhat mild, often more than a little tenuous, and sometimes faltering, but the fact that they could even broach the topic of Christian unity is stunning. They did not need to say anything about Christian unity—and as we have seen some of them did not (e.g., Taylor and Durham)—but despite that fact, most Pentecostals did give at least a nod in the direction of ecumenism. Taking into account the contentious colors of the world in which they lived, that nod jumps out like a shout from the page. It is not the strength of their comments in and of themselves, but the place of those comments in historical context that makes me think Christian unity was not a throw-away concern. Many first generation Pentecostal leaders believed that the struggle for Christian unity was somewhere close to the core of Pentecostal faith and life, even if they simultaneously knew that they themselves (like King David of old) would not be the ones to build that unified temple of faith in their own lifetimes.

A Second Context

As a second context, I would like to compare certain comments by the first-generation leaders of the movement to the comments or attitudes expressed by leaders in other churches and Christian traditions who have been involved in ecumenical work during the last century. In particular, I would like to examine the notion that when early Pentecostals discussed Christian unity they were not really being ecumenical as much as they were being evangelistic. That is, they welcomed Christian unity, if that unity was understood to mean that other Christians would simply become more like themselves—Pentecostal.

There is something to this critique. Many historic Pentecostal documents do seem much more evangelistic—at least on the surface—than they seem ecumenical. But I am not sure this is a criticism that is all that unique to Pentecostalism, whether in the past or today. Pentecostal attitudes in this regard mirror the attitudes of many others involved in the ecumenical movement. We all know change will be required from us, in some way. None of us thinks the road to Christian unity will be smooth or easy. But deep down inside, we hope and we pray, and perhaps we really believe, that our own tradition may hold the key. And that is exactly what the leaders of the early Pentecostal movement thought, too. The fact that they voiced those ideas may be more a sign of their commitment to honest speech than a sign of any lack in the area of ecumenical resolve.

The bottom line is that when all is said and done, and when context is taken into account, the bent of early Pentecostal thinking with regard to ecumenism leans more in the direction of support than opposition. It was weakly, but positively ecumenical. It is more than fair to say that ecumenical engagement is clearly not out-of-sync with the origins of the movement. Given that fact, and given the increasing sense in the world-wide Christian community that the struggle for Christian unity is no longer an optional calling, I would urge the leaders of the contemporary Pentecostal movement to become leaders in the ecumenical movement as well. In doing that, they may also discover new ways to celebrate and honor the deep roots of their own Pentecostal identities.

2

Global Pentecostalism and Ecumenism

Two Movements of the Holy Spirit?

Harold D. Hunter

In contrast to what is sometimes advertised as the monolithic character of classical Pentecostalism, it is the considerable diversity of Pentecostalism worldwide that complicates the process of clearly identifying what is "Pentecostal." The ubiquity of the international Pentecostal-Charismatic movement at the beginning of the twenty-first century outdistances attempts at classification and clarification. In the face of ecumenical designations, such as patchwork quilt, rainbow, kaleidoscope, or mosaic, it may be appropriate to apply Dom Gregory Dix's verdict on the Church of England, and to say that global Pentecostalism is truly an "amorphous mass of Pelagian good will." At a minimum, glossocentric definitions fall short of the mark when trying to stretch the canvas to cover Pentecostalism as a global and ecumenical phenomenon.

The twentieth century was variously labeled the century of Pentecostal revival and the century of the ecumenical movement. Among the ecumenical observers, Peter Staples identifies the ecumenical movement and the Pentecostal-charismatic renewal as the two most important and extensive social movements of the century, since both movements drew attention to the Holy Spirit.[1] Similarly, Jerry L. Sandidge concluded that

1. Peter Staples, "Ecumenical Theology and Pentecostalism," *Pentecost, Mission, and Ecumenism: Essays on Intercultural Theology: Festschrift in Honour of Professor Walter J. Hollenweger*, eds. Jan A. B. Jongeneel et al. (Frankfurt: Lang, 1992) 261–71.

both movements were born of the Holy Spirit.[2] This essay explores the possibility and extent to which these assessments are correct and the two movements converge. The overarching question is whether global Pentecostalism and ecumenism represent one or two movements of the Holy Spirit. In the first part, I outline the attitudes and advances of Pentecostalism toward ecumenical endeavors. In turn, the second part analyzes the openness of conciliar ecumenism toward the worldwide Pentecostal movement. I conclude with an examination of the prevalent models of ecumenism in the global Pentecostal and charismatic community.

IS THE PENTECOSTAL MOVEMENT INHERENTLY ECUMENICAL?

The claim that Pentecostalism is inherently ecumenical has been made, most prominently, by Walter J. Hollenweger, Peter D. Hocken, Cecil M. Robeck, Jr., and Patrick Granfield. Hollenweger's seminal work, *Pentecostalism: Origins and Developments Worldwide*, lists five roots of global Pentecostalism; the final root is ecumenism.[3] He concentrates on a few early Pentecostal leaders in Europe, moves on to David J. du Plessis, and finishes with conciliar ecumenism. From his perspective, early Pentecostals, 1960s charismatic Christians, and 1980s "Third Wavers" were inherently ecumenical. In the same way, Hocken calls Pentecostalism the "first instance of a mass movement for Christian unity."[4] Robeck points to the earliest Pentecostal publications to vindicate similar kinds of claims.[5] And Granfield highlights the assessment of the World Council of Churches (WCC) at its Nairobi Assembly in 1975 that considered the charismatic renewal "a major thrust of ecumenism in our time."[6]

2. See Jerry L. Sandidge, "The Pentecostal Movement and Ecumenism: An Update," *Ecumenical Trends* 18 (July–August 1989) 102–6.

3. Walter J. Hollenweger, *Pentecostalism: Origins and Developments Worldwide* (Peabody, MA: Hendrickson, 1997), chapter 25.

4. Peter D. Hocken, "Charismatic Renewal and Christian Unity," *America: The National Catholic Weekly* 70 (Dec. 1, 1979) 340–42, here 341.

5. Cecil M. Robeck, Jr., "Pentecostals and Ecumenism: An Expanding Frontier," paper read to Conference on Pentecostal and Charismatic Research in Europe, Kappel, Switzerland, July 3–6, 1991, 1. For European leaders, see David Bundy, "The Ecumenical Quest of Pentecostalism," *Cyberjournal for Pentecostal-Charismatic Research* 5 (February 1999), available at http://www.pctii.org/cyberj/index.html, accessed August 1, 2009.

6. Patrick Granfield, "The Ecumenical Significance of the Charismatic Movement," *Ecumenical Trends* 9.7 (1980) 97–99.

Granfield identifies three kinds of ecumenical activity: theological, social, and spiritual. Theological ecumenism deals with doctrinal matters; social ecumenism involves cooperation in the work for justice; and spiritual ecumenism, called by the Second Vatican Council "the soul of the whole ecumenical movement," is described as a "change of heart and holiness of life, along with public and private prayer and unity of Christians" (*Decree on Ecumenism*, no. 8). For Granfield, the charismatic renewal is primarily involved with spiritual renewal. As a reaction against what it believes to be an excessive formalism and preoccupation with externals in much of official Christianity, the charismatic movement stresses personal holiness rooted in scripturally-oriented public and private prayer. Charismatic Christianity affirms that the Holy Spirit is the source of Christian unity, and that all Christians, through the baptism of the Holy Spirit and the exercise of the charisms, can celebrate together the peace and joy that stem from Christ's victory over sin and death. The charismatic renewal is the most broadly-based ecumenical phenomenon in present-day Christianity that engages Christians of all traditions.

In response to this ecumenical idealism, one must reckon with the reality that to fight off its opponents, many participants and friends initially said that although there are unfortunate aspects of the Charismatic movement, these are outweighed by the fact that an ecumenism initiated by the Holy Spirit is arising that far exceeds the initial efforts of those who began dialogues and like meetings some time ago.[7] Much of enthusiastic pneumatomania with which I am familiar have made such claims, but the end result is the same—"ecumenism" often means nothing more than people of various denominations now adhering to doctrines distinctive to that movement. Even though a given charismatic prayer meeting may encompass a variety of people from different denominations, they may actually not have learned theological tolerance. It has become increasingly clear, especially in the Pentecostal movement, that we are witnessing the emergence of new denominations or related communities often defined on the basis of various formulas, personalities, cultures, traditions, and other variables. Even the renewal in the Roman Catholic Church has experienced much fragmentation. The demise of the North American Renewal Service Committee (NARSC) reflects this reality with particular sharpness.

7. See Peter Hocken, *One Lord, One Spirit, One Body* (Exeter: Paternoster, 1987); Kilian McDonnell, *The Charismatic Renewal and Ecumenism* (New York: Paulist, 1978); Robert Wild, *Enthusiasm in the Spirit* (Notre Dame: Ave Maria, 1975) 114–16.

Space limitations prohibit an adequate treatment of facets of the internal make-up of Pentecostals that generated tensions with the conciliar movement.[8] Not to be ignored, however, is the fact that the classical Pentecostal movement in North America is barely a century old. The person familiar with the formation of ecclesiastical movements can observe familiar stages of organizations in classical Pentecostalism. People become less comfortable with their existing churches, rallies give birth to annual conferences and parachurch organizations, while numerous independent churches appear at the same time. Before long, new, incorporated denominations appear. This development can be observed in the multiplied Calvary chapels, which have not been associated with the mainline charismatic movement, even though their theological orientation is much the same, as well as the Vineyard churches, Covenant churches, Word-Faith churches, Rock churches, Victory chapels, and even the Apostolic Reformation churches. At the same time, the Protestant charismatic movement spawned megachurches—many of which disappear as quickly as they appear—and saw the explosion of independent congregations, their fastest growing segment. Doctrinal distinctions are evident even in ecumenical ventures like NARSC, which sponsored major conferences in Kansas City, New Orleans, and elsewhere. Nor has the adage disappeared in North American Pentecostal ranks that a Roman Catholic, who becomes a charismatic Christian, should then join a classical Pentecostal denomination.[9] Since the Pentecostal movement at large has not come to judge genuine ecumenism as an important work of the Spirit, the future

8. See Jeffrey Gros, "An Ecumenical Perspective on Pentecostal Mission," in *Called and Empowered: Global Mission in Pentecostal Perspective*, ed. Murray W. Dempster, Byron D. Klaus, and Douglas Peterson (Peabody: Hendrickson, 1991) 285–98; Jean-Jacques Suurmond, "Van de Beek, Reiling in 'The Ecumenical Review,'" *Bulletin voor Charismatische Theologie* 26 (1990) 52–64; Henry I. Lederle, "The Spirit of Unity: A Discomforting Comforter. Some Reflections on the Holy Spirit, Ecumenism and the Pentecostal-Charismatic Movements," *The Ecumenical Review* 42.3–4 (1990) 279–87; Cecil M. Robeck, Jr., "Pentecostals and the Apostolic Faith: Implications for Ecumenism," *Pneuma: The Journal of the Society for Pentecostal Studies* 9.1 (1987) 61–84; Marta Palma, "A Pentecostal Church in the Ecumenical Movement," *The Ecumenical Review* 37.2 (1985) 223–29.

9. I first made this point in my 1984 Presidential Address to the Society for Pentecostal Studies under the title "What Is Truth?" It is the only presidential address never to have been published in *Pneuma*. Here I proposed three concentric circles as a premise for ecumenical and interfaith engagement. I expanded on these concepts in a paper read to the 1999 European Pentecostal Charismatic Research Association conference that convened in Hamburg, Germany.

could make the same judgment on it that Abraham Kuyper made of the proto-Pentecostal followers of Edward Irving: "It is already manifest that this movement, which started among us under the pretext of uniting a divided church by gathering together the Lord's people, has accomplished little more than to add another to the already large numbers of sects, thus robbing the Church of God of excellent powers that now are being wasted."[10] Critics of the Pentecostal movement in the early years decried Pentecostal examples of sowing disunity. Arthur T. Pierson complained about divisions created by Pentecostals in Europe. Holiness Pentecostal denominations in the United States had already fragmented the Holiness movement of the late nineteenth century. Robert Jaffray, a Christian and Missionary Alliance missionary in China, spoke in tongues in 1908. By the next year, he argued that the dogma of Spirit baptism that requires the evidence of speaking in tongues necessarily led to division. Jaffray further charged that Pentecostals separated themselves from others because of a spiritual superiority complex. Pentecostalism had swept his mission, but those claiming spiritual empowerment had separated from the community and gathered in small select meetings.[11]

Many of the North American Pentecostal platitudes about unity were born not in a vision of unity in diversity but in belief-systems, which stipulated that "all" needed to come around to "the" Pentecostal way. In other words: "once you can mirror my image or embrace me as normative, then we can all join together." The early Pentecostal leader, A. J. Tomlinson, was hardly alone in this posturing. While Tomlinson was driven by his ecclesiology, it seems to be often forgotten that the eschatological frenzy that gripped many early Pentecostals is not unrelated to some of those who wrote of Christian unity in platitudes. For some, such a prediction was another sign of the soon return of the Lord. The Pentecostal belief system at the Azusa Street Mission revival was so narrow that there were splits in the Mission before one year passed. Any defense of the ecumenical side of Pentecostalism has to cope with Roger Robin's quip that early Pentecostal ecumenism was nothing but "a commitment to proselytize all denominations, without discrimination."[12]

10. Abraham Kuyper, *Work of the Holy Spirit* (Grand Rapids: Eerdmans, 1975) 87.

11. Edith L. Blumhofer, *Restoring the Faith: The Assemblies of God, Pentecostalism, and American Culture* (Chicago: University of Illinois Press, 1993) 103–5.

12. Roger Glenn Robins, "Plainfolk Modernist: The Radical Holiness World of A. J. Tomlinson" (Ph.D. diss., Duke University, 1999) 47. Cf. Douglas Jacobsen, "United Church of Christ Response," *Pneuma: The Journal of the Society for Pentecostal Studies*

Even if the Azusa Street Mission intended to encourage genuine unity for the entire body of Christ, its influence on at least the Holiness denominations that turned Holiness Pentecostal was minimal on this point. Although the Pentecostal movement brought many "unchurched" persons into its fellowship, fledgling movements across the spectrum seeking converts have been known to "steal sheep." While this assessment is not to imply that other Christian traditions reached higher ground, there are instances, which support the judgment that what is lauded as "full communion" among magisterial churches is, at times, little more than the alignment of particular segments of likeminded orientation from varying fellowships.

IS CONCILIAR ECUMENISM EXCLUSIVE?

To use hyperbole, if Roman Catholics are not the only members of the church catholic, if the Greek Orthodox are not the only orthodox, are professional ecumenists the only ecumenists? Pentecostals do not diminish the importance of the day of Pentecost for other traditions, but conciliar ecumenists too often portray a belief that they are the only proponents of authentic ecumenism. The implications of setting a standard for genuine ecumenism have yet to be explored. Questioning this kind of standard begs the question if the staff of the WCC indeed reflects an equal representation of their total constituency. The discrepancy in question was particularly evident at the assembly in Harare, when the daily paper for the assembly sponsored by the Geneva headquarters became the object of heated discourse on the floor. Conciliar agencies have at times given birth to the "enlightened" elite. There are even cases where conciliar careers and institutions are made at the expense of genuine

23.1 (2001) 90–94. Absent here are comments about Spurling's link to Landmarkism and later to the Church of God of Prophecy. Doug Beacham, *Rediscovering the Role of Apostles & Prophets* (Franklin Springs, GA: LifeSprings Resources, 2003) 49, notes that it was in this context of leadership and organization that Ephesians 4:11–13 was referenced in an article calling for unity among Pentecostals. Paul Ham of Goldsboro, NC wrote in the *Bridegroom's Messenger* (December 1, 1909) that all the Pentecostal churches should be in unity and called "the Church of God" in each city or part of the city. A. J. Tomlinson replied in March 1, 1909, that "this unity obtained and churches established in every county and city where Pentecost has gone with the New Testament as our only faith and discipline, and the Church would shine and the world would see the glory of it as never before. This would keep out false teaching and fanaticism after a thorough order (Colossians 2:5) was reached. She (the church) should not only be one in name, but also one in doctrine and government."

ecumenical efforts. One has to also guard against Eurocentric tendencies of the major groups. Yet another arena would be the conciliar treatment of social justice, an issue too important to be commented on quickly here. These are exclusivist tendencies that should be avoided.

On the other hand, the official engagement of Pentecostal churches in the ecumenical movement is still virtually unknown. In 1961, the *Iglesia Pentecostal de Chile* and the *Misión Iglesia Pentecostal* joined the WCC as the first Pentecostal members.[13] They were the first of a yet undetermined number of Pentecostal churches that would cast their lot with the WCC. They were joined by a number of Latin American churches, Manuel de Mello and his *Igreja Evangélica Pentecostal*, "O Brasil para Cristo," in 1969, the International Evangelical Church in 1972, Bishop Gabriel O. Vacaro's Iglesia de Dios from Argentina in 1980, the *Missáo Evangélica Pentecostal de Angola* in 1985, and the *Iglesia Misiones Pentecostal Libres de Chile* in 1991. The Christian Biblical Church in Argentina joined the WCC in 1997. Hollenweger rightly adds to the group the African Church of the Holy Spirit, Kenya; African Israel Church, Nineveh, Kenya; Church of the Lord, Aladura, Nigeria; *Eglise de Jésus-Christ sur la Terre par le Prophète* Simon Kimbangu, Zaire; *Eglise Evangélique du Congo*; *Iglesia de Dios*; *Igreja Evangélica Pentecostal de Angola*; International Evangelical Church, USA; and the Union of Evangelical Christians/Baptists of USSR.[14] Word for the World Christian Fellowship, when still connected to the Church of God (Cleveland, Tennessee), joined the National Council of Churches in the Philippines, and the Korean Assemblies of God joined the Korean Council of Churches. The Pentecostal Christian Church of Cuba participates actively in the Ecumenical Council of Cuba.[15] The *Seminario Sudamericano*, a seminary of the Church of God in Ecuador has a positive relationship with the *Consejo Latinoamericano*

13. See the essay by Carmelo E. Alvarez in chapter 3 in this collection.

14. Ofelia Ortega, "Ecumenism of the Spirit," *In the Power of the Spirit: The Pentecostal Challenge to Historic Churches in Latin America*, ed. Benjamin F. Gutierrez and Dennis A. Smith (Arkansas City, KS: Gilliland, 1996); Cecil M. Robeck, Jr., "A Pentecostal Looks at the World Council of Churches," *Ecumenical Review* 47.1 (1995) 60–69; Ans J. van der Bent, ed., *Handbook: Member Churches World Council of Churches*, rev. ed. (Geneva: WCC Publications, 1985) 265–66; Hollenweger, *Pentecostalism*, 386–88.

15. Carmelo E. Alvarez, "Historic Panorama of Pentecostalism in Latin America and the Caribbean," Gutierrez and Smith, *In the Power of the Spirit*, 35. See also Alvarez' essay in this collection. Cf. Cecil M. Robeck, "Do 'Good Fences Make Good Neighbors'? Evangelization, Proselytism, and Common Witness," *Asian Journal of Pentecostal Studies* 2.1 (1999) 87–103.

de Iglesias (CLAI) and hosted *Consejo Latinoamericano de Estrabismo* (CLADE) IV. Frank Chikane, a minister of the Apostolic Faith Mission, spearheaded the South African Council of Churches, and the Apostolic Faith Mission eventually joined this council. Equally striking is the work of Wilfedro Estrada with the Council of Churches of Puerto Rico. Various Pentecostal churches belong to the Fédération Protestante de France, and its general secretary is Christian Seytre, a Pentecostal who belongs to the Apostolic Church (UK).[16]

Signs of change are in the air, as a growing group of Pentecostal scholars from several continents press forward into WCC circles, that the Pentecostal attitude embodied in the 1965 Assemblies of God General Council resolution, and reaffirmed in 1997, which disapproved of mainstream ecumenical efforts, is slowly eroding.[17] The high profile role, once played by David du Plessis in the WCC, is well known. Cho-Lak Yeow and Cecil M. Robeck Jr., serve on the WCC Commission on Faith and Order. A few Pentecostals were noticed for their contributions to the fifth world conference on Faith and Order at Santiago de Compostela in 1993, and a small band of Pentecostals were present in Canberra for the 1991 general assembly of the WCC.[18] The WCC hosted a Consultation with North American Pentecostals and Latin American Pentecostals in 1996 in Costa Rica. Not unlike the prior Consultation with Latin American Pentecostals, in Lima, Peru, in 1994, approximately twenty-five Pentecostals took part in the proceedings. Late in 1995, the WCC brought together African and African-Caribbean church leaders in Britain, most prominently Joe Aldred of the Church of God of Prophecy and *Jerisdan*

16. See Wilfredo Estrada, *Pastores o Políticos con Sotanas? Pastoral de la guardarraya en Vieques* (San Juan, Puerto Rico: Fundación Puerto Rico Evangélico, 2003); Raymond Pfister, "Pentecostalism and Ecumenism in France," paper presented at the 10th EPCRA conference (2001) in Leuven, Belgium, available at http://www.epcra.ch/papers_site/leuven2.html, accessed August 1, 2009. A 2009 survey revealed a significant expansion of PWF member churches involvement in national council of churches around the world led by the Church of God of Prophecy. The rationale in play, however, is not always altruistic.

17. See Rex Davis, *Locusts and Wild Honey* (Geneva: WCC Publications, 1978); Christian Lalive d'Epinay, *Haven of the Masses* (London: Lutterworth, 1969); Albert C. Outler, "Pneumatology as an Ecumenical Frontier," *The Ecumenical Review* 41.3 (1989); and *The International Review of Mission* 75.297 (1986) dedicated to Pentecostalism.

18. See Cecil M. Robeck Jr., "Taking Stock of Pentecostalism: The Personal Reflections of a Retiring Editor," *Pneuma: The Journal of the Society for Pentecostal Studies* 15.1 (1993) 35–60.

Jehu-Appiah of the *Musama Disco Christo* church. All these meetings were the initiative of Huibert van Beek, then Executive Secretary of the Office of Church and Ecumenical Relations at the WCC office in Geneva. A WCC-Pentecostal consultation was initiated at Bossey, Switzerland, in 1997. The highlight of the event was a morning session that featured Konrad Raiser, then general secretary of the WCC. A Pentecostal worship service was held at the WCC headquarters in Geneva. Twenty-nine Pentecostals were also present in Harare for the WCC General Assembly held in 1998. This assembly approved a joint consultative group with Pentecostals that commenced work during the summer of 2000.[19]

This litany of Pentecostal engagements of conciliar ecumenism is often coupled with the reductionist argument that member churches of the Pentecostal World Fellowship (PWF) should therefore join the WCC. Such a position sets aside the reality that the Pentecostal groups that belong to the WCC are different from those represented by PWF churches. As a friend of the many manifestations of Pentecostalism around the world, I find that the mission of the autochthonous and indigenous Pentecostals with regard to the WCC is quite different from that of the PWF. This reality was particularly well-displayed during the 2001 meeting of the WCC-Pentecostal Joint Working Group, hosted by the *Seminario Sudamericano*, in Ecuador. It is also evident in the limitations of ecumenical endeavors to academic circles.

Confounding the axiomatic antithesis between expressive narrative and reflective theology, the surge of Pentecostal scholars provokes a search for theological treatises that are global in scope and seek to rise above internal issues and controversies of the past. Pentecostal theologians have disavowed appellations such as precritical and submodern, yet are predictably drawn to the Apostolic Faith project of the WCC, in part because their inherited restorationist tendencies resonate with sensitivities to doxological and confessional orientations. In this re-

19. Samkwan Kim, "Transition Time of Christianity and Timely Attitude of Asian Pentecostals," *Challenges and Opportunities for Asian Pentecostals* (Makati City, Philippines: Asian Pentecostal Society, August 25, 2000) 54, points out that the host community at the Hautecombe monastery for the WCC-Pentecostal Joint Consultative Group (JCG) was influenced by Dr. Cho. A report on the Pentecostal presence at the 8th general assembly of the WCC and documents generated by the WCC-Pentecostal JCG meeting are available at http://www.pctii.org/wcc/index.html, accessed August 2, 2009. For earlier efforts see David Cole, "Pentecostal Koinonia: An Emerging Ecumenical Ecclesiology among Pentecostals," (Ph.D. diss., Fuller Theological Seminary, 1998).

spect, one can recommend conciliar documents like *Baptism, Eucharist, and Ministry* and *Confessing the One Faith*.[20] Pentecostalism has been rightly identified—by Juan Sepulveda and Bernardo Campos, among others—as a popular religion, that is a religion of the people.[21] Their vantage point is different from traditions governed by a magisterium. In bilateral and multilateral dialogues, others seem content to describe only grassroots Pentecostalism while making comparisons not to those in their own pews, but to their finest universities, and even here selectively. Pentecostals should not be influenced by these other traditions to distance themselves from their grassroots origins.

There is irony in the scholarly disdain heaped on the myths that are part of the fabric of classical Pentecostalism. Many of these same scholars highly esteemed sections of canonical materials they judge to be mythical. The inconsistency of valuing one set of myths, while unilaterally condemning all such things when associated with Pentecostalism, may demonstrate an ethnocentric view of reality. Analysis of the belief systems of ordinary people has often been held in disrepute by intellectuals and always provided an easy target of ridicule. Such mockery of popular religion is sometimes thinly disguised, as made clear by Peter W. Williams in *Popular Religion in America*.[22] The lack of interest in popular religiosity can be measured by the level of disinterest among theologians toward teachings prevalent among their own conclaves. Voices from the pew have been muffled or conveniently not heard. Theological tomes, erudite expositions, and conciliar documents virtually eliminate any concern for interacting with grassroots thinking.

MODELS OF ECUMENISM IN THE GLOBAL PENTECOSTAL-CHARISMATIC MOVEMENT

No one typology is at play in common usage to categorize the various models of ecumenism involving Pentecostal and charismatic Christians.

20. See Harold D. Hunter, "Reflections by a Pentecostalist on Aspects of *BEM*," in *Journal of Ecumenical Studies* 29.3–4 (1992) 317–45; Harold D. Hunter, "Musings on *Confessing the One Faith*," *Pneuma: The Journal of the Society for Pentecostal Studies* 14.2 (1992) 204–8.

21. See Edwin David Aponte. "Coritos as Active Symbol in Latino Protestant Popular Religion," *Journal of Hispanic/Latino Theology* 2.3 (1995) 57–66.

22. Peter W. Williams, *Popular Religion in America: Symbolic Change and the Modernization Process in Historical Perspective* (Englewood Cliffs, NJ: Prentice-Hall, 1980).

A particular distinction can be seen between academic and ecclesiastical efforts. This concluding analysis is merely suggestive.

There exist academic organizations in Pentecostalism spread across six continents that are committed to ecumenism on various levels. Chief among them are the Society for Pentecostal Studies (USA), the Asian Pentecostal Society (Asia), the European Pentecostal-Charismatic Research Association, GloPent (Europe), the Comisión Evangélica Pentecostal Latinoamericana (Latin America), the Fellowship for Pentecostal Studies in New Zealand (Oceania), and the Pentecostal Theological Association of Southern Africa (Africa).[23]

Organizations led by ecclesiarchs include the Pentecostal World Fellowship (PWF), International Charismatic Consultation (ICC), previously called International Charismatic Consultation on World Evangelization (ICCOWE), the North American Renewal Service Committee (NARSC), and the Pentecostal Charismatic Churches of North America (PCCNA). ICC and NARSC encompass various shades of Pentecostals, Charismatics, Roman Catholics, Orthodox, and other, conciliar ecumenists. The ecumenical scholar Dale Irvin described the ICCOWE conference, known as Brighton '91, as a "landmark in the emergence of the Pentecostal ecumenical consciousness."[24] The 2002 co-chairs of PCCNA demonstrated a similar openness to the forums initiated by the WCC and the NCCCUSA.

Related efforts include the international Roman Catholic-Pentecostal dialogue and the World Alliance of Reformed Churches-Pentecostal dialogue. As a result of my audience with the Ecumenical Patriarch Bartholomew on June 17, 2009, in Istanbul, Turkey, I have been asked to initiate an Orthodox-Pentecostal theological preparatory committee with a view toward becoming bilateral. National dialogues

23. Cf. Jerry L. Sandidge, "An Update on the Ecumenical Activities of Pentecostals," *Experiences of the Spirit/Conference on Pentecostal and Charismatic Research in Europe at Utrecht University 1989*, ed. Jan A. B. Jongeneel (Frankfurt: Lang, 1991) 245.

24. Dale T. Irvin, "'Drawing All Together in One Bond of Love': the Ecumenical Vision of William J. Seymour and the Azusa Street Revival," *Journal of Pentecostal Theology* 6 (1995) 26. As was reported in a special edition of *Ecumenical Trends* (nos. 3 and 4, 1992) and *Tychique* (no. 1, 1992), established organizations such as the World Council of Churches and pan-continental organizations serving Pentecostal and charismatic scholars (CEPLA/EPLA, ACTA, CPCRE, SPS) in addition to other international groups of some notoriety (WEF, Lausanne, PFNA, PWC, EPTA) were amply represented at Brighton '91. Mention is made of the forums in the disappointing "Whither Christian Unity?" by Thomas C. Oden in *Christianity Today* (August 3, 2002) 46–50.

involving Pentecostals have taken place in Finland, the Netherlands, and the USA. Also of interest is the Word, Kingdom, and Spirit Conference in Malaka, Malaysia, in 1994. The issue of *Transformation* featured at the conference concentrated on Pentecostal perspectives on social issues. A respectable showing was made by Protestant charismatics while classical Pentecostals were few in number.

The majority of Pentecostals engaging conciliar ecumenists are academicians. North American Pentecostal scholars, who freely criticize ecclesiarchs seeking the approval of the National Association of Evangelicals (NAE), should examine their broad support for Evangelical opinions and evaluations of the Pentecostal movement. Boundary lines were drawn clearly by the American Academy of Religion (AAR), when in the early 1980s I tried to organize an AAR section devoted to Pentecostalism.[25] It seemed that almost every group except Pentecostals could be allowed to speak for themselves. The Pentecostal movement does not need to be co-opted by those outside but should have the same right of self-determination exercised by historic traditions. An example is the special edition of *Concilium*, edited by Jürgen Moltmann and Karl-Josef Kuschel, that allowed Pentecostals to speak for themselves while engaging Christendom at large.[26] It is clear that a genuine model of ecumenism that engages the global Pentecostal and charismatic movements must come from inside the community.

Particular opportunities exist for cooperation in the arena of the WCC. Despite protestations to the contrary, the WCC is more than a mere "council" of churches. WCC officials and boards located in Geneva carry momentum and ecumenical influence of their own. It is in this arena where the stakes are high for Pentecostals, and invitations are not something that should be taken lightly. Conciliar ecumenists, and the WCC in particular, have increasingly been consumed by discussions on universalism. In whatever ways Pentecostals conceive of the Spirit outside the church, and however they might rightly engage in inter-faith conversations, they have generally not affirmed a ubiquitous salvific presence.[27] Outside of inflammatory issues, ecclesiarchs will ask what

25. A Pentecostal-Charismatic Movements Consultation was eventually established in 2008.

26. Jürgen Moltmann and Karl-Josef Kuschel, eds., *Pentecostal Movements as an Ecumenical Challenge*, Concilium 3 (London: SCM, 1996).

27. Jürgen Moltmann commends Tony Richie's reading of IPHC founder J. H. King's concept of the "religion of Christ." See the preface of Veli-Matti Kärkkäinen, *The*

benefits flow from joining such an organization. A representative of the Georgia Orthodox Church was permitted to speak during a business plenary session of the WCC General Assembly in Harare. He explained that his church was not made up of "fanatics," but nonetheless made the painful decision to leave the WCC in order to avoid schism. In similar ways, some Pentecostal denominations are connected on various levels with groups around the world that staunchly resist relations with the WCC and many of its member churches. The dividing question remains how a Pentecostal denomination can justify a major investment in conciliar ecumenism when their own concerns are generally under-represented and the engagement puts at risk their loyalties to the PWF.

Profoundly relevant for an answer to this question is the theological diversity contained in the canonical record. Ernst Käsemann brought to the 1963 Montreal conference on Faith and Order his publicized view that the New Testament canon does not dismiss but in fact contains "the basis for the multiplicity of the confessions."[28] Coping with the additional realities of diverse cultural and social contexts also strengthens the argument of Jürgen Moltmann that the church should not be seeking "uniformity but should be working through the ecumenical movement to expand its range of unlikeness."[29] Contact alone is not compromise. As has been said by the Waldensians in Italy, no one church has all the marks of the church, and the more we fellowship with other churches, the more we represent the body of Christ rather than compromise the unity of that body.

Although there is some merit to the idea of mere spiritual unification, I do not believe that the tangible work of theologians and church administrators is to be ignored. Perhaps, Emil Brunner's thoughts in his

---

Spirit in the World: Emerging Pentecostal Theologies in Global Contexts (Grand Rapids: Eerdmans, 2009). Richie's essay is entitled "Azusa-era Optimism: Bishop J. H. King's Pentecostal Theology of Religions as a Possible Paradigm for Today."

28. Käsemann quoted by James D.G. Dunn, *Unity and Diversity in the New Testament: An Inquiry into the Character of Earliest Christianity* (Philadelphia: Westminster, 1977), 376. This view compares favorably with Dunn's perspective that "there was no single normative form of Christianity in the first century." Cf. William G. Rusch, *Ecumenism: A Movement Toward Church Unity* (Philadelphia: Fortress, 1985), chapter 1; John R.W. Stott and Basil Meeking, eds., *The Evangelical-Roman Catholic Dialogue on Mission, 1977–1984: A Report* (Grand Rapids: Eerdmans, 1986) 19–20; Anton W. J. Houtepen, "Toward An Ecumenical Vision of the Church," *One in Christ* 25.3 (1989) 217–37.

29. Jürgen Moltmann, "Pentecost and the Theology of Life," in Moltmann and Kuschel, *Pentecostalism as an Ecumenical Challenge*, 123–34.

book, *The Misunderstanding of the Church*, serve as suitable encouragement for balanced work in this regard.[30] Brunner exerted a great deal of effort working on behalf of Christian unity even though his expectations seem somewhat low. Full unity could not be achieved, he thought, but at least progress could be made by avoiding hostilities, and helping rather than hurting one another. As a constant traveler, I believe the rate at which the world "decreases in size" demands that all traditions devote attention to living out the shared identity in Christ. Since the Pentecostal movement is global and significant, it cannot shrink from its ecumenical responsibilities. It cannot remain simply introspective. It must engage responsibly other Christians, other religions, and the whole of creation.

30. Emil Brunner, *The Misunderstanding of the Church* (Philadelphia: Westminster, 1953).

3

Joining the World Council of Churches

The Ecumenical Story of Pentecostalism in Chile

Carmelo E. Álvarez

The official commitment of Pentecostal churches to the World Council of Churches (WCC) begins in Latin America—not in the ecumenically rich and stable soil of the modern European or North American continents, but in the turbulent political and religious environment of Chile. This essay is an attempt to trace and analyze the ecumenical commitment of the first two Pentecostal churches that joined the WCC: the Pentecostal Church of Chile (*Iglesia Pentecostal de Chile*) and the Pentecostal Mission Church (*Misión Iglesia Pentecostal*) of Chile. I intend to show how these Pentecostal churches responded to their own ecumenical context and assumed a leading pastoral and prophetic stance in times of national crisis and confrontation. My analysis starts by identifying the roots and identity, both sociologically and historically, of these two Pentecostal denominations and their ecumenical commitment. Since this story is also related to the larger Latin American and Caribbean ecumenical movements, I begin by outlining the nature of indigenous Pentecostalism in Chile. I then describe some pioneering efforts of Chilean Pentecostals in the ecumenical movement of the twentieth century, and conclude with a brief analysis of Pentecostalism and the state of ecumenical affairs in Chile.

INDIGENOUS PENTECOSTALISM IN CHILE

Indigenous Pentecostalism[1] (known as "*criollo*" or *creole* in South America) grew out of the local mainline Protestant churches. At the same time, it holds strong roots in popular Catholic culture, has an indigenous pastorate, and is economically and structurally independent of foreign missions.[2] Between 1907 and 1909, in Valparaiso, Chile, missionary doctor, Willis C. Hoover, began a revival campaign in the Methodist Episcopal Church.[3] All-night vigils, bible studies, and prayer groups energized a movement that eventually reached the capital city of Santiago. Yet, the movement also provoked schism, and congregations in Valparaiso and Santiago eventually left the group to form the Methodist Pentecostal Church. Nonetheless, the growing movement continued to expand despite further schisms and the formation of new Pentecostal churches.[4]

1. Manuel Gaxiola in his valuable typology of Latin American Pentecostalism calls this group "Autochthonous Pentecostal Churches" and makes a distinction by separating the "Oneness Churches" into a distinct category. The only difference between these two categories is doctrinal. Sociologically and liturgically, they have more or less the same principles and reflect the same social status among poor people in Mexico and elsewhere in Latin America. See Manuel Gaxiola, "Latin American Pentecostalism: A Mosaic within a Mosaic," *Pneuma: The Journal of the Society for Pentecostal Studies* 13.2 (1991) 107–29. Bernardo Campos calls classical Pentecostalism "international," and he refers to Indigenous or Creole Pentecostalism as "national with intermixture of roots." See Bernardo Campos, *De la reforma protestante a la pentecostalidad de la iglesi*a (Quito, Ecuador: CLAI, 1997) 96. See also Carmelo E. Álvarez, "Los pentecostales en América Latina: Ecuménicos o evangélicos?" *Kairos* 1 (December 1988) 9–14.

2. Juan Sepúlveda, "Pentecostal and Liberation Theology: Two Manifestations of the Work of the Holy Spirit for the Renewal of the Church," in *All Together in One Place*, eds. Harold D. Hunter and Peter D. Hocken (Sheffield: Sheffield Academic Press, 1993) 53. See also Karl-Wilhem Westmeier, *Protestant Pentecostalism in Latin America: A Study in the Dynamics of Mission* (London: Associated University Presses, 1999) 17, 70–71.

3. The most important source for the beginnings of the Pentecostal movement in Chile is still W. C. Hoover, *Historia del avivamiento pentecostal en Chile* (a private edition by the *Comunidad Teológica de Chile,* n.d.). For the important role played by Hoover as a Methodist "self supporting missionary" sent by Bishop William Taylor, see David Bundy, "Unintended Consequences: The Methodist Episcopal Missionary Society and the Beginnings of Pentecostalism in Norway and Chile," *Missiology* 37.2 (1999) 211–29. See also Luis Orellana Urtubia, "Breve Historia del Movimiento Pentecostal Chileno en su Primera Etapa (1909-1932)," (Licenciate thesis, Comunidad Teológica de Chile, 1989).

4. Humberto Muñoz, *Nuestros hermanos evangélicos* (Santiago: Ediciones Nueva Universidad, 1974) 217–52. Narciso Sepúlveda, "Breve síntesis histórica del movimiento pentecostal en Chile," in *Pentecostalismo y liberación: Una experiencia latinoamericana*, ed. Carmelo E. Álvarez (San Jose: DEI, 1992) 37–45.

With Hoover at the helm, the revival spread throughout Chile at a dizzying pace during the early decades of the twentieth century. Hoover mobilized believers for street evangelism, and organized them into squads of militants, who shared songs, bible readings, open-air preaching, and personal testimony. The purpose of these efforts was to animate the poor and marginalized with a simple but demanding Christian faith.[5]

Ecumenical relations developed initially through partnership with churches in neighboring countries and the United States. The Christian Church (Disciples of Christ) and the United Church of Christ in the United States established close ecumenical partnerships with Pentecostal churches in Latin America, specifically in Argentina, Chile, Cuba, Nicaragua, and Venezuela. The churches in these partnerships exchanged missionary personnel and engaged in mutual collaboration for theological education, development projects, and the sharing of short-term volunteer missionaries and volunteer lay-people delegations. These churches played a particularly crucial role in the formation of the Latin American Evangelical Pentecostal Commission (CEPLA) during the 1960s, a regional commission to promote Christian unity between Pentecostal churches and other denominations in Latin America. Pentecostal churches also significantly contributed to the formation of the Latin America Council of Churches (CLAI) a decade later and to the continuing recruitment of new members for the Council at its general assemblies.

The theological context and framework for ecumenical relationships of Pentecostals with other denominations are what many interpreters (including some Pentecostals) have called an "ecumenism of the Spirit."[6] The phrase gained particular momentum during the organization of CEPLA in 1990 and, later, at the General Assembly of CLAI in Concepción, Chile, in 1995. Several historic churches have responded by taking seriously the importance and relevance of Pentecostalism in Latin America and engaging the Pentecostal churches in research and dialogues, exchanges, and forums.[7] The late American Methodist

5. Juan Sepúlveda, "El nacimiento y desarrollo de las iglesias evangélicas," in *Historia del pueblo de Dios en Chile: La evolución del cristianismo desde la perspectiva de los pobres,* ed. Mariano Salinas (Santiago: CEHILA-REHUE, 1987) 247–77.

6. See the essay by Raymond R. Pfister, "Ecumenism of the Spirit: Toward a Pentecostal Pedagogy of Reconciliation," chapter 5.

7. The Disciples of Christ started an ecumenical partnership with several Pentecostal churches in Latin America and the Caribbean, the Evangelical Pentecostal Union of Venezuela in 1963, the Pentecostal Christian Church of Cuba in 1976, and

theologian and ecumenist, Albert C. Outler, relates this idea to specific moments in which the Spirit acts in the "fullness of time" providing "ecumenical epiphanies," moments of unexpected divine revelation, which were loaded with joy and enthusiasm.[8] These "ecumenical epiphanies" are always opportunities to live intensely the promise of an ecumenical dialogue in which the Holy Spirit opens new "frontier spaces of pneumatology." Outler's definition strives for an ecumenical agenda in which the "ecumenism of the Spirit" is a concrete commitment to a praxis and life as witnesses in the world and an openness to the calling of God's Spirit to newness of life in all its fullness. The implications of this perspective can be observed with particular clarity among Pentecostals in Latin America. The Argentinean missiologist, Guillermo Cook, comments: "Christian unity, for Pentecostals, is a theological fact based upon the unity of the Trinity, the present and the future hope that drives them, both a factor in and a requirement for the growth of the church and—for an increasing number of perceptive leaders—an imperative in the contemporary era of the divine *kairós*."[9] Christian unity, as Cook sees it, provides an inclusive and holistic approach to Christian mission based on the action of the Holy Spirit, manifested in experience, and expressed in the commitment to promote unity in the church and the world. A particular case of this approach is the Assembly of the WCC in New Delhi, in 1961, which represented a turning point for the ecumenical movement, when both Pentecostal and Orthodox churches were received as full members of the WCC.[10] Two Pentecostal churches joined the WCC at that time: the Pentecostal Church of Chile and the Pentecostal Mission Church of

---

the Christian Mission Church of Nicaragua in the 1980s. The United Church of Christ established an ecumenical partnership with the Pentecostal Church of Chile in the 1980s. The Presbyterian Church (USA) has had relationships with several Pentecostal churches. See Benjamín Gutiérrez and Dennis A. Smith, *In the Power of the Spirit: The Pentecostal Challenge to Historic Churches in Latin America* (Louisville: Latin American Center for Pastoral Studies-Alliance of Presbyterian and Reformed Churches in Latin America, 1996).

8. Albert C. Outler, "Pneumatology as an Ecumenical Frontier," in *To the Wind of God's Spirit: Reflections on the Canberra Theme*, ed. Emilio Castro (Geneva: WCC Publications, 1990) 9–20.

9. Guillermo Cook, "Interchurch Relations: Exclusion, Ecumenism, and the Poor," in *Power, Politics, and Pentecostals in Latin America*, eds. Edward L. Cleary and Hannah W. Stewart-Gambino (Boulder: Westview, 1997) 77–96.

10. John A. Mackay, *Ecumenics: The Science of the Church Universal* (Old Tappan, NJ: Prentice Hall, 1964) 197–98.

Chile.[11] The process of ecumenical participation by these two Pentecostal churches needs to be analyzed within the larger picture of ecumenical cooperation and the image of an ecumenism of the Spirit. It is a story of ecumenical solidarity.

PENTECOSTAL PIONEERS IN THE ECUMENICAL MOVEMENT

The late Enrique Chávez was originally an active member of the Methodist Pentecostal Church, also known as Jotabeche, and a close collaborator of Presiding Bishop Umaña of the Methodist Pentecostal Church of Chile. In 1946, Chávez decided to leave Jotabeche because of discrepancies over the handling of finances in the church. He established a congregation in the city of Curicó that soon became the center of a new movement, the Pentecostal Church of Chile.[12] The next year, Chávez became General Superintendent of the Pentecostal Church of Chile. Later, in 1966, he became General Bishop and remained in that position until his death in 1990.[13]

The Pentecostal Church of Chile became a member of the WCC during the 1961 New Delhi Assembly. Chávez admitted that it was no easy task. Many pastors in the Pentecostal Church of Chile had reservations, particularly because other Pentecostal churches in Chile were very critical of the World Council. Many churches within the WCC also had reservations about the membership of Pentecostal churches, in general, and from the Third World, in particular.[14] But both sides took the risks involved as part of their ecumenical dedication. In addition, the Pentecostal Church of Chile sought to establish fraternal relationships

11. Marta Palma, "A Pentecostal Church in the Ecumenical Movement," *The Ecumenical Review* 37.2 (1985) 223–29.

12. Bishop Enrique Chávez, interview by Carmelo E. Álvarez, August-November 1983.

13. Carmelo E. Álvarez, Pedro Correa, and Manuel Poblete, *Historia de la iglesia pentecostal de Chile* (Santiago: *Editorial REHUE*, n.d.) 21–52. See Manuel Poblete, *Antecedentes para una historia: Iglesia pentecostal de Chile, conferencias anuales de 1984*. This is a short document with three important appendixes, the first ever written as a public document about the history of this church.

14. Walter Hollenweger, *El pentecostalismo: historia y doctrinas* (Buenos Aires: La Aurora, 1976) 441–44. In 1985 the author had two long conversations in Pasadena, California, with David du Plessis, who confirmed these observations. See David du Plessis, "Un pentecostalismo y el movimiento ecuménico," in *El espíritu habla a las iglesias*, comp. Theodore Runyon, trans. Alba Barosio (Buenos Aires, Argentina: La Aurora, 1978) 95–106.

with Pentecostal churches in North America, and Chávez decided to explore a relationship with the Pentecostal Holiness Church in the United States, but noted that "they were too conservative for us."[15] In turn, the Pentecostal Holiness Church did not like the fact the Pentecostal Church of Chile was a member of the World Council of Churches.[16] While conservative Pentecostal groups criticized the official ecumenism of the Chilean churches, membership in the WCC opened new doors to other ecumenical relations.

The United Church of Christ invited Chávez to its General Synod in 1982. The atmosphere was good, and "they were very respectful of our positions. They did not understand our doctrinal positions, but tried honestly to understand our Pentecostal experience."[17] Eventually, the United Church of Christ, and later the Disciples of Christ, through its "Common Ministry in Latin America and the Caribbean" program, became ecumenical partners with the Pentecostal Church of Chile. These relationships have been enhanced by the exchange of delegations, pastors, and missionary personnel.

Chávez worked throughout his life in the ecumenical movement. He admired many important figures in the established ecumenical circles.[18] He trusted many ecumenical leaders to the point of allowing their active participation in theological education, preaching, the training of Sunday school teachers, and leadership for youth and women's retreats.[19] Along with other Pentecostals from Chile, Chávez participated in the II Latin American Conference in Lima, Peru, 1961, and at the III Latin American Conference in Buenos Aires, where he met with Gabriel Vaccaro of the Church of God in Argentina. Vaccaro and Chávez became good friends and actively promoted the Pentecostal cause in ecumenical circles.[20] Vaccaro was first vice president of CLAI for many years,

15. Bishop Enrique Chávez, interview by Carmelo E. Álvarez, August-November 1983.

16. Ibid.

17. Ibid.

18. Irma Palma, ed., *En tierra extraña: Un itinerario del pueblo pentecostal Chileno* (Santiago: AMERINDIA, 1988) 155–70.

19. These were the experiences that the author and his wife Raquel shared with the Pentecostal Church of Chile the second semester of 1983 as fraternal workers on behalf of the Disciples Division of Overseas Ministries during a sabbatical year.

20. Bishop Enrique Chávez, interview by Carmelo E. Álvarez, August-November 1983.

while Chávez was second vice-president for six years. Both were actively involved in the Evangelical Union in Latin America (UNELAM) and the process that led to the formation of CLAI.

According to pastor Narciso Sepúlveda of the Pentecostal Mission Church, he and his family first joined the Evangelical Pentecostal Church in 1935. It was a process of conversion to the Pentecostal faith in the context of a serious personal crisis. His father abandoned the family and his mother was left alone as the sole provider. The Pentecostal community became their second family and provided a welcoming and accepting experience for his mother and siblings.[21] Sepúlveda embraced the Pentecostal experience "for life." At one time, his father even tried to be an obstacle, opposing his active participation in a local Pentecostal congregation. But Sepúlveda persevered and eventually became convinced that pastoral ministry in a Pentecostal congregation was an important call.[22]

Over the years, Sepúlveda realized that the Evangelical Pentecostal Church of Chile had a very authoritharian and rigid leadership. He and other leaders decided that the intolerance, lack of dialogue, and disrespect for lay persons in the denomination, as well as an anti-intellectual attitude, were pushing them out of the church. In contrast, they desired a denomination of "open doors," including a strong ecumenical vision and commitment. The Pentecostal Mission Church of Chile represented these ideas when it was founded in 1952 and that same year began to join the membership of different ecumenical organizations in Chile and throughout Latin America. The church joined the Evangelical Council of Chile, the Union of Latin American Evangelical Youth, the Union of Evangelical Women of Chile, and became the first Pentecostal church along with the Pentecostal Church of Chile to join the WCC.[23] The decision to join the WCC represented an international ecumenical gesture that began a fruitful period of ecumenical solidarity among Pentecostals and other churches in Chile.

21. Palma, *En tierra extraña,* 199–200.

22. Ibid., 201–3.

23. Ibid., 204–6. See also Frans Kamsteeg, "Prophetic Pentecostalism in Chile. A Case Study on Religion and Development Policy" (Ph.D. diss., Free University, Amsterdam, 1995) 85–89.

PENTECOSTALS AND ECUMENICAL SOLIDARITY IN CHILE

The antecedents to the process of ecumenical solidarity can be found in 1941, when the Evangelical Council of Chile was established, and important Pentecostal churches began to participate actively in ecumenical matters. In 1960, a new entity, Evangelical Christian Aid (*Ayuda Cristiana Evangélica*, herafter ACE), was formed as an organization to extend interdenominational cooperation. Many Pentecostal churches joined the venture, and ACE ultimately became a main platform for membership in the WCC. The fact that UNELAM, a Latin American ecumenical organization promoting unity among the churches, had its headquarters in Santiago, helped in providing space for cooperation and coordination, particularly in national emergencies.[24]

The event that triggered an immediate commitment to ecumenical solidarity in Chile was the 1960 earthquake, a national crisis that provided opportunities for interaction and joint organization by both Pentecostal and Evangelical groups. According to Juan Sepúlveda, ecumenical solidarity in Chile was theologically based on "the defense of life and the promotion of human rights."[25] Several Pentecostal churches and mainline denominations started a program for theological education in Chile known as the Theological Community of Chile.[26] The joint activities received a further boost in 1973 with the coup d'etat against president Salvador Allende. The churches celebrated an ecumenical *Te Deum* at the Roman Catholic Cathedral of Santiago that promoted unity among the churches and gave high visibility to their willingness to help in promoting the unity of the Chilean people.[27]

On August 9, 1973, one month before the coup d'etat, the Ecumenical Fraternity of Chile (*Fraternidad Ecuménica de Chile*) was founded amidst serious political polarization. The Roman Catholic Church, the Orthodox Churches, historic Protestant churches, the Jewish community, and some Pentecostal churches decided to form this body as an attempt to improve and promote Christian unity and reconciliation in times of political

24. Ibid., 22

25. Juan Sepúlveda, "La defensa de los derechos humanos como experiencia ecuménica," *Persona y Sociedad* 17.3 (2003) 21–22.

26. CEPLA, ed., *Proceso de unidad y cooperación pentecostal en América Latina, 1960-1992* (Maracaibo: CEPLA, 1992) 3.

27. Sepúlveda, "La defensa de los derechos humanos," 21–22.

confrontation.[28] Some conservative churches were praying for a military intervention.

Roman Catholic Cardinal, Raúl Silva Henríquez, and Lutheran Bishop, Helmut Frenz, became key figures in responding immediately after the coup d'etat to the national crisis that included massive violation of human rights and the disappearance of many Chilean citizens. It was a time of turmoil and confusion. The Cooperation Committee for Peace (*Comité de Cooperacion para la Paz*) soon organized a network of solidarity and cooperation with ecumenical organizations in the United States and Europe, including the National Council of Churches of Christ in the USA and the WCC.

However, these efforts provoked serious confrontations with the Pinochet regime to the point that, due to the consistent and continuous pressures from the government, it was decided to close the Committee. Henríquez then established by decree the Vicary of Solidarity (*La Vicaría de la Solidaridad*) in the Diocese of Santiago. Even though the Vicary was mainly a pastoral entity in the diocese, it maintained and pursued a visible ecumenical commitment and strategy.[29] Father Santiago Tapia, Vicar General, was respected and revered as a true ecumenist, pastor, and person of integrity and passion for justice. He attended both the assembly of churches that decided to form the Latin American Council of Churches in Oaxtepec, Mexico, in 1978, and the official constitution of that body in Huampaní, Peru, in 1982. He remained a trusted friend and colleague for many in the ecumenical movement in Latin America.[30]

On the Pentecostal side, ACE was reactivated, and the Evanglical Service for Ecumenical Development (SEPADE) was founded by the Pentecostal Mission Church in 1978. The main emphasis centered on responding to the lingering national crisis with food aid, and the promotion of health and education. But the ecumenical activities among the Pentecostal churches also moved into the area of leadership formation, community development, organization, and theological education. SEPADE remains a significant institution among Pentecostals in ecumenical scope and purpose to this day.[31]

28. Ibid., 23.

29. Ibid., 24.

30. "Conversando con Monseñor Santiago Tapia, Vicario de la Solidaridad," *Evangelio y Sociedad* 3 (July 1986) 4–8.

31. Kamsteeg, *Prophetic Pentecostalism in Chile*, 87–89.

An important culmination of this process of ecumenical solidarity is the formation of the Christian Confraternity of Churches (*Confraternidad Cristiana de Iglesias*). This body provided the space and the option for a public prophetic role played by the historic Protestant churches and Pentecostal churches in Chile. In many ways, it provided for the majority of believers in Chile a hope much needed in times of confrontation and rigid dictatorship as well as the necessary reflection to envision the return of democracy.[32] The Pentecostal churches in Chile were key protagonists in the process.

In 1982, at the founding of CLAI, in Huampaní, Peru, three Pentecostal leaders were elected to the new board, including Enrique Chávez as second vice-president. Other Pentecostal churches from Chile joined the Council.[33] Roger Cabezas, President of the Faith and Holiness Pentecostal Church of Costa Rica, summarizes the process by which these Pentecostal churches committed to an ecumenical vocation within the ecumenical movement in Latin America.[34]

1. Investigation and deepening of the understanding of the origins of the Pentecostal faith and the particular contribution of Pentecostal identity as a catalyst agent for social changes.
2. Examination of the theological heritage from Christianity in the West as an individualistic ethical approach to social problems.
3. Christian formation through theological reflection.
4. The experience of an "ecumenism of the Spirit" as an integral approach of action at the personal level, in the church, and for the whole of creation.
5. Promotion of a new consciousness of the role of Pentecostal churches as servants of the people.
6. A sharing of the Pentecostal experiences in daily life from the testimonial perspective.
7. Examination of the critical aspects of televangelism and the radio as a possible disfigurement of the Pentecostal message and ecumenical commitment.

32. Sepúlveda, "La defensa de los derechos humanos," 25–28.

33. Carlos A. Valle, ed., *Semilla de comunión* (Buenos Aires: CLAI, 1983) 155–64.

34. Roger Cabezas, "Despertar ecuménico del pentecostalismo latinoamericano," in *CEPLA. Jubileo: La fiesta del Espíritu. Identidad y Misión del Pentecostalismo Latinoamericano* (Maracaibo: CEPLA, 2001) 111.

8. Welcoming other Pentecostal churches in joining an ecumenism of the Spirit.
9. Continuation of the process of Latin American encounters (*encuentros*) that propitiate and contribute to ecumenism, Pentecostal identity, and mission in Latin America.
10. Creation of spaces for critical thinking, dialogue, and challenge to Pentecostalism in Latin American.
11. Theological reflection on Pentecostalism in Latin America with its unique testimonial-experiential approach.

In light of this process, it can be said that the two Pentecostal churches in Chile made several important contributions to the Pentecostal and ecumenical movement in Latin America. The Pentecostal Church of Chile and the Pentecostal Mission Church of Chile are pioneer churches of a movement that is committed to the ecumenical dialogue but often rejected by many conservative churches and isolated from traditional mainline denominations. Both churches advanced the struggle for a genuine Pentecostal identity, even though they did not have the theological sophistication or education of other ecumenical leaders. They worked to provide a solid theological education for their national communities, and the leaders and their churches were active participants in the formation of the Latin American Council of Churches, paving the way for the organization of Latin American Pentecostal Commission. The legacy of the Pentecostal Church of Chile and the Pentecostal Mission Church of Chile is a Pentecostal movement in Latin America that is faithful to the fundamental principles of a Pentecostal identity, profoundly Evangelical, deeply committed to an ecumenical vocation, and clearly identified with the poor and marginalized. A new generation of Pentecostal leaders is making a significant contribution along these same lines, with remarkable success.[35]

35. A number of articles and books written by a new generation of Pentecostal leaders involved in CLAI, WCC, Centro Medellín, SEPADE, and other ecumenical organizations illustrates this point: Roger Cabezas, *CLAI: Experiencia de un ecumenismo latinoamericano de base* (Lima: CLAI, 1982); Gamaliel Lugo, "*Base docial del pentecostalismo latinoamericano*," *Revista Cevej* 11.27 (1989) 10–14; Juan Sepúlveda, "Reflections on the Pentecostal Contribution to the Mission of the Church in Latin America," *Journal of Pentecostal Theology* 1 (1992) 93–108; Daniel Godoy, "Pentecostalismo: Signo de unidad," *Pastoral Popular* 227 (April 1993) 30–33; Daniel Farfán, "Somos ecuménicos los pentecostales," *Pastoral Popular* 235 (December 1993) 30-31; Fernando Oshige, "Entrevista con Rev. Orlando Silva," *Signos de Vida* 3 (1993) 3–5;

These churches united their efforts to inspire a movement toward unity among Pentecostals in Latin America, and thus created the conditions and confidence necessary to challenge the churches to participate actively in the ecumenical movement through their membership in the WCC. The process that started in 1960 as a response to a national crisis evolved to become a more consistent attempt to create an atmosphere of mutuality and respect, the discernment of a Pentecostal identity, and promotion of an integral and holistic evangelism that includes an openness to dialogue and ecumenical cooperation. Today, these churches continue their struggle as Pentecostals in the ecumenical agenda and vocation for service and commitment to life and the defense of human rights. They have expanded their ministry to ecological projects, for example, the Shalom Project of the Pentecostal Church of Chile, co-sponsored with the Common Global Board Ministries of the United Church of Christ and the Christian Church in the USA and Canada. SEPADE continues its role as a ministry of social service and leadership formation from an ecumenical perspective.[36] The history of ecumenism among the Pentecostal churches in Chile has cast a bold image for the future of the ecumenical movement in Latin America. It is marked by a willingness to be changed for the purpose of a common goal: unity and solidarity among the churches in times of crisis and as a testimony to the world.

Juan Sepúlveda, *The Andean Highlands: An Encounter with Two Forms of Christianity* (Geneva: WCC Publications, 1997); Bernardo Campos, *De la reforma protestante a la pentecostalidad de la iglesia: Debate sobre el pentecostalismo en América Latina* (Quito: CLAI, 1997).

36. Edward L. Cleary and Juan Sepúlveda, "Chilean Pentecostalism: Coming of Age," in Cleary and Stewart-Gambino, *Power, Politics, and Pentecosatls in Latin America*, 97–121.

4

Guidelines for Ecumenical Dialogue with Pentecostals

Lessons from the Netherlands

Paul van der Laan

When I finished my dissertation in 1988 on an ecumenical perspective of Pentecostalism, one could hardly have envisioned how relevant this topic would become in the following decades.[1] Today, the international dialogue between the Roman Catholic Church and some classical Pentecostals is in its sixth quinquennium, and the international dialogue between Pentecostals and representatives of the World Alliance of Reformed Churches just entered its second quinquennium.[2] The Pentecostal chair of both dialogues, Cecil M. Robeck Jr., aptly summarizes the situation: "Pentecostal interest and participation in ecumenism are still in their infancy. Those who enter the field at this time will help to define the field for the future of Pentecostal participation. A variety of churches and organizations exist that are open to Pentecostal participation. The building of bridges between denominations is a rewarding challenge that can bear good fruit."[3] Beyond my wildest dreams, the ecumenical dialogue with Pentecostal participation also flourished in the Netherlands. Various national dialogues began of which two are still

1. Paul van der Laan, "The Question of Spiritual Unity: The Dutch Pentecostal Movement in Ecumenical Perspective" (Ph.D. diss., University of Birmingham, 1988).

2. See chapter 11 in this collection.

3. Cecil M. Robeck Jr., "Pentecostals and Christian Unity: Facing the Challenge," *Pneuma: The Journal of the Society for Pentecostal Studies* 26.2 (2004) 307–38, here 338.

ongoing. The dialogue with the Re-Reformed Churches in the Netherlands (*Gereformeerde Kerken in Nederland*, hereafter RRCN) lasted for three years (1992–95), and dialogue with a number of interdenominational missionary organizations began in 1998. The most recent dialogue with the Roman Catholic Church started in 1999. I was privileged to participate in all of these dialogues as a Pentecostal delegate. Other important developments were the growth of the indigenous migrant-churches, the Alpha-courses, the merge of the two largest Pentecostal denominations and the integration of the Azusa Theological College, including the establishment of an Academic Chair in Pentecostalism, at the Free University of Amsterdam. In this essay, I propose that the Netherlands can serve as a model for fruitful ecumenical dialogue with Pentecostals. I will begin by presenting a brief overview of the most significant ecumenical interchanges that have taken place in the Netherlands. This synopsis then allows me to assess the relationship of Pentecostalism and Christian unity and to offer guidelines for ecumenical dialogue with Pentecostals from the perspective of the lessons learned from the Netherlands.

THE NETHERLANDS: AN ECUMENICAL MODEL

The Netherlands occupied a leading role in the development of the ecumenical movement in the twentieth century. The World Council of Churches (WCC) was established in Amsterdam in 1948, and the Dutchman Willem A. Visser 't Hooft served as its first General Secretary. J. A. Hebly has suggested that "many call the Netherlands an 'ecumenical model,' an example worthy of imitation, while others, watching from afar, register shock at the changes taking place in the Lowlands."[4] W. Nijenhuis adds to this assessment, "Nowhere in the world outside the USA is the picture of the history of the Reformation as varied as it is in the Netherlands. This spiritual and ecclesiastical diversity is matched by a corresponding diversity of cultural, social, and political organizations."[5] The Pentecostal movement, however, initially did not experience the tolerance and ecumenical openness characteristic of the country. On the contrary, in spite of the fervent plea for unity by the pioneer and leader

4. J. A. Hebly, ed., *Lowland Highlights: Church and Oecumene in the Netherlands* (Kampen: Kok, 1972) 5.

5. W. Nijenhuis, "The Dutch Reformation," in Hebly, *Lowland Highlights-Church and Oecumene in the Netherlands*, 22–31, here 23.

of the Dutch Pentecostal movement, Gerrit Polman,[6] Pentecostals initially were looked down upon as an insignificant, fanatic sect that would soon disappear. Only a few open-minded Dutch Reformed ministers took some personal interest.[7] Polman himself had expressed that it was his desire that the Pentecostal movement would ultimately "loose itself in the body of Christ."[8] At the end of his ministry he continued to stress the goal of unity.

> We belong to everybody, we are not a sect and avoid every sectarian spirit, we want to be a blessing for everybody and do not aim to become big ourselves, but to help the common cause. May the Pentecostal Spirit be poured out in every church of whatever name, that is our prayer.[9]

The controversy about divine healing in the 1950s opened up an unexpected interest by the Netherlands Reformed Church (*Nederlands Hervormde Kerk*) that seemed to answer Polman's prayer.

The Pastoral Letter of the Netherlands Reformed Church

When David J. du Plessis visited Holland in 1959, he observed clear signs of the movement of the Holy Spirit:

> My visit to Holland in June gave me the opportunity to observe at first hand the mighty work of the Holy Spirit in the Netherlands Reformed Church. I felt a movement in that country that can only be sensed by people who are truly filled with the Spirit. A genuine Pentecostal tide is rising within that church . . . I am convinced that America cannot boast of a further and deeper reaching movement of God than Holland.[10]

A year later, the Netherlands Reformed Church published a remarkable pastoral letter, entitled "The Church and the Pentecostal Groups" (*De Kerk en de Pinkstergroepen*). In spite of its brevity and relatively simple content, it was received with enthusiasm and approval by most main-

6. Cornelius van der Laan, *Sectarian Against His Will: Gerrit Roelof Polman (1868-1932) and the Birth of Pentecostalism in the Netherlands*, Studies in Evangelicalism 21 (Metuchen: Scarecrow, 1991).

7. See van der Laan, *The Question of Spiritual Unity*, 52–63.

8. G. R. Polman, "Uit den Arbeid," *Spade Regen* 18.1 (April 15, 1925) 14.

9. [G. R. Polman], "Spade Regen," *Spade Regen* 22.12 (March 15, 1930) 190–91.

10. David J. du Plessis, "Echo van de Opwekking in de Kerken," *Kracht van Omhoog* 23.2 (July 25, 1959) 7–8.

line churches as well as by Pentecostals. It is probably the earliest official publication in which a mainline church acknowledges the important contributions of the Pentecostal movement to the church and which seeks answers within its own denominational context. Nevertheless, the original intent was rather protective, as is demonstrated by the initial letter of the Synodal Board to the proposed committee members:

> The Synodal Board is of the opinion that a to be published writing should not only contain teaching and guidance to the church, but also investigate the reasons for the origin of these movements in the life, confession and work of the Netherlands Reformed Church and show a means by which the growth of these movements could be prevented.[11]

Du Plessis did not believe that the time was ripe for the Pentecostal movement to consider the question of membership in the WCC, but he did notice a remarkable openness. He compared the Pentecostals with a busy, annoying child and the church with an old man sleeping in a chair and concluded that "they both have their own downsides, but at least the baby is very much alive!"[12] In December 1960, the pastoral letter was finally published, with an introduction from the Synodal Board. Over a period of nine years, it reached four reprints and a total circulation of 12,000 copies.[13]

In 1962, Feitse Boerwinkel, the chairman of the committee who wrote the initial draft of the pastoral letter, wrote a pamphlet entitled "The Pentecostal Groups" (*De Pinkstergroepen*) in which he stressed the ecumenical challenge succinctly:

> The Pentecostal movement asks the people of the church to read their Bible again concerning the promises of God towards His assembly. She is asking the people of the church whether they are satisfied with the present situation of impotence and if not, if it would not be a good thing to simply, but strong in faith, pray for the powerful manifestation of the Spirit who is already given to the church.[14]

11. Synodal Board, "Letter to the Committee for the Study of Sectarianism," The Hague (February 13, 1958).

12. J. Swijnenburg, "Verslag van het gesprek met ds. du Plessis op woensdag 24 juni 1959 op de Horst te 9 uur v.m.," report of meeting with David du Plessis, June 24, 1959, 2.

13. *Herderlijk schrijven van de Generale Synode der Nederlandse Hervormde Kerk, De Kerk en de Pinkstergroepen* (Den Haag: Boekencentrum, 1960).

14. F. Boerwinkel, *De Pinkstergroepen*, Oecumenische Leergang 5 (Den Haag: Stichting Plein, 1962) 13.

The "Brotherhood of Pentecostal Assemblies in the Netherlands" (hereafter "Brotherhood"), which later affiliated with the Assemblies of God, decided to issue an official answer to the pastoral letter, presented on October 13, 1962, to the Synodal Board of the Netherlands Reformed Church. The Committee for the Study of Sectarianism, which had written the "Pastoral Letter," met once with the committee that prepared the answer of the "Brotherhood." Though none of the participants who are still alive seem to remember much of this historic meeting, the minutes reveal an interesting and promising discussion.[15] The main theme chosen was the question, "What prevents us to be the church of Jesus Christ together?" A report in the Pentecostal periodical, *Pinksterboodschap*, mentions that the meeting took place "in a spirit of mutual frankness which resulted in some new perspectives."[16] When questioned about their attitude towards the WCC, the Pentecostal delegation answered that they objected to its liberal elements. Indeed, the group feared that the Bible was not fully accepted as the Word of God and that the WCC was too sympathetic to communism.[17]

The Pentecostals did not expect the Brotherhood to join the WCC, but were open to cooperation in practical areas. At the end, it was agreed to have two more meetings, one concerning the "exegesis of certain scriptures," and the other concerning "the work of the Holy Spirit." However, these meetings never took place. Eventually, the Committee for the Study of Sectarianism asked the Synodal Board whether it was desirable that the committee should continue this dialogue. The Board, which seemingly never expected this dialogue to last longer than one meeting, answered that the committee could consider its task completed.[18] Interest in the dialogue gradually diminished, because the Netherlands Reformed Church was caught up too much in political issues like nuclear armament, while the Pentecostals were focused on handling some

15. J. Swijnenburg, "Verslag van het gesprek van de Commissie voor het Herderlijk Schrijven 'De Kerk en de Pinkstergroepen' met enige vertegenwoordigers van de Broederschap van Pinkstergemeenten in Nederland," unpublished report, Driebergen, 28 May, 1963.

16. "Gesprek Nederlandse Hervormde Kerk-Broederschap van Pinkstergemeenten," *De Pinksterboodschap* 4.7 (1963) 11.

17. Minutes of meeting of the Netherlands Reformed "Committee for the Study of Sectarianism" and the Brotherhood delegates, Driebergen, May 28, 1963, 4.

18. Synodal Board, "Letter to the Committee for the Study of Sectarianism," The Hague, May 26, 1964.

turbulent divisions in their own ranks. Thus a promising dialogue was quenched before it really got started.

The Reference Document of the Re-Reformed Churches in the Netherlands

In 1967, the General Synod of the RRCN accepted a reference document entitled "The Work of the Holy Spirit in the Assembly." The subtitle reveals that it was really intended as a "reference document about the Pentecostal churches." In contrast to the pastoral letter of the Netherlands Reformed Church, this document resembled a classical refutation of the Pentecostal movement. From a Pentecostal perspective, the document was much more conservative than the pastoral letter. Nevertheless, it is meaningful that the second largest Reformed denomination in the Netherlands felt the need to supplement the pastoral letter with a document that promised to "pursue the Scriptural data in a more profound way." The motivation for the reference document were letters from various local churches of the Regional Synod of South Holland to the General Synod of the RRCN in which they requested " . . . clear guidance concerning the Pentecostal movement, and if possible general guidelines with reference to the pastoral and ecclesiastical handling of these church members; so as to further the unity of action in these churches."[19]

The RRCN decided to install a study committee, which would prepare a reference document on the Pentecostal groups. At the General Synod at Lunteren, on September 14, 1967, the document was accepted with hardly any question or comment and was published in 1968.[20] In spite of the fact that Kilian McDonnell called it "a major document from the historic churches" and included a complete translated version in his collection, *Presence, Power, Praise*, the text was hardly noticed in the Netherlands.[21] The publication raised little interest and there proved to be no need for a reprint.[22] Even the authors of the reference document

19. Particuliere Synode Zuid-Holland (Oost) der Gereformeerde Kerken in Nederland, letter by W. G. Scheeres of April 16, 1962 (!) to the General Synod of the Gereformeerde Kerken in Nederland.

20. *Acta van de Generale Synode van Amsterdam, Utrecht en Lunteren 1967–1968*, (Kampen: Kok) 123, art. 163.

21. Kilian McDonnell, *Presence, Power, Praise: Documentation Charismatic Renewal*, vol. 1 (Collegeville, MN: Liturgical, 1980) 147.

22. H. C. Endedijk, A. G. Kornet and G. Y. Vellenga, *Het werk van de Heilige Geest in de Gemeente" Voorlichtend geschrift over de Pinkstergroepen* (Kampen: Kok, 1968).

had to admit retrospectively that "it did not make an impact."[23] From amongst the Pentecostals, only the Brotherhood issued a serious response. In a letter to the General Synod of the RRCN they expressed their appreciation and stated:

> We regard ourselves attached to all who accept and confess Jesus Christ as the Son of God and Savior and with all who pray and reach out for "the Spirit of truth and revelation to know Him truly." We hope to discuss this document in our midst and inform you about the results in due time together with a stand and view of the Brotherhood of Pentecostal Assemblies.[24]

The fact that the Brotherhood gave a positive response to such a critical document can only be explained by the assumption that, at the same time, the Brotherhood was at its pinnacle of ecumenical openness. Their general superintendent, Dick Voordewind, had started a column in their periodical, *De Pinksterboodschap*, entitled "Between Church and Pentecost," in which he openly pleaded for dialogue with other denominations.[25] In their information booklet, the Brotherhood stated:

> We are grateful for the change in attitude in many churches with regard to the revelation of the Holy Spirit in our days. Whenever a talk with the churches and its representatives is possible, we will like to do so. On a local level the assembly is free to be represented as an observer on the local Council of Churches.[26]

The letter of the Brotherhood was read during the General Synod of the RRCN in 1968, but its receipt was merely noted.[27] The Brotherhood also published the letter partially in *De Pinksterboodschap* and advised Pentecostals to read the document. The only critical note raised was the fact that the historical information about the Brotherhood was not up to

23. H. C. Endedijk, personal interview at Velp, September 23, 1987. A. G. Kornet (interview December 9, 1987) and Prof. H. N. Ridderbos (December 14, 1987) agreed with this statement.

24. H. Ch. Sleebos on behalf of the Executive Council of the Broederschap van Pinkstergemeenten, Letter to the General Synod of the RRCN at Lunteren, March 2, 1968.

25. See D. Voordewind, "Tussen Kerk en Pinksteren," *De Pinksterboodschap* 8 (October 1967) 6.

26. Committee for literature of the Brotherhood, *Het zal zijn in de laatste dagen* (Den Haag: Broederschap van Pinkstergemeenten, 1968) 6.

27. *Acta van de Generale Synode van Amsterdam, Utrecht en Lunteren 1967 en 1968* (Kampen: Kok) 277 (art. 359).

date.[28] During the General Council of the Brotherhood, the same year, a committee was installed to prepare an official answer to the reference document, but the project was never finished.[29]

This unfortunate development can serve as an example of what may happen if opportunities for a genuine dialogue are not taken seriously. The sociological phenomenon of the Pentecostal movement was hardly recognized, and the brief historical perspective was already full of mistakes. Even worse, however, was the caricature made of Pentecostals in the reference document. The Synodal board refuted a movement, which only existed in their imagination. In the preface, the board stated "they expected that church councils and community members would obtain a correct viewpoint concerning the nature and background of the Pentecostal movement."[30] However, the booklet gave a shamefully distorted picture. If one realizes that this report was prepared over a period of three years and was checked twice by over a hundred people, including many scholars, one could almost doubt the academic standard in the Netherlands. The document leaves the impression that hardly any authentic Pentecostal literature was read. This ignorance concerning (Dutch) Pentecostal literature is even more embarrassing, when one considers that in 1964 an excellent bibliography of Pentecostal literature had been published in the renowned periodical, *Nederlands Theologisch Tijdschrift*.[31] The committee of the RRCN committed a major omission by not inviting any Pentecostals for a hearing. In the meeting with the Netherlands Reformed Church, the Brotherhood had shown itself to be eager to enter into mutual dialogue. In light of this intention, the opening phrase of the reference document that the authors "hoped to contribute towards a positive exchange of thoughts with supporters of the Pentecostal movement"[32] seems rather surprising. One of the main goals of the reference document was to stop the exodus from RRCN to the Pentecostal assemblies. Yet, the statistics show that the reverse was accomplished;

28. D. Voordewind, "Tussen Kerk en Pinksteren—Het werk van de Heilige Geest in de gemeente," *De Pinksterboodschap* 9.5 (May 1968) 12.

29. The minutes of the Executive Council of 14 September 1970 simply stated that "the manuscript has been mislaid." See "Minutes of the Executive Council of the Brotherhood," September 14, 1970, 1.

30. Endedijk, *Het werk van de Heilige Geest in de Gemeente*, 5.

31. Walter J. Hollenweger, "Literatur von und über die Pfingstbewegung," *Nederlands Theologisch Tijdschrift* 18.4 (1964) 289–306.

32. Endedijk, *Het werk van de Heilige Geest in de Gemeente*, 7.

in the year of publication, the number almost doubled.[33] As a result, the RRCN failed to enter into a genuine dialogue with Pentecostals.

Dialogue with the Re-Reformed Churches in the Netherlands

In 1976, the Synod of the RRCN decided to appoint some delegates for the study of the charismatic movement, in particular with reference to the questions of church-offices and water baptism.[34] This task resulted in a positive evaluation of the Charismatic movement and finally in the decision to give the committee a more permanent appointment to sustain the dialogue with the charismatic movement in the Netherlands, which had been organized as the so-called CWN (*Charismatische Werkgemeenschap Nederland*).[35] In 1992, I challenged this committee to open a dialogue with the Brotherhood, which had at that time appointed a committee for the same purpose. To my surprise, they reacted positively to my suggestion.[36] In this dialogue, a representative from the RRCN committee for Ecumenism and a representative of the CWN also participated. In their report to the Synod of the RRCN, the Ecumenism committee concluded that "they had experienced these conversations as open and fruitful."[37] The committee met seven times with a number of representatives of the Brotherhood over a period of more than two years and discussed such topics as the perception church members have of the Pentecostal movement, the perception Pentecostals have of the church, the transfer of members from the mainline churches to Pentecostal denominations and vice versa, prophecy, ethics, and pastoral care. Let me summarize the main conclusions of these discussions, which may serve as an illustration of how mutually beneficial an open dialogue can be, if we only engage it.[38]

33. See van der Laan, *The Question of Spiritual Unity*, 476.

34. *Acta van de Generale Synode van Maastricht 1975–1976 van de Gereformeerde Kerken in Nederland* (Kampen: Kok) 216 (art. 332).

35. See Vurig van Geest, "Een handreiking voor gesprekken over en met de charismatische beweging," Series Toerusting (Driebergen: Centrale voor vormingswerk, 1984).

36. *Bijlagen bij de Acta van de Generale Synode van de Gereformeerde Kerken in Nederland - Aalten 1993* (Kampen: Kok, 1995) 155.

37. *Bijlagen bij de Acta van de Generale Synode van de Gereformeerde Kerken in Nederland - Haren 1995* (Kampen: Kok, 1997) 499.

38. The following is a summary of *Bijlagen bij de Acta van de Generale Synode van de Gereformeerde Kerken in Nederland—Haren 1995*, 500–504.

1. The Perception Church Members Have of the Pentecostal Movement

- The Pentecostal movement holds great attraction for people who are looking for fulfillment in their lives.
- Pentecostals sing enthusiastically and use a variety of musical instruments.
- There is earnest prayer and experiential preaching.
- Pentecostals pray for the sick and have a practical involvement of their faith.
- Pentecostals tend to look upon themselves as superior over other church-members.
- In many Pentecostal churches, there is rivalry between the pastor, elders, and members.
- In ethical issues, the Bible is used too quickly and univocally.
- The preaching is quite elementary.
- Infant baptism is not accepted, and believers who want to join a Pentecostal church need to be re-baptized.

2. The Perception Pentecostals Have of the Church

- Pentecostals seem to have a more negative perception of the church.
- There is little spiritual life, especially with regard to prayer and relationship with God.
- There is insufficient openness to the work of the Holy Spirit.
- There is a great lack of sanctification.
- The theological education is too much geared toward the intellectual.
- Biblical exegeses and hermeneutics is too liberal.
- The liturgy is too static, old-fashioned, and impersonal.
- There is too little personal contact among members.
- The churches are too much engaged in politics and social help, instead of emphasizing the vertical relation with God and evangelization of the world.
- The distance between God and man is too big in the church.

3. Transfer of Members

Reasons why members of the RRCN transferred to a Pentecostal church:

- Enthusiastic Christianity
- Songs and music in the Pentecostal church
- Adult baptism by immersion
- Appealing sermons and call to conversion
- Warm social involvement with one another
- The security of life offered
- Active church-programs for children
- Former personal experiences with the Holy Spirit, which are acknowledged by the Pentecostals

Reasons why Pentecostals join the RRCN:

- More liberty and tolerance
- More openness to different opinions
- Room for homosexuals and acceptance of their lifestyle
- More profound preaching and biblical exposition
- A broader view on the church and its tradition.

4. Prophecy

Pentecostals indicated that they were suspicious when a prophet is re-affirming himself or herself or his/her position. The community of believers should test the prophets, and a prophet who does not want that his/her prophecies are tested cannot be trusted. Prophecies have a tendency to confirm the status quo and loose their critical effect. The routine of having prophecies sometimes results in not taking them too seriously.

The RRCN delegates added that Pentecostals only seem to be open to a specific type of prophecy. According to them, a consistent urge by one of the church members or a particular section of a sermon may also be of a prophetic nature. The pacifists, who demonstrated for nuclear disarmament, also experienced the prophetic nature of their manifestations. Pentecostals are generally reluctant to give prophetic utterances about political issues, but there is an increasing awareness of social and political abuses.

5. Ethics and Pastoral Care

Pentecostals have a strong sense of community and provide shelter for many who have social or psychological problems. As a result of their holiness heritage, many Pentecostals have ethical reservations on issues, such as sex before marriage or divorce. There is a tendency to spiritualize or demonize a social or psychological problem. It was acknowledged that the mainline churches usually provide more balanced and professional care in these cases.

At the end of the dialogue, the committee of the RRCN concluded that this has been ". . . a genuine dialogue. From both sides there was a readiness to critically observe one's one denominational tradition and to hold the other 'party' accountable for the questions and criticism that is raised."[39] They recommended to continue this dialogue, but unfortunately this never happened. Similarly, the Pentecostals also did not initiate a continuation. From my personal observation, the dialogue was the most intensive and genuine conversation with Pentecostals in the Netherlands so far. There was indeed a surprising openness, and Pentecostals were treated as equal partners. However, all meetings were held in the headquarters of the RRCN and chaired by their committee, which created a feeling of ownership and dominance by the RRCN. I personally challenged the RRCN members to integrate time for mutual worship in order to "get a taste of our spiritual life." Although some of the Reformed delegates were open to this challenge, its realization never materialized. Thus the dialogue remained merely an intellectual exchange. Essential topics like pneumatology, water baptism, divine healing, signs and miracles, evangelism and missions, and others were never touched. The Pentecostals could also have reflected on the various documents the RRCN committee had produced.[40] There remains plenty of material to talk about.

Missiological Interaction and Vision

In 1996, the delegates of the Netherlands Missionary Council[41] (*Nederlandse Zendingsraad*, hereafter NZR) were astonished that there were no representatives of the (black) Pentecostal Churches, who took part in the Conference on World Mission and Evangelism (CWME) at Salvador, Brazil. When the group asked critical questions about this neglect, they

39. *Bijlagen bij de Acta van de Generale Synode van de Gereformeerde Kerken in Nederland—Haren 1995*, 504.

40. See *Bulletin voor Charismatische Theologie* 4.7 (1981) 2–16; *Bulletin voor Charismatische Theologie* 6.11 (1983) 3–19; *Bulletin voor Charismatische Theologie* 9.18 (1986) 3–14; *Bijlagen bij de Acta van de Generale Synode van de Gereformeerde Kerken in Nederland - Haren 1995*, 474–98.

41. The NZR is a platform of about 15 Dutch denominations and organizations for the exchange of reflections and ideas in its broadest meaning. Most of the affiliated organizations are Dutch Reformed or Evangelical. See http://www.zendingsraad.nl.

were challenged by the leadership of the conference and the WCC to initiate dialogue with the national Pentecostal and charismatic organizations. The general secretary, Wout van Laar, had already taken up a personal interest in the Pentecostal movement during the years he worked and lived in Chile. Together with the Evangelical Missionary Alliance (*Evangelische Zendingsalliantie*, herefter EZA)[42] and the Netherlands Mission Council (*Nederlandse Missieraad*, hereafter NMR)[43] the NZR organized a "day of meeting and consultation" on May 12, 1998. The goal for this meeting was "to get to know and recognize Christians of the Ecumenical, Charismatic and Pentecostal traditions, in the hope that in this meeting and celebration a new vision may grow for cooperation and unity in the unified mission of God (*missio Dei*)."[44] More than fifty representatives of these various traditions, including members of the migrant Pentecostal churches, participated. This meeting resulted in the formation of the Mission Quarterly Council (*Missionair kwartaalberaad*). During its first session, in January 1999, Water J. Hollenweger made a number of suggestions for an effective dialogue. The group agreed to pursue the following goals:

- The Mission Quarterly Council aims to create a forum where 15–20 participants meet informally in a hospitable environment.
- The meetings must include moments of celebration and prayer. Heart and mind, worship and discussion need to be pursued in a fruitful balance.
- The Council wants to initiate a learning process in which we get to know one another in such a way that it will eliminate our prejudices and will lead to possible ways of cooperation in a missiological perspective.
- The meetings cannot be merely investigative and noncommittal. It is our goal to develop a framework for a combined missiological strategy for the twenty-first century.[45]

42. In the EZA about 70 evangelical missionary organizations in the Netherlands cooperate. For a complete list of their participants, see http://www.eza.nl.

43. The NMR coordinates the activities in the Dutch Roman Catholic Church with regards to mission, development aid and dialogue. See http://www.missieraad.nl.

44. Wout van Laar, "Missionair Kwartaalberaad–Een terugblik," *Nederlandse Zendingsraad* 123.1 (May 10, 2001) 1.

45. Ibid., 2.

During subsequent meetings, a wide range of topics was discussed, including the strength and weakness of Pentecostal mission, eschatology as a motive for mission, intercultural theology and narrative exegesis, testimony and witness, as well as African Pentecostalism, and non-Western Pentecostalism in the Netherlands. One of the most significant features of this dialogue has been the time of worship and prayer, usually at the beginning of each session. In his report on the fist three years of these meetings, Wout van Laar described the events succinctly:

> What cannot be reported are the experiences during the moments of celebration and fellowship, which are the heart of the Missionary Quarterly Council. These repeating moments, when we light the candle and are silent together in the face of God and call out His name. When we worship Him, it brings the participants closer to one another, and these moments are invaluable.[46]

The discussion of many issues still seems to be in an exploratory phase. It will be interesting to see whether a combined missiological strategy can be formulated. The mutual recognition, dialogue combined with worship and balanced participation, may prove to be the right ingredient to reach this challenging goal.

The Holy Confusion of Roman Catholic Charismatics

In 1997, Peter Hocken visited the Catholic Charismatic Renewal in the Netherlands. His lecture stimulated the National Pastoral Core Group (*Landelijk Pastorale Kerngroep*) to invite the Brotherhood to appoint a delegate who would attend their annual conferences. The Brotherhood responded positively and appointed me as their delegate to represent them at their annual conference. This contact, and the desire to discuss the report of the fourth phase of the international dialogue 1990–1997 between the Roman Catholic Church and some Classical Pentecostal Churches and leaders on "Evangelization, Proselytism and Common Witness,"[47] resulted in the decision to start a national dialogue between representatives of the Roman Catholic Charismatic Renewal and the Brotherhood in the Netherlands. We decided to meet every four months with about ten representatives from each denomination. The delegates include clergy and laity and represent different age groups. Each denomination hosts the

46. Ibid., 9.

47. See chapter 10 in this collection.

meeting alternately. A core-group with two representatives from each denomination prepares the meetings and sets up the agenda. Every meeting starts with a time of worship, personal testimony, prayer, and prophecy. I insisted on these aspects because I knew that many Pentecostals were prejudiced against the Charismatic Catholics. They could not figure out how somebody could be baptized in the Spirit and still pray to Mary or, even more horrific, smoke a pipe. I knew by experience that the best way to overcome this prejudice was to have charismatic interaction. The holy confusion would result in the undeniable acknowledgement that the same Spirit and the same gifts are active in both groups. After the worship, a delegate of each denomination would introduce the topic for the day, which is then discussed in small-groups and/or in a plenary session. This set-up has worked remarkably well. The dialogue is still ongoing and so far eight meetings have taken place.[48] These meetings were also attended by a delegate the Catholic Society for Ecumenism (*Katholieke Vereniging voor Oecumene*). In 2002, the Brotherhood merged with the Full Evangelical Communities in the Netherlands (*Volle Evangelie Gemeenten in Nederland*), the second largest Pentecostal denomination in the Netherlands, into the United Pentecostal Evangelical Communities (*Verenigde Pinkster Evan-geliegemeenten*, herafter VPE), which resulted in a broader representation of the Dutch Pentecostals in the dialogue.

In his chronological overview of the dialogue, Kees Slijkerman concluded that the goal of the first phase "to recognize and appreciate one another as belonging to the same Lord, to further respect and mutual understanding and to exchange the work of the Holy Spirit in each denomination" has been met.[49] During the last meeting, Peter Hocken stressed that a dialogue with the Pentecostal movement should "focus on the essence of faith and Church, in line of the Second Vatican Council, (and result in) an appeal for conversion and renewal."[50] He recognized that this conversation in the Netherlands, which is less academic and more personal, had many elements of a model ecumenical dialogue.

48. Kees Slijkerman, "Chronologisch overzicht van de eerste fase van dialoog in Nederland, 1999–2002," available at http://home.hetnet.nl/~stucom/document/0093.htm.

49. Slijkerman, "Chronologisch overzicht van de eerste fase van dialoog in Nederland," 3.

50. "Persbericht, Oecumenische dialoog naar een nieuw model. Achtste Dialoogdag van katholieken en pinkstergelovigen," available at http://home.hetnet.nl/~stucom/document/0094.htm.

Current Ecumenical Efforts

Current ecumenical efforts extend particularly in the dialogue between Pentecostals and the Roman Catholic Church. Since 2003, six annual meetings were organized in the Netherlands on a variety of themes, including the experience of the Eucharist and Holy Communion in both traditions, revival and renewal in the churches: what went right and what went wrong, how to become a Christian, the appeal of the Pentecostal movement after 100 years, water baptism, repentance, and faith. Various other ecumenical gatherings and initiatives have taken place in this period as well, of which the following are probably the most significant:

On November 30, 2007, a symposium on the theme "On Becoming a Christian" was organized by the professorial chair for Pentecostal Studies, headed by Cees van der Laan, and by the professorial chair for the Charismatic Movement in the Netherlands (CWN), headed by Cees van der Kooij, at the Free University of Amsterdam. Cecil M. Robeck, Jr., was the keynote speaker.[51] The symposium focused on the results of the international Roman Catholic-Pentecostal dialogue. At the official centennial celebration of the Pentecostal movement in the Netherlands, on September 15, 2007, in the Olympic Stadium at Amsterdam, the general secretary of the merged Dutch Reformed and Lutheran Churches (PKN), Bas Plaisier, asked forgiveness for the haughtiness of the Reformed Churches towards the Pentecostals. The Roman Catholic bishop J. van Burgsteden and André Rouvoet, vice president of the Dutch government, also spoke and congratulated the Pentecostals. In November 2007, Peter Sleebos, the general superintendent of the Dutch Pentecostals organized in the largest Pentecostal denomination (VPE), addressed the National Synod of the PKN and asked forgiveness for the arrogant and exclusive attitude of the Pentecostals over the years. The confession of Plaisier and response of Sleebos resulted in the publication of the book, *We Choose Unity*,[52] in which various leaders of the Roman Catholic, Protestant, Pentecostal, and Evangelical denominations issue a joint ecumenical

51. Cecil M. Robeck Jr., "On Becoming a Christian": Some Thoughts on the International Roman Catholic–Pentecostal Dialogue," available at http://www.stucom.nl/document/0205uk.pdf.

52. Wilkin van de Kamp and Joke Tan, *Wij kiezen voor eenheid* (Aalten: Crosslight, 2009).

plea. On the internet, one is invited to support this initiative by signing a "Manifest for Unity."[53]

On June 6, 2008, the Historical Documentation Center for Dutch Protestantism organized a conference on "100 Years of Cross Connections between Pentecostal and Protestant Churches."[54] During this conference, I proposed that the Dutch Protestants unite with us Pentecostals. This deliberately premature proposal was turned down, however, a dialogue with the now united Protestant churches (PKN) and the Dutch Pentecostals was initiated. The first meeting took place in 2008 at the PKN Service Center in Utrecht and was attended by the chosen dialogue members, six representatives of each denomination, and representatives of the boards of the PKN and the VPE. It was agreed to aim for five meetings per year for a period of two years, after which the results of the dialogue will be evaluated. The chair will alternate by denomination every other meeting. The most recent meeting was conducted on the theme of salvation, which in the connotation of the Dutch word "Heil" also implies "wholeness." The third meeting took place in 2009 on the theme "Onheil," which literarily translated means "Un-wholeness" or "Un-salvation," but in the Dutch language also means "disaster" or "casualty." These meetings open with a time of worship and prayer. After an introduction by representatives from each denomination, the theme is discussed in small groups. Participants of this dialogue seem to appreciate the openness and cross-fertilization.

Finally, it must be mentioned that the Centre for Intercultural Theology (Centre IIMO)[55] published an evaluation of the Global Christian Forum (GCF)[56] which was discussed at a conference in Utrecht in 2009. The Global Christian Forum is an international initiative that started in 1998 to promote ecumenical encounters between Ecumenical, Evangelical, Charismatic and Pentecostal Christians. It is headed by the Dutchman Hubert van Beek, who serves as their general secretary. The GCF has held international meetings in the USA (2002), Asia (2004), Africa (2005), Europe (2006), and Latin America (2007).

53. Manifest voor Eenheid, ed., *Wij kiezen voor eenheid*, available at http://www.wijkiezenvooreenheid.nl.

54. On the theme and lectures of the conference, see http//www.hdc.vu.nl/hdc/hdc-contact.htm.

55. See http://www2.hum.uu.nl/godgeleerdheid/onderzoek/centrumiimo/centre-iimoenglis.

56. See http://www.globalchristianforum.org/evaluation.

GUIDELINES FOR ECUMENICAL DIALOGUE WITH PENTECOSTALS

All of the above initiatives, of which some are still an ongoing process, underline that the Netherlands can indeed serve as a model for a fruitful ecumenical encounter with Pentecostals. The lessons learned from the historical development of ecumenical relations can be summarized as follows.

1. All participants must have a willingness to look critically at one's own tradition and be enriched by the tradition of the denomination with which they are in dialogue.
2. False presuppositions and prejudices must be eliminated as soon as possible. This can best be done by creating an inventory of the mutual perception in small-groups, during the first session. In a plenary sessions, these perceptions can be corrected where necessary. This exercise also helps to set the right tone for the following sessions.
3. It is essential that there is an equal participation in all elements of the dialogue: in the preparation and determination of the agenda, the number of delegates, liturgical elements in the worship, equal number of presenters and respondents, alternate chairs of the meetings, etc. It is also advisable to host the meetings alternately by each denomination in different locations that represent the variety of each tradition.
4. Worship and prayer should always be included in the dialogue, preferably at the beginning or at the end of each day. During this time, there should be room for charismatic utterances, intercession, silence, and testimonies. Some may get annoyed by the noisy worship of Pentecostals, and others may get upset by some liturgical elements of the other group, but this risk must be taken. The experience of the Netherlands shows that all participants felt blessed and enriched by this part of the dialogue.
5. There must be clear mutual understanding of the goal that is to be accomplished by the dialogue. This goal must regularly be evaluated and updated. The topics that are discussed should be chosen in the perspective of the goal that has been set.

6. The selection of the participants is crucial. Ideally it is a healthy, balanced mix of various ages, clergy, laity, ethnic variety, and gender. All should authentically represent their denomination or tradition and exhibit an ecumenical spirit.
7. The group must be big enough to represent the various streams, but small enough in order to build personal relationships among the participants. The ideal number is between twenty and thirty participants.
8. The lectures and the reports of the dialogue must be made accessible and, when possible, published on the internet.

A fruitful ecumenical dialogue with Pentecostals can follow the suggestions proposed already in 1987 by Cecil M. Robeck, Jr.[57]

1. Acknowledge the universal nature of the church and allow room for one another in it.
2. Forgive and ask forgiveness of each other for the hurts we have inflicted and received.
3. Begin to treat one another as sisters and brothers, rather than as people outside the common household of faith.
4. Affirm each other's strengths and acknowledge our own weaknesses.
5. Encourage one another to live up to our expectations.
6. Seek mutual review of our priorities and practices to reveal helpful information.

The lessons learned from the Netherlands further add the following suggestions:

7. Realize the biblical and universal implications of spiritual gifts, enriched by the integration of our various denominational traditions.
8. Tackle the powers of war and injustice in this world in Jesus' name and by the power of the Holy Spirit.
9. Discover the essence of our mutual driving force.
10. Build up a critical and lasting friendship.
11. Pray together for genuine and visible Christian unity.
12. Worship and celebrate together.[58]

57. Cecil M. Robeck Jr., "A Proposed Pentecostal/Ecumenical Movement Dialogue Agenda," *Ecumenical Trends* 16.11 (1987) 185–88.

58. van der Laan, "The Question of Spiritual Unity," 450.

13. Develop an ecumenical theology that integrates oral tradition.
14. Establish a community of believers from various Christian denominations that serves as a global model of the kingdom of God and exemplifies relevant contemporary Christianity.
15. Work out a unified plan to disciple every ethnic group according to the example of Jesus Christ.

I realize that these combined goals are extremely idealistic. The most significant step to be taken is to engage in dialogue in the first place. For everything else, we acknowledge the need for the baptism of the Holy Spirit and all the spiritual gifts we can get to accomplish at least some of them. The lessons from the Netherlands join in the ecumenical hymn: Veni Creator Spiritus!

5

Ecumenism of the Spirit

Toward a Pentecostal Pedagogy of Reconciliation

Raymond R. Pfister

The twentieth century has been referred to as the "century of the Holy Spirit"[1]and has seen millions of lives affected by the worldwide Pentecostal and Charismatic renewal.[2] Men and women came from various different ecclesiastical backgrounds, yet all believed that God "moves sovereignly by the power of His Holy Spirit in the lives of human beings, bringing new life, or revival."[3] However, one of the great weaknesses of the Pentecostal and Charismatic movements[4] during the last century has been their disregard for the Spirit's ministry of unity. More divisions and separations have devastated the Christian churches and affected their credibility than ever before. The church is desperately in need of a Pentecostal spirituality that is rooted in an understanding of the ministry of unity of the Holy Spirit. Only if the call for a pedagogy of reconciliation is heard and understood, can an ecumenism of the Spirit

1. Vinson Synan, *The Century of the Holy Spirit: 100 Years of Pentecostal and Charismatic Renewal* (Nashville: Nelson, 2001) ix.

2. An earlier version of this essay appeared under the title "An Urgent Plea for a Real Ecumenism of the Spirit" in *The Journal of the European Theological Association* 19.1 (2009) 8–25 and is used here with kind permission.

3. Ruth N. B. McGavin, *Running for Revival: The Life and Times of Henry Brash Bonsall* (Fearn: Christian Focus, 1999) 203.

4. In this article I am using the words "Pentecostal" and "Pentecostalism" in a generic sense as referring to a great many different Pentecostal and Charismatic movements around the world, and not limited to classical Pentecostal denominations.

be articulated for the whole of the people of God as the one people of one Spirit. The central question on the following pages is, if the Pentecostal movement is a movement of the Spirit, how is the Spirit likely to move among Pentecostals for the sake of Christian unity?

A fundamental aspect of this concern is the question, if ecumenical theology is best understood as a lifelong learning and conversation within the fellowship of the Spirit, what kind of theological thinking is needed to promote such a spiritual journey? Pentecostal theology needs to enable believers to be disciplined learners who are prepared to move from indoctrination (told what to think) to education (learning how to think), from system-thinking (theology as a finished product) to creative thinking (theology as a ongoing dynamic enterprise), from systematic theology (formulating propositional truth) to historical theology (critical understanding of our heritage), from a "God-in-the-box" theology (reducing God's revelation to manageable, predetermined categories) to an innovative, constructive, and prophetic theology (serving the needs of today's church in today's world, by allowing for change and responding to new challenges), from a monopoly of the Spirit (a spirit of chauvinism advocating uniformity) to an ecumenism of the Spirit (a spirit of diversity advocating unity).

In this essay I address these challenges by rethinking how we use the words "Evangelical," "Ecumenical," "Pentecostal," and "Charismatic"—all of which, though familiar, have been used or rejected by different segments of the Christian church, at different times, in different places, and for various reasons. Words have a history, which is certainly also true for theological terminology. My goal is to look at the broader historical and theological factors that determine a Pentecostal involvement in the ecumenical agenda. I suggest that a pedagogy of reconciliation uses and teaches a language of dialogue that promotes new communication processes and relational models through a fresh understanding of both what separates and divides, and what unites and brings together.

REVISITING EVANGELICALISM

One way of defining "Evangelical" has been simply to take its basic root meaning, the Greek word, *euangelion*, or "good news." For this definition, all that is required to be an Evangelical is that one believes in the gospel, the good news of Jesus Christ. However, it goes without saying that this definition is contingent on what one means by "gospel," and what the "good news" really is. Another way to define "Evangelical" has been according to geography. In Europe, historically, an "Evangelical" was a follower of Luther ("*evangelisch*"),[5] as opposed to "Reformed," which implied a follower of Calvin. In Latin America, "*evangélico*" means Protestant, as opposed to the majority Catholic population (i.e., *all* Protestants, whether liberal or conservative, are *evangélicos*). An even more expansive definition also includes Pentecostals. Thirdly, "Evangelical" was coined as a moderate counter-term to fundamentalism.[6] Ironically, although "Evangelical" was supposed to differentiate itself from fundamentalism, often in the media "Evangelical" is taken to mean "fundamentalist" (or at least "conservative"). A fourth way to define "Evangelical" is in opposition to the word "ecumenical," where the word "ecumenical" has come to mean "liberal" or "compromising one's faith." However, this understanding begs again the question of what "ecumenical" really means. A fifth usage of the word "Evangelical" can be found in the contemporary Catholic understanding of mission, what some call the "evangelical mission of the Catholic Church."[7]

Evangelicalism as a historical movement is a modern phenomenon reaching back to the nineteenth and twentieth centuries of Protestant history. Historical links explain why some would define themselves as Pentecostal Evangelicals, although not all Pentecostals are Evangelicals, just as not all Evangelicals are Pentecostals.[8] Many early Pentecostals have seen themselves as "fundamentalist with a plus" (i.e., baptism of the Holy Spirit),[9] thus essentially equating a fundamentalist mindset with Evangelicals. Others wonder how Evangelical Pentecostals can be for the sake of Christian unity without giving up what is unique about them.

5. In today's usage of the German language, one distinguishes between *evangelisch* (referring to the pluralistic Protestantism found in Lutheran and Reformed Churches) and *evangelikal* (referring to conservative Protestantism, mostly found in free churches, comparable to Evangelicalism in the Anglo-Saxon world).

6. In the first half of the twentieth century, the fundamentalist-modernist controversy erupted, polarizing opposing camps.

7. Jeffrey Gros, Eamon McManus, Ann Riggs, *Introduction to Ecumenism* (New York: Paulist) 90.

8. Sébastien Fath, *Du ghetto au réseau: Le protestantisme évangélique en France (1800–2005)* (Geneva: Labor et Fides, 2005) 300–302.

9. Leonard Steiner, *Mit Folgenden Zeichen: Eine Darstellung der Pfingstbewegung* (Basel: Verlag Mission für das volle Evangelium, 1954) 169–82.

Beyond Fundamentalism: Caught between Calvinism and Dispensationalism

One of the most crucial problems with Evangelical theology is that it has allowed itself to be trapped by its own distinctive theological systems.[10] Modern Evangelicalism cannot be understood apart from Protestant fundamentalism. That is where its roots can be found, but is it where its future lies? Doing theology through unilateral, cultural lenses will always bring a special concern for salvaging one's restricted worldview, instead of engaging the world, under the guidance of the Holy Spirit, in a proactive and constructive way. We may want to pay attention to Ben Witherington III's lucid observation: "Those who do theology while constantly looking longingly into the rearview mirror are going to crash sooner or later." [11]

During much of the twentieth century, dispensationalism has been very influential, not only in North America, but also in European Evangelicalism and Pentecostalism. It would seem that, in the twenty-first century, Calvinism is now playing a similar role. Both represent a system of thought that developed a set of principles for the "proper" understanding of Scripture and, therefore, of salvation history. Both have developed a basic hermeneutical pattern of interpretation with its respective theological presuppositions. Each holds very different views on the church and eschatology, but both claim to be faithful to biblical Christianity and/or Reformed theology. Pentecostals may ask if they can escape preconceived dogmatic schemes or develop an approach to the Christian faith and theological education with a high view of Scripture, yet non-fundamentalist in outlook.[12]

The fundamentalist mindset is no longer limited to its historical starting point—North-American Protestant Christianity, more specifically dispensationalism—but, wherever it is found, it conveys the same

10. See the debate on the center of Evangelicalism, Stanley J. Grenz, *Renewing the Center: Evangelical Theology in a Post-Theological Era*, 2nd ed. (Grand Rapids: Baker Academic, 2006); Millard J. Erickson, Paul Kjoss Helseth, and Justin Taylor, *Reclaiming the Center: Confronting Evangelical Accommodation in Postmodern Times* (Wheaton, IL: Crossway, 2004).

11. Ben Witherington III, *The Problem with Evangelical Theology: Testing the Exegetical Foundations of Calvinism, Dispensationalism and Wesleyanism* (Waco: Baylor University Press, 2005) 249.

12. James Barr, *Beyond Fundamentalism: Biblical Foundations for Evangelical Christianity* (Philadelphia: Westminster, 1984) 156–62.

mentality and shares the same characteristics. The complexity of late modernity has produced fears and anxieties. The challenges of postmodernist pluralism have generated insecurities which go beyond the issue of mere faithfulness to scriptural evidence and the gospel. Moving beyond fundamentalism means that it must be possible to be Evangelical without remaining attached to a dualistic worldview plagued by narrow-mindedness, isolationism, authoritarianism, and reductionism. A view of reality, which is kept alive by a permanent polemical tone, ultimately will not allow for real dialogue.[13]

Beyond the Bebbington Quadrilateral

In seeking the essentials of Evangelical belief, most roads today lead back to David Bebbington's "quadrilateral of priorities that is the basis of Evangelicalism,"[14] which many use as a basis for common ground: biblicism, crucicentrism, conversionism, and activism. Biblicism is a belief in the Bible's divine inspiration, truth, and ultimate authority, and led Evangelicals to encourage the devotional use of the Bible. Crucicentrism is a belief in the atoning death of Christ for sinners. Conversionism is the belief that one becomes a Christian by repentance of sin and acceptance by God through faith alone, not works. Finally, activism refers to the dedication and energy of Evangelicals in their quest to convert others, and frequently also involves social engagement.

Similarly, I believe that there is evidence for a Pentecostal quadrilateral: experience, resurrection, baptism, and community. Experience is the belief that the actual "receiving of the Spirit" and its accompanying life transformation takes precedence over any doctrinal formulation or statement of faith. Resurrection is a belief that Christ's overcoming death is what is most significant for the believer's faith and life, since it is resurrection power—not the death of Christ on a cross as such—which establishes both the "now" of divine righteousness in his life and the "then" of his eschatological hope. Baptism is the belief that a conscious identification with Jesus and his followers—expressing what it means to become a new person "in Christ"—is best demonstrated by a requested

13. Wolfgang Beinert, "Der «Katholische» Fundamentalismus und die Freiheitsbotschaft der Kirche" in *«Katholischer» Fundamentalismus: Häretische Gruppen in der Kirche?* (Regensburg: Pustet, 1991) 67–71.

14. David W. Bebbington, *Evangelicalism in Modern Britain: A History from the 1730s to the 1980s* (Grand Rapids: Baker, 1992).

physical immersion into water. Finally, community refers to the involvement of God's people with God's worldwide project of a new society characterised by kingdom ethics, i.e., a desire for justice, compassion and equality.

In order to understand better how the Pentecostal approach differs from the Evangelical, we should consider in particular how and why Evangelical crucicentrism is replaced by what one might call "moving beyond the cross." In his classical presentation, *The Cross of Christ*,[15] John Stott, who is considered one of the most influential clergymen in the Church of England during the twentieth century, establishes the centrality of the cross for the Christian faith. The central focus on the crucifixion has brought about a cross-centred theology leading to a cross-centred life. This idea seems to be backed up by Paul's writing to the Corinthians that "we proclaim Christ crucified" (1 Cor 1:23) and "I decided to know nothing among you except Jesus Christ, and him crucified" (1 Cor 2:2). At the same time, Stott reminds us that "it is often asserted that in the book of Acts the apostle's emphasis was on the resurrection rather than the death of Jesus," but believes that "although they emphasised it, it would be an exaggeration to call their message an exclusively resurrection gospel."[16] Pentecostals would readily question if such a statement is supported by the apostolic witness.

From a Pentecostal perspective, there is no Christian redemption story without a suffering Jewish messiah dying so that the Scriptures might be fulfilled,[17] or without making clear that "the ultimate purpose for which Jesus gave up his life in obedience to God was the redemption of God's people, of which Jewish and Gentile believers . . . now form part . . . , that those belonging to God's people might practice the righteousness God desired and demanded . . . with the help of the Holy Spirit."[18] It must be said that this goal was not only the result of Christ's death but also of his incarnation, his ministry, and his resurrection. To isolate the cross from the resurrection has had a number of most unfortunate

15. John Stott, *The Cross of Christ* (Nottingham: InterVarsity, 2006) 23–56. Incidentally, the French translation of this book interpreted Stott's *exclusively* by *essentially*, suggesting therefore that the apostolic message was not fundamentally a resurrection message.

16. Stott, *The Cross of Christ*, 41, 43–44.

17. David A. Brondos, *Paul on the Cross: Reconstructing the Apostle's Story of Redemption* (Minneapolis: Fortress, 2006) 55.

18. Brondos, *Paul on the Cross*, 74.

consequences, as it has been rightly pointed out by Michael Green in his book, *The Empty Cross of Jesus*. I agree with him when he says that with such a separation "the way is paved for a powerless orthodoxy."[19] You may get the doctrine right, but not necessarily find life transformation; the creed affirmed, yet no divine encounter secured.

The disciples believed indeed that Jesus had died, but such "belief" resulted in a most severe crisis until they realized that "God raised him up, having freed him from death, because it was impossible for him to be held in its power" (Acts 2:24; see 1 Cor 6:14). As a result of his resurrection, Jesus is alive as lord and has been given the power to bring about the promised redemption. The gospel is the power of God for the salvation of everyone who believes in a resurrected messiah: first for the Jew, then for the Gentile (cf. Rom 1:16).

Consequently, salvation through Jesus does not result *directly* from Jesus' death, nor *automatically* from his resurrection, but by following him as members of his new community of God's new people. It is a personal life-changing encounter with the living God, producing something radically and completely NEW: a new association with Christ:

- a new faith (identification with Christ = confession),
- a new mind (repentance towards God, turning from one's own way to Christ's way)
- a new life-style (righteousness of Christ = sanctification), and
- a new family (incorporation into the body of Christ = baptism).

In order to understand how God was reconciling the world to himself in Christ . . . so that in him we might become the righteousness of God (see 2 Cor 5:18, 21), Christians need to contemplate the twofold reality of an empty cross and an empty tomb (see 2 Cor 5:15; Rom 4:25; 10:9).

A fresh look at Paul's baptismal theology makes it clear that the theme of "death" and "burial" underlines the radical changes inherent in a life bound to freedom. There is an old life which is no longer in existence and a former identity which is no more relevant, since both belong to the past. There is a new life which is graciously given and a new identity freely received by association with the resurrection of Jesus that belongs to both present and future (Rom 6:3–8).

19. Michael Green, *The Empty Cross of Jesus* (London: Hodder & Stoughton, 1984) 13, 16.

Christian identity is centered on the resurrecting work of the Spirit, first of all in Christ and then in the believer's life. It is all about moving from a "because of sin" dead-end street to a "because of righteousness" start of a new-life journey. Resurrection power is at the heart of the Easter message, which in turn gives meaning and purpose to the Christian faith (see Rom 8:9–11; 1 Cor 15:14; Phil 3:10–11).

"To be an Evangelical Christian," says John Stott rightly, "is not just to subscribe to a formula, however orthodox . . . The Evangelical faith reaches beyond belief to behavior."[20] Theological education today can help redefine being "Evangelical" simply as being "good-news people" of the reconciliation available in Jesus Christ, who are enabled to distinguish between essentials and *adiaphora* (i.e., things that do not matter as much) for the sake of unity, to learn the lessons from history (including from Evangelicalism) with greater appreciation, in order to take better possession of a new future without being trapped by any glorious past.

REVISITING ECUMENISM

At its root meaning, *oikumene* is the whole household or community of God. Pentecostalism has greatly affected most every Christian tradition across the world and has become inherently a grass-root level ecumenical movement in its own right. Nevertheless, Pentecostalism is itself a divided world in which one is likely to associate with a particular group and therefore disqualify for fellowship with another group; we are all likely, in somebody's eyes, to be connected with the *wrong* people for the *right* reasons, or vice-versa. Ecumenism has become for many Pentecostals synonymous with the World Council of Churches (WCC) or the notion of "liberalism," both used to describe an attitude of compromises with regard to the essentials of the Christian faith. At the very beginning of the third millennium, the feeling of Orthodox scholar Constantine Cavarnos, that "'ecumenistic Orthodoxy' . . . is a *betrayal* of the Holy Orthodox Church, a *negation* of its essence"[21] is shared in a

20. John Stott, *Evangelical Truth: A Personal Plea for Unity* (Leicester: InterVarsity, 1999) 135.

21. Constantine Cavarnos, *Victories of Orthodoxy: Homilies in which are discussed in a forthright and analytical manner Iconoclasm, Orthodox Mysticism, the False Union of Florence, the Calendar Change, Traditional Iconography, Sacred Music, and Ecumenism; and the stand of the Orthodox Church regarding these* (Belmont: Institute for Byzantine and Modern Greek Studies, 1997) 81.

similar way by many church leaders and their flocks when it comes to their own Christian traditions.

There are many misunderstandings about what the word "ecumenism" actually means and about what the WCC actually is. Pro- and anti-ecumenical positions usually back two contrasting approaches to one's understanding of the Christian church. The latter places its emphasis on the *exclusiveness* of the church in light of one's own tradition. Here one defines the church and its life by what it is not and looks at the other with suspicion, noting almost exclusively what is wrong. The former approach considers the *inclusiveness* of the Christian church in light of one's own tradition. It rejoices in all truth found outside one's own tradition and looks at the other to see what is right and true despite real differences, and seeks also to work constructively on what is believed to be untrue.[22]

For Pentecostals, the question therefore remains, what is true ecumenism and what is pseudo-ecumenism? According to Lesslie Newbigin, "the word 'ecumenical' . . . properly speaking refers to the task of the whole church to bring the gospel to the whole world."[23] He believed that it is important to recover the correct meaning of the term and deplored that many communities call themselves *interdenominational* when they actually mean *undenominational,* because they do not allow for real participation and are not seriously interested in the particular witness of the separate confessions.[24] What kind of ecumenical commitment can be drawn from the prayer of Jesus in John 17:21–22? How can both unity and legitimate diversity in the church be accounted for when dealing with the relations with other Christian churches like the Roman Catholic Church and the Orthodox Church? Just as the views on unity are many, so are the opinions on how the Holy Spirit is likely to bring the church(es) together. The historical reasons behind the divisions within Christianity are manifold, some of which are the result of political and cultural factors, some the result of real doctrinal differences. What kind of theological education is needed to help all Christians grow out and beyond such divisions? How can the church experience full communion, the *koinonia* of the Spirit, which reflects the life eternal from God

22. Peter Bouteneff, "Orthodox Ecumenism: A Contradiction in Terms?" *Sourozh* 69 (August 1997) 1–7.

23. J. E. Lesslie Newbigin, "Missions in an Ecumenical Perspective" (1962) 9; unpublished document, available at http://www.newbigin.net/assets/pdf/62mep.pdf.

24. Newbigin, "Missions in an Ecumenical Perspective," 9.

above, truly faith, hope and love? The answers seem to lie in a universal pedagogy of reconciliation.

Pentecostal theological education needs to help learners-students-disciples in understanding the distinctive ecumenical contribution of the Pentecostal and Charismatic movements to the church at large. In order to be able to share its benefits, the churches will need, first of all, to recognize that:

- in each Christian community the Holy Spirit has been active even during the centuries of separation;
- the missionary movement has been one of the earliest stimuli for collaboration in the history of ecumenism;
- missionary outreach is one of the central dimensions of the pilgrimage toward unity;
- the complex and often tension filled journey toward the unity for which Christ prayed demands responsiveness to the Holy Spirit;
- the accomplishment of the ecumenical task requires the power of the Holy Spirit;
- comparing Christian communities by emphasizing the achievements of one and the weaknesses of the other is not an expression of God's grace and mercy.

Ecumenical Church History: Facing Theological, Cultural, Political, and Ecclesiastical Tensions

The study of church history is also the study of the history of ecumenism. Such study has to start with an honest look at the development of Christian divisions from New Testament times onwards, as much as to the impulses toward ecumenical reconciliation over the centuries.[25] Central to the development of a pedagogy of reconciliation is an understanding of the alienation caused by the perceived opposition between Judaism and Christianity, East and West, and Catholic and Protestant Christianity.

Judaism versus Christianity: Alienation from the Jewish Roots of the Christian Faith

The Jewish character of early Christianity has long been overlooked. The Jewishness of the messiah Jesus, his Jewish apostles and community of

25. Gros, *Introduction to Ecumenism*, 9–34.

Jewish believers have been widely perceived—wrongly so!—as a relatively small chapter in church history, closing shortly after the destruction of Jerusalem in A.D. 70. It is commonly believed that Christianity became quickly a Gentile (i.e., non-Jewish) majority movement. The Christian attitude towards its Jewish roots has definitively not been a positive one for most of its history. Sad to say, the drama of Christian anti-Judaism—a story of hostility and rejection—is well documented.[26] The often marginalized modern Messianic Jewish movement is instrumental in raising anew vital questions that have long been omitted. For Pentecostals, the question remains if it is possible to acknowledge the legitimacy of a Jewish identity for Jewish followers of Jesus. Is it possible to accept that both Jewish history and Jewish theology can positively challenge and nurture the faith of Jewish and non-Jewish believers in Jesus alike? Is it possible to overcome a negative reading of Mosaic law that leads to its becoming *terra incognita* of Christian theology? Is it possible for the Torah to be relevant for a Judaeo-Christian faith (righteousness) and lifestyle (holiness)?[27] Despite the basic nature of these questions, many of them have remained unanswered.

Eastern versus Western Christianity: Alienation between the Latin West and the Byzantine East

The so-called Great Schism is often dated at A.D. 1054, but differences between the East and the West were many and separation was a gradual process. Their approaches to liturgy, spirituality, theology, or church order were dissimilar, and most historians would now admit that it is not the debate around the *filioque*, nor Patriarch Cerularius' excommunication by Cardinal Humbert, but the sacrilegious cruelty of the fourth crusade of A.D. 1204 that issued the final blow.[28] In countries where the majority of the population is Catholic or Protestant, Western Europe is still viewed as being synonymous with Western Christianity. This was never true, however, for Eastern European nations like Greece, Romania, or Bulgaria, and it is certainly challenged by today's rapidly growing migration movements from Eastern to Western Europe. It is most interesting

26. Oskar Skarsaune, *In the Shadow of the Temple: Jewish Influences on Early Christianity* (Downers Grove, IL: InterVarsity, 2002) 442–43.

27. David H. Stern, *Messianic Judaism: A Modern Movement with an Ancient Past* (Clarksville: Messianic Jewish Publishers, 2007) 126. Cf. Marvin Wilson, *Our Father Abraham: Jewish Roots of the Christian Faith* (Grand Rapids: Eerdmans, 1989).

28. Gros, *Introduction to Ecumenism*, 16.

how Michael Harper, now Dean of the Antiochian Orthodox Deanery of the United Kingdom and Ireland, argues that "the original roots of Christianity in Britain are more Eastern than Western, and the sources of the Celtic Church were more Byzantine than Roman."[29] Overcoming today the rupture of East and West within the Christian church is a challenge raised by a deep longing for Christian unity and renewed experience of the Holy Spirit, but also by the construction of Europe which is bringing East and West together in a new way.[30]

Catholic versus Protestant Christianity: Alienation within the Latin Church of the West

When Catholicism gave birth to Protestantism in the sixteenth century, it was but the beginning of ecclesiastical and theological developments that will bring forward a multiplication of new traditions and spiritualities. By way of reformation(s), revival(s) and renewal(s), it allowed more and more separate paths to define the faithful, both individually and corporatively. It seemed more and more difficult to resist the swinging pendulum of truth as it goes back and forth between authority and autonomy, austerity and liberty, dependence and independence, separation and integration, clergy and laity, Scripture and tradition, Word and Spirit, law and grace, sovereignty and freewill, symbolism and literalism, liberalism and conservatism. If to be Protestant, for example, can be "translated" by a Lutheran, Reformed, Anglican, Methodist, Mennonite, Quaker, Baptist, or Pentecostal, one should not be too easily tempted to believe that Protestant pluralism is now facing a monolithic Catholicism. There are, besides Roman Catholics (with various different spiritualities and liturgical rites), Eastern Catholics, Old Catholics, Anglo Catholics, and various independent Catholics. If true ecumenism is not likely to result in a single "super-church" organisation, can it help build bridges where there are none between Christians of all horizons? Theological education should be a constructive ecumenical education, helping replace clichés with understanding, condemnation with commendation,

29. Michael Harper, *A Faith Fulfilled: Why Are Christians Across Great Britain Embracing Orthodoxy?* (Ben Lomond: Conciliar, 1999) 56. Harper describes his personal journey from Anglicanism to Orthodoxy.

30. Raymond Pfister, "Does Europe Matter? Towards a European Agenda for the Church in the 21st Century," *Evangelical Review of Society and Politics* 3.1 (2009) 37–56.

and disdain with respect. Pentecostal theological education in particular can help to realize that where the Holy Spirit is at work there is a degree of tension, and that not all tension is destructive.[31]

Ecumenical Theology: Overcoming Divisions with a Spirituality of Dialogue

Are we willing in the twenty-first century to engage in "a kind of Christian activity in which each of the different confessions is invited to participate, bringing the full truth of that confession as its people understand it without compromise or dilution?"[32] In the past, the concern for truth has often led to a pretended monopoly of truth, a fabricated ownership of truth, and thus a fictional golden age of Christianity. For Newbigin, here is the question which we finally have to face: "Is the truth ultimately in the Name of Jesus and there alone, or is the truth only to be known by adding something else in the Name of Jesus?"[33] If indeed only Christ can be seen as the absolute, what guiding principles will bring about "a more authentic sharing of diverse gifts in a Christ-given unity?"[34]

Helpful guidelines can be found in various Christian traditions and should be seriously reflected upon. Not least among them are those found in John Paul II's encyclical, *Ut Unum Sint* (1995), in which he delineated four among the various dimensions of ecumenical dialogue in the Christian community:

- dialogue of charity: demonstration of mutual love;
- dialogue of conversion: openness to being changed by a receptivity to new dimensions of understanding;
- dialogue of truth: discerning and speaking the truth;
- dialogue of salvation: participation in the saving mission of the church in the world.[35]

31. See Philip Zampino, "An Ecumenical Bridge," Life In Jesus Community (2002), available at http://www.lifeinjesus.org/art_bridge.html.

32. Newbigin, "Missions in an Ecumenical Perspective," 9. This is Newbigin's definition of the word "interdenominational."

33. Newbigin, "Missions in an Ecumenical Perspective," 9.

34. Newbigin, quoted in Gros, *Introduction to Ecumenism*, 71.

35. Gros, *Introduction to Ecumenism*, 114–15.

Grass-root Ecumenism and Ecumenical Institutions

Having been for almost 15 years an active member of the theological commission of the Council of Christian Churches of Hamburg, Germany, I realize that one could easily aim at mere institutional interchanges. I know, however, the importance of reminding ourselves that "ecumenical life is not something that comes from the summit but will always come from the grassroots."[36] A real *ecumenism of the Spirit* demands openness and responsiveness of the people of God to the ministry of unity of the Holy Spirit: to grow in Christ is also to come close in Christ in mutual appreciation, respect, and love.[37] Such Spirit-led inner transformation (change of heart!) and community encounter (caring exploration!) needs an ongoing process of ecumenical formation.

Unity and Uniformity

It is a great temptation to look at the Christian faith with our preconceptions and oversimplifications. We may think that because people look alike that they are the same, that because they talk the same way, they think the same way. We like to think that it is easier to be bound together by the allegiance to a perceived uniformity. Are we aware how much syncretistic thinking in our pluralistic world is affecting our own theology and therefore our ministry as educators? Theological education needs to help us look positively at Christian unity, producing a faith lifestyle, which is different because it looks positively at diversity, rather than a frail manufactured ideology despite diversity. In plain language, it should help us learn to agree how we can best disagree.

CONCLUSION

The experiential worldview of Pentecostals has not only opened wide the gates for a renewed understanding of Spirit baptism, signs, and wonders, it has also opened the gates for various ecclesiastical streams to wander in different directions, causing many hurtful divisions and dramatic separations. We urgently need to rediscover the gospel message, not any longer as an individualistic salvation message guaranteeing one's ticket to heaven, but as life-changing reconciliation with the creator affecting all

36. Jean-Arnold de Clermont, a French Protestant who is president of the Conference of European Churches, quoted in "European Pan-church Assembly Seeks a Fresh Unity Impetus," *Ecumenical News International* (7 September 2007) 12.

37. Gros, *Introduction to Ecumenism*, 91.

of one's relationships. This transformation is always divinely appointed by God who "has given us the ministry of reconciliation" (2 Cor 5:18). Theological education can help face the challenge of how to be agents of reconciliation rather than agents of one's culture and tradition. It can provide the necessary resources in order to build bridges rather than to build walls of partitions. To cultivate a sense of belonging together "in Christ" (acceptance) rather than highlighting boundary lines of differences (rejection) is our choice to make as we now conceive the curriculum of our theological schools and training centres for our common future.

Jesus Christ is God's reconciler par excellence. Christian unity will be experienced only in proportion to how much the churches become agents of his reconciliation, reshaping Christians who practice "reconciliation as an action word."[38] As early as 1969, Fr. John Meyendorff had commented on this problem:

> The future of true ecumenism lies in asking together true questions instead of avoiding them; in seeking the unity God wants, instead of settling for substitutes; in invoking the Spirit of God, which is not the Spirit of the world. Councils, assemblies, conferences and consultations provide the opportunities for doing so and should not therefore be altogether discarded. However, they will not create unity because unity 'in Christ' is not man-made; it is given in the church and can be only there discovered and accepted.[39]

If the unity of Christians is not, in the end, a human task, but a work of the Holy Spirit, it is, nonetheless, our responsibility to yield to the Spirit. Obedience to Christ here means actively "being diligent to preserve the unity of the Spirit" (Eph 4:3) with the clearly outlined objective to have Christians—followers of Jesus—"all attain to the unity of the faith, and of the knowledge of the Son of God, to a mature man, to the measure of the stature which belongs to the fullness of Christ" (Eph 4:13).[40] If Christian

38. See Samuel Georges Hines and Curtis Paul DeYong, *Beyond Rhetoric: Reconciliation as a Way of Life* (Valley Forge, PA: Judson, 2000) 147–50. Cf. Ronald Habermas and Klaus Issler, *Teaching for Reconciliation: Foundations and Practice of Christian Educational Ministry* (Grand Rapids: Baker, 1992) 33–57.

39. Quoted in: Vladimir Vukašinović, "Toward New Ecumenism", *Iskon* 4.24, available at http://www.iskon.co.yu/4/ekumenizam_e.html.

40. Cf. Alessandro Iovino, "The Pentecostal movement and ecumenism of the Spirit", paper presented at the 2007 International Conference of CESNUR, Centre for Studies on New Religions: *Globalization, Immigration, and Change in Religious Movements*, Bordeaux, France, 7–9 June, 2007.

education has to do with helping others understand the broader picture of church and society, it is not an option also to help them get involved in that broader picture. Such determination will "strengthen the ecumenism of the Spirit moving in us for the transformation of women and men, society and creation in God's great purpose of reconciling and gathering in all things in Christ Jesus."[41] Those who believe that we need to make ourselves available to the ministry of unity of the Holy Spirit will most certainly want to equip a new generation of men and women with such a renewed mind (Rom 12:20), that is, a new capacity to think and judge things providing the foundation for a new mentality, for a true ecumenism of the Spirit.

41. "Living in the Unity of the Spirit," Latin American Pentecostal Consultation, Peru, 14–19 November, 1994, available at http://www.pctii.org/wcc/unity94.html.

6

Lessons from the International Roman Catholic–Pentecostal Dialogue

Cecil M. Robeck Jr.

Some years ago, my friend and former colleague, Father Kilian McDonnell, OSB, shared a story with me that I will never forget.[1] When Pope John XXIII announced that he would convene a Second Vatican Council, it came as a complete surprise even among Vatican employees. In a sense, he opened it as early as September 1959 with a simple prayer: "Renew in our own days your miracles as of a second Pentecost,"[2] although the first meeting of Vatican II was not held until October 11, 1962. While he did not live to see the end of the council (December 8, 1965), his successor, Paul VI carried Vatican II to its conclusion in keeping with the hopes of John XXIII.[3] Working together with the bishops, these two popes brought about some enormous changes in how the Roman Catholic Church now views itself and its relationship to other Christians.[4]

1. An earlier version of this paper was presented at a meeting of the European Pentecostal-Charismatic Research Association (EPCRA) in conjunction with the Society for Pentecostal Studies (North America) at the Assemblies of God Bible College, Mattersey Hall, Mattersey, Doncaster, England, on July 11, 1995.

2. *Pope John XXIII, Journal of a Soul*, trans. Dorothy White (New York: McGraw-Hill, 1964) 391.

3. See Peter Hebbelthwaite, *Pope John XXIII: Shepherd of the Modern World* (Garden City: Image Books, 1984), and Peter Hebbelthwaite, *Paul VI: The First Modern Pope* (New York: Paulist, 1993).

4. See the Dogmatic Constitution on the Church (*Lumen gentium*), and the Decree on Ecumenism (*Unitatis redentigratio*).

In keeping with the prayer of John XXIII, Vatican II also made ample room for the Holy Spirit to blow more freely throughout the Church in different ways than it had prior to the Council.[5] These changes surely made possible and ultimately contributed to the rise and success of the Charismatic Renewal within the Catholic Church, a movement of the Holy Spirit through which many lives were touched.[6]

It was during the period when this renewal was in full swing that Kilian McDonnell was invited to South Africa to share with some Pentecostals a first-hand account of what was then taking place. During his stay in South Africa, Fr. McDonnell was invited to the home of a Pentecostal pastor to share a meal. As they were eating, his hostess turned to him and asked, "Tell me, Kilian, with all these changes going on in the Catholic Church, do Catholics still worship Mary?"

Kilian hesitated for a moment, and then responded with the kind of response that Jesus often used. "Will you answer my question first?" he asked. She, of course, encouraged him to do so, hoping that he would enlighten her further. She was not, however, prepared for the question he would ask "Tell me," invited Kilian, "do Pentecostals still handle snakes?"[7]

5. See Austin Flannery, ed., *Vatican Council II*, 2 vols. (Northport: Costello, 1975; rev. ed. 1996).

6. See Kilian McDonnell, ed., *Open the Windows: The Popes and Charismatic Renewal* (South Bend: Greenlawn, 1989); Richard J. Bord and Joseph E. Faulkner, *The Catholic Charismatics: The Anatomy of a Modern Religious Movement* (University Park: Pennsylvania State University Press, 1983); René Laurentin, *Catholic Pentecostalism* (Garden City: Image Books, 1978); Meredith B. McGuire, *Pentecostal Catholics: Power, Charisma, and Order in a Religious Movement* (Philadelphia: Temple University Press, 1982); J. Massyngberde Ford, *Which Way for Catholic Pentecostals* (New York: Harper & Row, 1976); Joseph H. Fichter, *The Catholic Cult of the Paraclete* (New York: Sheed & Ward, 1975); Kilian McDonnell, ed., *The Holy Spirit and Power: The Catholic Charismatic Renewal* (Garden City, NY: Doubleday, 1975); Edward D. O'Connor, ed., *Perspectives on Charismatic Renewal* (Notre Dame: University of Notre Dame Press, 1975); Léon Joseph Suenens, *A New Pentecost?* (New York: Seabury, 1974); Donald L. Gelpi, *Pentecostalism: A Theological Viewpoint* (New York: Paulist, 1971); Edward D. O'Connor, *The Pentecostal Movement in the Catholic Church* (Notre Dame: Ave Maria, 1971); Kevin Ranaghan and Dorothy Ranaghan, *Catholic Pentecostals* (Paramus, NJ: Deus, 1969).

7. On the snake handling tradition in the southern United States, see Weston La Barre, *They Shall Take Up Serpents: Psychology of the Southern Snake-Handling Cult* (Prospect Heights: Waveland, 1962, repr. 1992); W. Pelton and Karen W. Carden, *Snake Handlers: God-Fearers? Or, Fanatics?* (Nashville: Nelson, 1974); Karen W. Carden and Robert W. Pelton, *The Persecuted Prophets* (South Brunswick: Barnes, 1976); Thomas Burton, *Serpent-Handling Believers* (Knoxville: University of Tennessee Press, 1993);

Kilian's hostess stiffened, flushed with embarrassment, and then volunteered rather sheepishly, "Well, I suppose that there might be a few who do so," quickly distancing herself from those who did, "though I've never met one." Kilian responded to his hostess in kind. "There might also be a few Catholics who mistakenly worship Mary," he said, "but I've never met one."

This story makes a telling point about why it is that Pentecostals and Roman Catholics need to talk *with* one another. All of us who are part of these two great traditions, Pentecostal and Catholic, claim to be Christians. We claim to be members of the "one, holy, catholic, and apostolic church" established by our Lord Jesus Christ. Each of us claims that we serve the same God. We claim that our salvation is deeply dependent upon what God accomplished on our behalf through the life, death, and resurrection of Jesus Christ. Each of us claims that the church of which we are a part has been given the task of bearing witness to what God has done for us. Yet, within our respective circles that are typically isolated from one another, we fail to see how many or most of these claims could possibly be true for those outside of our respective circles. We fail to discern the body of Christ among us and alongside us. And our attitudes and actions leave us open to judgment (1 Cor 11:27–32).

It is not difficult for us to understand why we take such positions. We are all heirs to the historic divisions of the Church—West and East, Protestant and Catholic, liberal and conservative, and a multitude of others. Many of our perceptions of "the other" come from the stories, caricatures, and stereotypes that we have inherited from our forebears as far back as the eleventh century. Others stem from the period of the Reformation in sixteenth-century Europe. Because of these stories, stereotypes, and resulting splits and schisms, many Pentecostals have failed to recognize the genuine Christian character of the Roman Catholic Church and its members. Sometimes their positions have been reinforced by experiences in which they have been the brunt of alleged Catholic abuse and persecution in places where they are the minority, but just as often they have been hardened through fear and suspicion based upon seemingly timeless stories from the distant past. Today, many Pentecostals harbor deep levels of distrust toward the Catholic

---

Scott Schwartz, *Faith, Serpents, and Fire: Images of Kentucky Holiness Believers* (Jackson: University Press of Mississippi, 1999); Fred Brown and Jeanne McDonald, *The Serpent Handlers: Three Families and their Faith* (Winston-Salem, NC: John F. Blair, 2000).

Church, suggesting that virtually no Catholic is a Christian.[8] And in many cases, Catholics have refused to recognize the genuine Christian character of Pentecostals and their denominations. From their perspective, Pentecostals are little more than heretical schisms or troublesome sects that should simply be suppressed or ignored.[9]

Pentecostals have unquestioningly accepted choices and judgments made on their behalf by their forebears and contemporaries. They have made past decisions about Catholics on the basis of this legacy, and they have made subsequent decisions not to pursue a relationship with Catholics because they believe the Roman Catholic Church to be in error. The same can be said about the way that many Catholics have come to view Pentecostals. In many parts of the world, we live in virtual ignorance of one another, if not in a state of war.

In 1996, an American professor of Latin American Studies, Phillip Berryman, spent a year in Brazil and Venezuela. He observed that within six weeks of his arrival in these two countries, he had learned more about both the Pentecostal and the Catholic communities there than either of them knew about the other, even though they had lived side by side for most of a century. Because of their perceived differences, they had chosen simply to ignore one another. The resulting lack of first-hand knowledge and their willingness to rely upon outdated reports led them to continue their long-held misgivings, suspicions, and fears of the "other."[10] It is as though, when some historic rupture in the distant past occurred, they embraced a way of thinking that now suggests that God had stopped working with the "other" at that specific moment in time, while God has continued to work with and among *them*.

Sadly, almost all of us have become comfortable with such realities. The problem with this way of responding is that we have never tried to find out whether or not these stories are true. Some of them may be, though many are not. Nor have we tried to find out whether anything has

8. Cf. Terry Peretti, "Proclaiming the Gospel in Italy," *The Pentecostal Evangel*, no. 4220 (March 26, 1995) 18; and Terry Peretti, "Learning from the Past, Looking to the Future," *The Pentecostal Evangel*, no. 4220 (March 26, 1995) 19; Jimmy Swaggart, *Catholicism and Christianity* (Baton Rouge, LA: Jimmy Swaggart Ministries, 1986).

9. Ken Serbin, "Latin America's Catholics: Postliberationism?" *Christianity and Crisis* 52.18 (1992) 405–6; Gary Haynes, "Brazil's Catholics Launch 'Holy War,'" *Charisma* 19.10 (1994) 74–75; Benjiamin Bravo, "Sectas," in *Vocabulario de la religiosidad popular*, ed. Benjamín Bravo (Mexico City: Ediciones Dabar, 1992) 173.

10. Phillip Berryman, *Religion in the Megacity: Catholic and Protestant Portraits from Latin America* (Maryknoll, NY: Orbis, 1996) 147–50.

changed on the other side of the wall, on the side where we have assumed that God has stopped working. We prefer to tuck our stories away until the opportune moment, and then pluck them out to impress our friends or instill our own fears and insecurities within the hearts of our children. The end result is that many Pentecostals can see in the Roman Catholic Church only a mission field, and many Catholics can see in Pentecostals only insensitive, aggressive, sectarian competitors. Neither can see the other as an army of *potential allies* with whom they might better face an increasingly secularized and often pagan, postmodern world.

PENTECOSTALS AND PROSELYTISM AS AN EXAMPLE

One of the results of this kind of thinking is proselytism. It is an ugly word, a word fraught with emotion, anger, and estrangement. At some levels, all Pentecostals would agree that proselytism, popularly called "sheep stealing," is abhorrent to them. Almost every Pentecostal denomination or group has bylaws that govern the conduct of its ministers in this regard. While they do not always use the term proselytism, their descriptions of actions of which they do not approve leave little doubt that this is what they mean. Most every Pentecostal group restricts the freedom of one minister in a denomination from raiding the congregation of another minister within the same denomination. The reason for this behavior seems obvious.[11]

At the same time, both ministers are in the same business, that of making disciples. And both of them are employed by the same company, that is, by the same denomination. Both ministers are bound to one another not only by an invisible *koinonia* but also by a visible one that is generally legally incorporated, with a name, a building, and a physical address. Hence, the bylaws that disallow such unhealthy competition, that condemn the taking of unfair advantage over the "other" within the denomination, and that censure such actions as bearing false witness, or engaging in cajolery, bribery, intimidation, coercion, or uncharitableness against "the other" in any attempt to move members from one congregation to another within the same Pentecostal denomination, also promise appropriate discipline.

Such inappropriate actions are viewed as violations of a trust, of collegial responsibility, of preferring the other over oneself. The inclusion in

11. See "Articles of Faith, the Individual Believer," no. 7, available at http://worldwidepf.com/go/default/index.cfm/about-us/articles-of-faith/.

the bylaws of the infringements that are not tolerated and the discipline that will be meted out if the infringements are performed forms a code of ethics for those who participate in that common community. By these means, then, Pentecostals condemn all explicit acts of proselytism within their own ranks already. It is, after all, an issue of *koinonia*, that is, of Christian unity.[12]

However, once Pentecostals move beyond their own denomination or some other comfortable circle of fellowship, a problem often quickly emerges. The rules seem to change, not only for Pentecostals, but for Roman Catholics as well. "This is a sign," as G. R. Evans has insightfully observed, "that the sense of sharing a common mind has broken down . . ."[13] Even the basic assumptions that we make, and which undergird our definitions of one another, are not shared, for as Evans goes on to argue, "If I think you are already in Christ in his Church where you are, I shall not want to win you for my Church. Indeed, I shall regard you as already a member of it."[14] But we do not think in this way.

Most Pentecostals say that they expect very little by way of theological competence for a person to become a Christian. After all, what is required? It is little more than a public admission that God loves us, that we are sinners, that God alone can forgive us, and that comes by exercising faith in the atoning work of Jesus Christ. It is a simple, time-worn formula of evangelization. It does not require a potential candidate to understand and defend a thoroughly developed trinitarian theology. It does not demand an intricately woven defense of a specific view of the atonement. It does not anticipate a certain prior commitment to a spiritual discipline or a demonstration of some level of sanctification. Pentecostal altar calls are as simple as the message of the gospel that the apostle Peter declared on the day of Pentecost. "Repent, and be baptized every one of you in the name of Jesus Christ so that your sins may be forgiven; and you will receive the gift of the Holy Spirit" (Acts 2:38). The apostle Paul put it just as simply when he wrote, "if you confess with your lips that Jesus is Lord and believe in your heart that God raised

12. See, for example, Article IX, Doctrines and Practices Disapproved, B, Section 8, Violations of Ministerial Courtesy in the *Minutes of the 51st Session of the General Council of the Assemblies of God convened at Denver, Colorado, August 2–5, 2005 with Revised Constitution and Bylaws* (Springfield: General Secretary's Office, 2005) 125.

13. G. R. Evans, *The Church and the Churches: Toward an Ecumenical Ecclesiology* (Cambridge: Cambridge University Press, 1994) 70.

14. Evans, *The Church and the Churches*, 70.

him from the dead, you will be saved" (Rom 10:9). These are very simple actions that promise profound results!

But when it comes to recognizing Roman Catholics fully as sisters and brothers in Christ, even those who claim to have repented and who have been baptized, that is, Catholics who have confessed and believed, many Pentecostals and Evangelicals seem suddenly to put a very different standard into place. The message of the gospel suddenly becomes something quite different from what has just been described. It becomes a complex message with all sorts of caveats, requirements, and expectations, not a simple one. As a result, the profundity of the gospel's power seems greatly reduced. In addition to repentance for one's sinfulness and faith in Christ, it also expects a sudden and complete renunciation of much, if not all of their Christian past, and a complete and total acceptance of a new one. Let me share a few examples with you of how I have seen this scenario at work in both communities.

In 1987, when John Paul II visited the United States, I was invited to sign my name to an open letter of welcome to him, which would simply give my name and the name of my denomination. I sent copies of the open letter in draft form to my denominational leaders before I signed my name. I waited for what I felt was a reasonable length of time without getting any response, and then I signed my name. I was completely unprepared for the resulting outcry that ensued.

The provocative anti-Catholic pamphleteer, Jack Chick, read the welcome letter and decided that he could not sit by and allow such a thing to be published without an appropriate Christian warning to the faithful. He authored a caustic piece in his tabloid, *Battle Cry*, condemning the letter and those of us who had signed it. His article opened with the claim that "Leaders of non-Catholic denominations throughout the United States are tripping over each other to show that they really don't stand for anything at all."[15] Chick subsequently noted that while many of us who had signed this welcome letter belonged to genuine Christian churches, our signatures on this letter, which lamented the lack of unity between Christians in the United States as "an intolerable scandal which hinders the proclamation of the Good News in Jesus Christ," were deemed incompatible with what our denominations actually believed. By calling attention to this disunity, he contended, we were actually call-

15. Jack Chick, "Church Leaders Welcome Pope to U.S.," *Battle Cry* (September/October 1987) 4.

ing for the reunification of all Christians under the leadership of the pope, who from Chick's perspective was nothing more than an idol worshipper.[16]

Soon, I was deluged with telephone calls from Assemblies of God ministers who informed me, sometimes in very heated and passionate language, that the pope was not a Christian, that I was a pawn in a Jesuit scheme to infiltrate and crush true Christianity, and that they were going to demand that my ordination with the Assemblies of God be revoked. I had no idea so many Assemblies of God ministers were subscribers to Jack Chick's anti-Catholic rhetoric. I had naively thought that unity, and the vitality of our Pentecostal witness before the world, somehow went together, just as Jesus had prayed in John 17:20–23 (italics mine).

> I ask not only on behalf of these, but also on behalf of those who will believe in me through their word, *that they may all be one*. As you, Father, are in me and I am in you, may they also be in us, *so that the world may believe that you have sent me*. The glory that you have given me I have given them, *so that they may be one*, as we are one, I in them and you in me, that they may become completely one, *so that the world may know that you have sent me and have loved them even as you have loved me*.

Apparently, a number of my sisters and brothers did not agree with me. Their fear that the Roman Catholic Church was being recognized as a genuine Christian church and that the head of that denomination, John Paul II, might be portrayed as being part of a genuine Christian church, in some way played into their deepest eschatological fears.

16. Chick, "Church Leaders Welcome Pope to U.S.," 4. Chick clearly misstated what we had said, "We join Pope John Paul's conviction that Christian divisions are 'an intolerable scandal which hinders the proclamation of the Good News in Jesus Christ'" in "Witnessing Together to a Divided and Hurting World," 1. The charge of idolatry is the single most repeated charge that Pentecostals in Latin America make of Catholics in that region. See Luisa Jeter Walker, *Peruvian Gold* (Springfield: Assemblies of God, Division of Foreign Mission, 1985) 19–20; Luisa Jeter de Walker, *Siembra y Cosecha: Las Asambleas de Dios de Argentina, Chile, Peru, Bolivia, Uraguay y Paraguay* (Deerfield, FL: Editorial Vida, 1992) 2:163–64. The "Regulamento Interno" of the Igreja Pentecostal Deus É Amor classifies Catholic baptism under the category Batismo – pagão. Item B 6 reads. '*O batismo Católico é sacrifício aos ídolos, o batismo bíblico é de pessoas adultas, libertas e transformadas, que prometem ser fiéis até a morte, cumprindo a justice de Deus. Assim sendo, é proibido ir a batismo Católico, por ser Sacrifício aos ídolos. 1 Cor. 8.1 a 13 = Sal. 115.1 a 18 e is. 45.20.* This rule is found in "Regulametno Interno: Igreja Pentecostal Deus É Amor," appended to *A Bíblia Sagrada* (São Paulo: Sociedade Bíblica do Brasil, 1969) 4.

The following year, I preached a sermon in a Pentecostal church in which the pastor invited me to mention my involvement in a recent meeting of the international Roman Catholic–Pentecostal dialogue. I agreed to do so enthusiastically. I took as my text Luke 9:49–50, and I raised the possibility that Pentecostals might view themselves as John and the disciples, while Roman Catholics might be viewed as the one who does not "follow us," but who nonetheless were doing the Lord's work. Jesus' word that we are not to stop them from doing their work was not well received by two men at the close of the service. They approached the pastor and demanded to have their offering contributions returned because it was apparent that the church supported the building of bridges with the antichrist.

In May 1994, I received a telephone call from the National Conference of Catholic Bishops in the United States. "The Pope will release his latest encyclical *Ut Unum Sint* on May 30," I was told. I was asked if I would you be willing to read an embargoed copy as an ecumenical specialist and give my name to the news media for possible comment. I readily agreed to do so.

When the encyclical was finally released, I was contacted by a number of individuals, church leaders, and media personnel. I told them that I thought that the encyclical made a positive contribution toward the unity of the church, that I thought the pope was genuinely attempting to build bridges with other Christians, that he had invited specific conversations on unresolved issues left over from the time of the Protestant Reformation, and that he was even willing to engage in discussion on the nature of the papacy that could serve the whole church. A number of my reflections subsequently appeared in newspapers around the country.

Following their publication, I received several letters in their wake, one of them unsigned. They were unanimous in their criticism of me simply for speaking to the press about what I had read in this encyclical. I had been far too positive. All of them told me that I needed to read some church history, never mind that this is my field of expertise. All of them informed me that I was naïve if I were willing to take the pope at face value. Each of these letters was full of suspicion and fear. All of them spoke of Catholic plots and of Catholic duplicity, and all of them condemned me for compromising the Church of Jesus Christ.

There is another side to this discussion also. Catholics have similar problems as well. In 1991, I was invited to preach the annual "Week of

Prayer for Christian Unity" sermon at St. Vibiana's, the Roman Catholic Cathedral in Los Angeles at that time. The procession was led by the Archbishop of Los Angeles, to be named Cardinal three months later, Roger Mahony, and I viewed the opportunity as a wonderful and providentially appointed one.

We arrived at the Cathedral in a rainstorm of diluvial proportions. But as the parishioners and guests arrived at the Cathedral to worship our Lord and to be addressed by the Word of God, they were required, as was I, to pass through a gauntlet of slicker-clad, tract-passing pickets. As my wife, Patsy, and I crossed the picket line, one of them grabbed my arm and thrust some papers into my hand. I took them and quickly entered the Cathedral. As I sat there trying to collect myself, I opened one of the tracts and began to read it. It quickly became apparent to me that these were not Protestant or Pentecostal "fundamentalists" such as I might have expected to be picketing an ecumenical service, but Catholic "Fundamentalists," who were damning the changes of Vatican II, censuring Archbishop Mahony for participating in such a gathering, and most of all condemning the very thought that a Protestant—a "Protester" who had rejected the truth of the Roman Catholic Church—was featured as the preacher! The tract made it very clear that I was desecrating the pulpit.

In 2002, I again faced this kind of criticism from former Catholics. This time it came because I had accepted the invitation of John Paul II to travel with him to the town of Assisi to pray for peace in the world. Had they attended that prayer meeting, they would have found something far different from that which they imagined. They had decided that John Paul II was the antichrist, probably because he had made the controversial decision to invite non-Christians to pray in other venues in Assisi, at the same time that the Christians gathered together to pray. I came home to find that my photograph was now featured on a website titled "Antichrist's Family Photo Album."[17]

Elsewhere, Pentecostals have been portrayed as sectarians, members of that host of non-Roman Catholic groups throughout Latin America that is frequently portrayed at the local level as part of that larger problem known as "sects, cults, and new religious movements."[18]

17. See Cecil M. Robeck, Jr., "John Paul II: A Personal Account of His Impact and Legacy," *Pneuma: The Journal of the Society for Pentecostal Studies*, 27.1 (2005) 3–34.

18. "Vatican Reports on Sects, Cults and New Religious Movements," *Origins: CNS Documentary Service* 16.1 (1986) 2–10.

Pentecostals are charged with proselytism simply "to increase . . . their membership at any cost," or to further some North American political agenda.[19] Bishop Sinesio Bohn of Brazil has been quoted as calling for a "Holy War" against Evangelicals among whom Pentecostals are usually numbered as contributing some 80–85 percent of their members.[20] Even John Paul II, at the opening of the Episcopal Conference of Latin American Bishops, on 12 October, 1992, in Santo Domingo, Dominican Republic, spoke of the "rapacious wolves" that were busy among the Catholic faithful, a comment that most journalists and many church leaders read as an obvious reference to Pentecostals.[21]

These stories are not unique. Many of us have participated on one side or the other of this very exhausting and often very painful debate. "When will it ever end?" we might ask. When everyone becomes Roman Catholic and we are back in the arms of "mother church" where we belong? Or perhaps it is when everyone becomes Pentecostal, when we freely embrace the Holy Spirit who sanctifies and leads us into holiness, when we accept the full, unadulterated gospel in a unified babble of tongues. My fear is that Pentecostals will prove, in the end, that they are no better than the Roman Catholics they attempt to displace. The day is coming in one or another place when Pentecostals will outnumber Roman Catholics and the balance of power will shift.[22] At that time it will be too late for dialogue. Those who now claim to be oppressed will become the newest oppressor and it will be done, as it has always been done, in the name of the gospel.

I believe that it is critical to begin to expand Pentecostal–Roman Catholic dialogue. It should come into play at all levels of life, from fam-

19. Alta/Baja California Bishops, ed., "Dimensions of a response to proselytism," *Origins: CNS Documentary Service* 19.31 (1990) 667; *New Christian Movements in Africa and Madagascar (Meeting for African Collaboration – MAC) Symposium of the Episcopal Conferences of Africa and Madagascar* (Rome: Typograti, 1992) 11–12; Florencio Galindo, "Fundamentalism in Latin America," *Theology Digest* 40.1 (1993) 12–13. But see contra David Stoll, *Is Latin America Turning Protestant? The Politics of Evangelical Growth* (Berkeley: University of California Press, 1990) xiv–xv.

20. Gary Haynes, "Brazil's Catholics Launch 'Holy War,'" *Charisma* 19.10 (1994) 74–75.

21. John Paul II, "Opening Address to Fourth General Conference of Latin American Episcopate," *Origins: CNS Documentary Service* 22.19 (1992) 326 (no. 12); Edward L. Cleary, "John Paul Cries 'Wolf': Misreading the Pentecostals," *Commonweal* 119.20 (1992) 7–8; Cecil M. Robeck Jr., "What the Pope Said," *Commonweal* 119.22 (1992) 30–31.

22. See Stoll, *Is Latin America Turning Protestant*, appendix. 3, 337–38.

ily, friends, and neighbors to local parishes, from regional dioceses to national conferences. It is time to move past our mutual fears, misunderstandings, hatreds, mistrusts, and bad doctrines. According to the apostle Paul, all of us, even at our best, have only a partial knowledge of reality. And ultimately, even that will be taken from us. Now we see in a mirror, dimly, but then we shall see, face to face." And at present we are urged forward in faith, hope, and especially in love (1 Cor 13:8–13).

HARD LESSONS LEARNED

I have learned a number of what I believe to be important lessons in the many years that I have spent in dialogue with Roman Catholics at the level of the Archdiocese of Los Angeles, where I have participated in an Evangelical-Roman Catholic Dialogue since 1987 and have co-chaired it since 1992, to the international Roman Catholic–Pentecostal dialogue in which I have participated since 1985, and which I have co-chaired since 1992.

The Past Cannot and Should Not Be Forgotten

Those who have paid a price because of our disunity need to be remembered, and their witness, their *martyria*, needs to be valued for what it is. If we fail to remember these people and their witness, we do two things. First, we run the risk of doing once again what we have done before, repeating history because we have failed to learn its lessons. Second, we have simply glossed over something that needs to be resolved. Covered over, it soon festers and the initial injury becomes an infection that may yield worse than the initial injury. I am reminded of the very difficult situation in which Pentecostals found themselves in Italy, for instance, when during the 1920s, 30s, and 40s many of them were imprisoned, allegedly for their faith. Pentecostals in Italy were not allowed to possess or to distribute Bibles until 1959. These claims are currently unresolved issues and demand further investigation.

Memories and official accounts need to be reconciled. It is not necessary, nor is it a good thing to remain in the past, but past injustices and mistreatments need to be acknowledged before anyone can truly move on. It is equally important to assess where we are in the present situation. Much of where we find ourselves stems from the past. Vatican II gave us a very clear lesson, when in the *Decree on Ecumenism* the Catholic bishops acknowledged that at the time of the Reformation, "Men of both sides were to blame" for the separation that had occurred.[23] That statement alone made it possible for Catholics and Protestants to take another look at the sixteenth century, and clearly, such a statement, made for the first time in the twentieth century, made it possible for Catholics and Protestants to take another look at each other. Many are the positive results that have come as a result of that admission.[24]

Pentecostals who engage in dialogue need to put these unresolved issues on the dialogue table. The witness of those caught in this plight should not have been borne in vain.[25] It needs to be addressed. Resolution needs to come. But it is not a simple process. It requires the knife, a paring back of accounts until the table arrives at the whole truth and not merely a part of it. By refusing to come to the table, the infection only spreads. By refusing to come to the table, healing is not possible. By not allowing others to represent those who refuse to come to the table, resolution is impossible. The offences need to be remembered and studied so that apologies can be offered and forgiveness communicated. When insurmountable walls are allowed to dictate the state of affairs, nothing good can come of it. Apart from dialogue, healing will never take place.

Sometimes My "Friends" Are Actually My Enemies, and My "Enemies" Are Sometimes My Friends

Those who are closest to us theologically are often those who cannot see across the wall that has for so long separated us from the "other."

23. The Decree on Ecumenism (*Unitatis redintegratio*), I. 3.

24. William G. Rusch and Jeffrey Gros, eds., *Deepening Communion: International Ecumenical Documents with Roman Catholic Participation* (Washington, DC: United States Catholic Conference, 1998); Jeffrey Gros, Harding Meyer, and William G. Rusch, eds., *Growth in Agreement II* (Grand Rapids: Eerdmans, 2000); Jeffrey Gros, Lorelei F. Fuchs, Thomas Best, eds., *Growth in Agreement III* (Grand Rapids: Eerdmans, 2007).

25. See David A. Womack and Francesco Toppi, *Le radici del Movimento Pentecostale* (Roma: A.D.I.-Media, 1989) 123–88, especially 134–61; Giorgio Rochat, *Regime fascista e Chiese Evangeliche: Direttive e articolazioni del controllo e dilla repression*, Collana Della Societa di Stud Valdesi 12 (Torino: Claudiana, 1990) 113–26, 241–73, and 317–29. Cf. "Religious Liberty," *Minutes of the Twenty-First General Council of the Assemblies of God convened at Springfield, Missouri, September 13–18, 1945* (Springfield: Office of the General Secretary, 1945) 39; "Religious Liberty in Italy," *Minutes of the Twenty-Fourth General Council of the Assemblies of God convened at Atlanta, Georgia, August 16–21, 1951* (Springfield: Office of the General Secretary, 1951) 28; "Mr Rosapepe of Italy," *Minutes of the Twenty-Fifth general Council of the Assemblies of God convened at Milwaukee, Wisconsin, August 26-September 2, 1953* (Springfield: Office of the General Secretary, 1953) 27.

Frank Bartleman said it well when he likened God's dealings with the church as occurring in waves. If you watch the shoreline of the ocean, waves come in, and then they recede. At the point where an incoming wave and a receding wave meet, the water boils. So it is each time God attempts something new. God's most recent movement is often the most vehement in opposing "the next forward movement."[26] It is difficult for a Pentecostal to look across the wall, appreciate what he or she sees, and then to share it with other Pentecostals. Anyone who can see across the wall and appreciate what he or she sees, anyone who reaches across the wall in an attempt to change the status quo, anyone who travels to the other side of the wall to bring healing, is all too quickly mislabeled as being part of the enemy. Friends must first trust one another. Dialogue allows for friendships to develop between previously disparate parties, and together they can work on issues that have previously separated them. Apart from dialogue, a twisted version seems to prevail of the old adage that any enemy of mine must be my friend's enemy as well. This stereotype flies in the face of Jesus' command to "Love your enemies and pray for those who persecute you, so that you may be children of your Father in heaven" (Matt 5:44–45a).

Those Who Condemn Ecumenical Dialogue Most Vehemently Often Have Never Had a Single Experience of Ecumenical Dialogue

The ecumenically inexperienced frequently hide behind their fears or their untested stereotypes rather than become vulnerable in dialogue. What dialogue has taught me is that those who fear it the most are those who might most benefit from participating. There, in the safety of a room of people that they have come to know, they can be encouraged to learn, allowed to change, and enabled to act in new ways. In order to benefit from dialogue, however, one must be willing to enter it. Having never experienced genuine dialogue, they are on very thin ice when they attempt to judge its outcome.

Many of Our Fears Are Often Institutional Rather Than Personal, but the Church Is Made Up of People

Every denomination is a mixture of people and institution. What has become clear to me through dialogue is that the Roman Catholic Church is

26. Frank Bartleman, "Pentecost—Or No Pentecost," 5. This tract was published about 1928.

every bit as much human as it is an institution. At the same time, it must be admitted that Pentecostal fellowships are often more institutional than many would like to admit. The Catholic Church has a hierarchy, but the human side of the hierarchy has names like Jean Paul, Roger Mahony, and Kilian McDonnell. Similarly, Pentecostal denominations have leaders who are known by name, but who also very often disappear into or hide behind their institutional offices. In the end, it is still human beings who make up the church, the Body of Christ. At the same time, the institutionalization of Pentecostalism is no secret, and while it can be disappointing and at times even dangerous, it also has a valid role of bringing and nurturing a measure of order to an otherwise often chaotic Movement.[27]

Dialogue Is the End of Fiction, and Confrontation Is the Beginning of Truth

Dialogue is a form of community. Those who sit around the table in order to speak with one another are also there to listen. If they are to bear any fruit at all, the acts of speaking and listening require that all participants enter into the dialogue fully. As they do so, they become a new community—a community in dialogue, partners in a discussion, people who give and receive, a group that is no longer made up of "us" and "them," but only of *a new us*. It is not a place where one can go and expect to remain unchanged. It is not a place for the faint of heart. It is a place where truth is sought within this new community. It is a place where community is built when the truth is exposed and embraced. Truth is sometimes difficult to accept without change. At the same time, "truth" that cannot be defended is not worth maintaining. It requires change, and change is often frightening. As a result, dialogue always holds the potential of changing the status quo.[28]

27. Margaret M. Poloma, *The Assemblies of God at the Crossroads: Charisma and Institutional Dilemmas* (Knoxville: The University of Tennessee Press, 1989); Margaret M. Poloma, "Charisma, Institutionalization and Social Change," *Pneuma: The Journal of the Society for Pentecostal Studies* 17.2 (1995) 245–52; Margaret M. Poloma, "The Future of American Pentecostal Identity: The Assemblies of God at a Crossroad," in *The Work of the Spirit: Pneumatology and Pentecostalism*, ed. Michael Welker (Grand Rapids: Eerdmans, 2006) 147–65.

28. See Michael Kinnamon, *Truth and Community: Diversity and Its Limits in the Ecumenical Movement* (Grand Rapids: Eerdmans, 1988).

In May 1993, I was invited by the Pontifical Council for Promoting Christian Unity to attend a meeting of the National Episcopal Commissions for Ecumenism. I went as one of a half-dozen Protestants in the category of "fraternal delegate." I was given voice and the bishops were told that we "fraternal delegates" were to be treated as peers, as equal to the bishops. Our criticism and affirmations would be entered into the official minutes with all the rest and our conclusions would be carried forward to the pope. Several things stand out in my mind from that meeting, but I shall note only one: On the first morning of the meeting, Edward Idras Cardinal Cassidy informed all the bishops who were present that Pentecostals are not to be lumped under the category of "sect," because, as he put it, they "do not deserve that title." The Pontifical Council has had fruitful dialogue and significant contacts with . . . Pentecostals," he went on. "Indeed, one can speak of a mutual enrichment as a result of these contacts,"[29] he finished.

We might wonder of what these enrichments consist. For one, the very next day, Cardinal Cassidy reproved the Latin American bishops in that meeting because they had protested my presence as a peer. "I am tired of your complaining to Rome about the Pentecostals," he told them. "If you would instead go home and talk with them, perhaps something good would begin to take place in Latin America," he said. I wondered how we would respond if suddenly they raced to embrace us in Christian love. Of what do these enrichments consist?

In Order to Arrive at Truth, We Must Confront Our Dialogue Partners in Love

Love is a genuine enrichment. In the fall of 1993, Archbishop Iakovos of the Greek Orthodox Churches in North and South America issued an encyclical directing all priests not to bless any marriage between an Orthodox and a Pentecostal. Why did he do this? Because, he wrote, "Religious groups which are not of the Christian tradition include Adherence [sic!] of Judaism and Islam; Buddhism, Hinduism and other Far eastern religions . . . Assemblies of God, [and other] Pentecostal[s]."[30]

29. Edward Idris Cardinal Cassidy, "Prolusio," [Given at the meeting of Representatives of the National Episcopal Commissions for Ecumenism, Rome, May 5–10, 1993] *Information Service* no. 84 (1993/III–IV) 122.

30. Iakovos, Archbishop of the Greek Orthodox Church of North and South America to the Pastors and Reverend Priests of the Greek Orthodox Archdiocese of

The Roman Catholic dialogue taught me how to address His Eminence, Archbishop Iakovos in a way that challenged or confronted him in love. Then I waited—for five months. On May 22, his office issued what is now known as Protocol No. 13 in which the following was stated: "A note of clarification must be made as to those religious groups cited in the September encyclical; in particular . . . it must be noted that most congregations of the Assemblies of God [and other] Pentecostals . . . are of the Christian Tradition. Some are not."[31] So the exchange continues, but at least most of us in this meeting are now viewed as Christian by Archbishop Iakovos, whose aide, Fr. Milton Efthimiou, has assured me that their relationship "with the Assemblies of God has always been a good one, and [they] hope that it will continue as such."[32]

More Than Any Other Single Event in My Life, the International Roman Catholic–Pentecostal Dialogue Has Helped Me Understand Who I Am as a Pentecostal

We can teach courses in Pentecostal history, polity, ethos, and theology, but until our convictions get challenged in an open and honest way, as frequently it does in this dialogue, our doctrine is without the meaning and value that we ascribe to it. If it fails under this pressure, it probably is not worth keeping. Fear, more than any other thing, will keep it from the ecumenical test. This test, however, will only enlarge our vision and make us better fit to be teachers and scholars of the Pentecostal movement. We need these loving but firm confrontations, and so do our Roman Catholic sisters and brothers. Together we, who have stood apart from one another for so long, can now bear witness to the world, something of the boundless, reconciling love which God has extended to us in Jesus Christ. And as a result of our growing reconciliation to one another, it can be done in a way that is profoundly believable. Hard lessons, difficult steps, tentative touches, warm embraces—the world as we know it needs to hear this message.

North and South America, "Concerning Interfaith Marriages," (September 1994) 1; "Archbishop Calls Pentecostals non-Christians," *Christianity Today* 39.1 (1995) 42.

31. The Rev. Dr. Milton B. Efthimiou, Director, Ecumenical Office to the Reverend Fathers of the Greek Orthodox Archdiocese of North and South America, *Protocol No. 13* (May 22, 1995) 1.

32. Personal Correspondence from Rev. Dr. Milton B. Efthimiou to Cecil M. Robeck, Jr. (May 23, 1995).

Part Two

International Ecumenical Documents with Pentecostal Participation

7

Final Report of the Dialogue between the Secretariat for Promoting Christian Unity of the Roman Catholic Church and Leaders of Some Pentecostal Churches and Participants in the Charismatic Movement within Protestant and Anglican Churches

1972–1976

INTRODUCTION[1]

1. The series of talks described as the Roman Catholic-Pentecostal dialogue had its beginning in the contacts made by individual members of the Pentecostal Churches with the Vatican Secretariat for Promoting Christian Unity in 1969 and 1970. With the assistance of Rev. David J. du Plessis, an international Pentecostal leader, noted figure among Pentecostals and a guest at the Second Vatican Council, and Fr. Kilian McDonnell, OSB, Director of the Institute for Ecumenical and Cultural Research, Collegeville, USA, the initial impulse was clarified and concrete proposals began to emerge.

2. In 1970, the first of two exploratory meetings was held to see if a serious theological discussion between Roman Catholics and Pentecostals on the international level would be possible. The first gathering was largely an occasion for beginning to know one another. At the second meeting in 1971 each side put "hard" questions to the other, a more purposeful conversation resulted, and it became clear that it would be possible to undertake discussions of a more systematic kind.

1. The final report was published in *Pneuma: The Journal of the Society for Pentecostal Studies* 12.2 (1990) 85–95, and is printed here with kind permission.

3. Therefore, later in 1971, a small steering committee with members from both sides worked out a program of topics which could be treated at meetings over a five-year period.

4. The dialogue has a special character. The bilateral conversations which the Roman Catholic Church undertakes with many world communions (e.g., the Anglican Communion, the Lutheran World Federation, etc.) are prepared to consider problems concerning church structures and ecclesiology and have organic unity as a goal or at least envisage some kind of eventual structural unity. This dialogue has not. Before it began, it was made clear that its immediate scope was not "to concern itself with the problems of imminent structural union," although of course its object was Christians coming closer together in prayer and common witness. Its purpose has been that "prayer, spirituality, and theological reflection be a shared concern at the international level in the form of a dialogue between the Secretariat for Promoting Christian Unity of the Roman Catholic Church and leaders of some Pentecostal Churches and participants in the charismatic movements within Protestant and Anglican Churches."[2]

5. The dialogue has sought "to explore the life and spiritual experience of Christians and the Churches," "to give special attention to the meaning for the Church of fullness of life in the Holy Spirit," attending to "both the experiential and theological dimensions" of that life. "Through such dialogue" those who participate "hope to share in the reality of the mystery of Christ and the Church, to build a united testimony, to indicate in what manner the sharing of truth makes it possible . . . to grow together."

6. Certain areas of doctrinal agreement have been looked at with a view to eliminating mutual misunderstandings. At the same time, there has been no attempt to minimize points of real divergence. One of these, for example, is the importance given to faith and to experience, and their relation in Christian life.

7. The dialogue has been between the Roman Catholic Church and some Pentecostal churches. Here, too, there have been special features. On the Roman Catholic side, it has had the usual authorization given by the Secretariat for Promoting Christian Unity to such meetings on an international scale and the participants were appointed officially by the

2. Quotations in this documents are from the "Report of Steering Committee Meeting," Rome, 25–26 October, 1971.

Secretariat. The Pentecostal participants were either appointed officially by their individual churches (and in several cases are leaders of these churches), or else came with some kind of approbation of their churches. Therefore, it has been a dialogue with some Pentecostal churches and with delegates of others. These are churches which came into being over the last fifty or sixty years when some Protestant churches expelled those who made speaking in tongues and other charismatic manifestations an integral part of their spirituality.

8. In addition, there were participants in the charismatic movement who were invited by the Pentecostals. They belong to Anglican or Protestant churches which already have bilateral dialogues in progress with the Roman Catholic Church. Therefore, it is as participants in the charismatic movement and not primarily as members of their own churches that they share in the dialogue.

9. It was also pointed out in the beginning that "this dialogue is not directly concerned with the domestic pastoral question of the relationship of the charismatic movement among Catholics to the Catholic Church. The dialogue may help indirectly to clarify this relationship, but this is not the direct concern of our deliberations."

10. At the first meeting of the dialogue in Horgen, Switzerland, June 1972, an exegetical approach was taken in order to study "baptism in the Holy Spirit" in the New Testament, its relation to repentance, and the process of sanctification and the relation of the charismata to it. At Rome, in June 1973, the second meeting was devoted to the historic background of the Pentecostal movement, the relation of baptism in the Holy Spirit to the rites of Christian initiation, and the role of the Holy Spirit and the gifts of the Spirit in the mystical tradition. The third meeting, held at Schloss Craheim, West Germany, June 1974, focused on the theology of Christian initiation, the nature of sacramental activity, infant and adult baptism. At the fourth meeting held in Venice, May 1975, the areas of public worship (especially eucharistic celebration), the human dimension in the exercise of the spiritual gifts, and discerning of spirits were the main concern. In Rome, May 1976, the final session was devoted to the topic of prayer and praise.

BAPTISM IN THE HOLY SPIRIT

11. In the New Testament, the expression "to baptize in the Holy Spirit" (Mark 1:8) is used to express, in contrast to the baptism of John

(John 1:33), the baptism by Jesus, who gives the Spirit to the new eschatological people of God, the Church (Acts 1:5). All men are called to enter into this community through faith in Christ, who makes them disciples through baptism and sharers of his Spirit (Acts 2:38–39).

12. In the Pentecostal movement "being baptized in the Spirit," "being filled with the Holy Spirit," and "receiving the Holy Spirit" are understood as occurring in a decisive experience distinct from conversion whereby the Holy Spirit manifests himself, empowers, and transforms one's life, and enlightens one as to the whole reality of the Christian mystery (Acts 2:4; 8:17; 10:44; 19:6).

13. It is the Spirit of Christ which makes a Christian (1 Cor 12:13) and that life is "Christian" inasmuch as it is under the Spirit and is characterized by openness to his transforming power. The Spirit is sovereignly free, distributing his gifts to whomsoever he wills, whenever and howsoever he wills (1 Cor 12:11; John 3:7–8). There is also the human responsibility to seek after what God has promised (1 Cor 14:1). This full life in the Spirit is growth in Christ (Eph 4:15–16) which must be purified continually. On the other hand, due to one's unfaithfulness to the promptings of the Spirit (Gal 6:7–9; 1 John 3:24) this growth can be arrested. But also new ways open up, and new crises occur which could be milestones of progress in the Christian life (2 Cor 3:17–18; 2 Cor 4:8–11).

14. The participants are conscious that during the nineteen centuries other terms have been used to express this experience called "baptism in the Holy Spirit." It is one used today by the Pentecostal movement. Other expressions are "being filled with the Holy Spirit," "receiving the Holy Spirit." These expressions should not be used to exclude traditional understandings of the experience of and faith in the reality of Christian initiation.

15. The Holy Spirit gratuitously manifests himself in signs and charisms for the common good (Mark 16:17–18), working in and through but going beyond the believer's natural ability. There is a great variety of ministries in which the Spirit manifests himself. Without minimizing the importance of these experiences or denying the fruitfulness of these gifts for the church, the participants wished to lay stronger stress on faith, hope, and charity as sure guides in responding to God (1 Cor 13:13–14:1; 1 Thess 1:3–5). Precisely out of respect for the Spirit and his gifts it is necessary to discern between true gifts and their counterfeits

(1 Thess 5:22; 1 John 4:1–4). In this discernment process the spiritual authority in the church has its own specific ministry (1 John 4:6; Acts 20:28–31; 1 Cor 14:37–38) because it has special concern for the common good, the unity of the church, and her mission in the world (Rom 15:17–19; Acts 1: 8).

GIVING OF THE SPIRIT AND CHRISTIAN INITIATION

16. From the earliest non-canonical texts of the church there is witness to the celebration of Christian initiation (baptism, laying on of hands/chrismation, eucharist) as clearly expressing the request for and the actual reception of the Holy Spirit. The Holy Spirit dwells in all Christians (Rom 8:9), and not just in those "baptized in the Holy Spirit." The difference between a committed Christian without such a Pentecostal experience and one with such an experience is generally not only a matter of theological focus, but also that of expanded openness and expectancy with regard to the Holy Spirit and his gifts. Because the Holy Spirit apportions as he wills in freedom and sovereignty, the religious experiences of persons can differ. He blows where he wills (John 3:8). Though the Holy Spirit never ceased manifesting himself throughout the entire history of the church, the manner of the manifestations has differed according to the times and cultures. However, in the Pentecostal movement, the manifestation of tongues has had, and continues to have, particular importance.

17. During times of spiritual renewal when charismatic elements are more manifest, tensions can arise because of prejudice, lack of mutual understanding and communication. Also, at such times as this, the discerning of spirits is more necessary than ever. This necessity should not lead to discernment being misused so as to exclude charismatic manifestations. The true exercise of the charisms takes place in love and leads to a greater fidelity to Christ and his church. The presence of charismatic gifts is not a sign of spiritual maturity and those who lack experience of such gifts are not considered to be inferior Christians. Love is the context in which all gifts are rightly exercised, love being of a more definitive and primary order than the spiritual gifts (1 Cor 13). In varying degrees all the charisms are ministries directed to the building up of the community and witness in mission. For this reason, mystical experiences, which are more generally directed toward personal communion with God, are distinguished from charismatic experiences which, while

including personal communion with God, are directed more to ministerial service.

GIVING OF THE SPIRIT AND CHRISTIAN INITIATION

18. The Holy Spirit, being the agent of regeneration, is given in Christian initiation, not as a commodity but as he who unifies us with Christ and the Father in a personal relationship. Being a Christian includes the reception of grace through the Holy Spirit for one's own sanctification as well as gifts to be ministered to others. In some manner, all ministry is a demonstration of the power of the Spirit. It was not agreed whether there is a further imparting of the Spirit with a view to charismatic ministry, or whether baptism in the Holy Spirit is, rather, a kind of release of a certain aspect of the Spirit already given. An inconclusive discussion occurred on the question as to how many impartings of the Spirit there were. Within classical Pentecostalism, some hold that through regeneration the Holy Spirit comes into us, and that later in the baptism in the Spirit the Spirit comes upon us and begins to flow from us. Finally, charisms are not personal achievements but are sovereign manifestations of the Holy Spirit.

BAPTISM

19. Baptism involves a passing over from the kingdom of darkness to Christ's kingdom of light, and always includes a communal dimension of being baptized into the one Body of Christ. The implications of this concord were not developed.

20. In regard to baptism, the New Testament reflects the missionary situation of the apostolic generation of the church and does not clearly indicate what may have happened in the second and following generation of believers.

21. In that missionary situation, Christian initiation involved a constellation normally including proclamation of the gospel, faith repentance, baptism in water, the receiving of the Spirit. There was disagreement as to the relationship of these items, and the order in which they may or should occur. In both the Pentecostal and Roman Catholic tradition, laying on of hands may be used to express the giving of the Spirit. Immersion is the ideal form which most aptly expresses the sig-

nificance of baptism. Some, however, regard immersion as essential, others do not.

22. In discussing infant baptism, certain convergences were noted: (a) Sacraments are in no sense magical and are effective only in relationship to faith.

23. (b) God's gift precedes and makes possible human receiving. Even though there was disagreement on the application of this principle, there was accord on the assertion that God's grace operates in advance of our conscious awareness.

24. (c) Where paedobaptism is not practiced and the children of believing parents are presented and dedicated to God, the children are thus brought into the care of the Christian community and enjoy the special protection of the Lord.

25. (d) Where paedobaptism is practiced it is fully meaningful only in the context of the faith of the parents and the community. The parents must undertake to nurture the child in the Christian life, in the expectation that, when he or she grows up, the child will personally live and affirm faith in Christ.

26. Representatives of the charismatic movement in the historic churches expressed different views on baptism. Some agreed substantially with the Roman Catholic, others with the classical Pentecostal view.

27. Attention was drawn to the pastoral problem of persons baptised in infancy seeking a new experience of baptism by immersion later in life. It was stated that in a few traditions rites have been devised, involving immersion in water in order to afford such an experience. The Roman Catholics felt there were already sufficient opportunities within the existing liturgy for reaffirming one's baptism. Rebaptism in the strict sense of the word is unacceptable to all. Those participants who reject paedobaptism, however, explained that they do not consider as rebaptism the baptism of a believing adult who has received infant baptism. This serious ecumenical problem requires future study.

SCRIPTURE, TRADITION, AND DEVELOPMENTS

28. The church is always subject to sacred Scriptures. There was, however, considerable disagreement as to the role of tradition in interpretation of Scripture.

29. The Pentecostal and charismatic movements have brought to the understanding of Scripture a new relevance and freshness to confirm

the conviction that Scripture has a special message, vital to each generation. Moreover, these movements challenge the exegetes to take a new look at the sacred text in the light of the new questions and expectations the movements bring to Scripture.

30. It was agreed that every church has a history and is inevitably affected by its past. Some developments in that past are good, some are questionable; some are enduring, some are only temporary. A discernment must be made on these developments by the churches.

CHARISMATIC RENEWAL IN THE HISTORIC CHURCHES

31. The dialogue considered that in the context of the charismatic movement in the historic churches, there was justification for new groups and communities within the churches. Though such movements have a legitimate prophetic character, their ultimate purpose is to strengthen the church, and to participate fully in her life. Therefore, the charismatic movement is not in competition with the churches, nor is it separate from them. Further, it should recognize the church authorities. In a word, the charismatic renewal is a renewal in the Body of Christ, the church, and is therefore in and of the church.

PUBLIC WORSHIP

32. Public worship should safeguard a whole composite of elements: spontaneity, freedom, discipline, objectivity. On the Roman Catholic side, it was noted that the new revised liturgy allows for more opportunities for spontaneous prayer and singing at the Eucharist and in the rites of penance. The Pentecostal tradition has come to accept a measure of structure in worship and recognizes the development in its own history toward some liturgy.

33. In the Roman Catholic context, the phrase *ex opere operato* was discussed in relation to the celebration of the sacraments. The disquiet of some participants was removed by the explanation of the Roman Catholic doctrine of grace, which stresses that the living faith of the recipient of a sacrament is of fundamental importance.

PUBLIC WORSHIP AND THE GIFTS

34. Corporate worship is a focal expression of the worshiper's daily life as he or she speaks to God and to other members of the commu-

nity in songs of praise and words of thanksgiving (Eph 5:19–20; 1 Cor 14:26). Our Lord is present in the members of his body, manifesting himself in worship by means of a variety of charismatic expressions. He is also present by the power of his Spirit in the Eucharist. The participants recognized that there was a growing understanding of the unity, which exists between the formal structure of the eucharistic celebration and the spontaneity of the charismatic gifts. This unity was exemplified by the Pauline relationship between chapters eleven to fourteen of 1 Corinthians.

THE HUMAN ASPECT

35. There exists both a divine and human aspect to all genuinely charismatic phenomena. So far as concerns the human aspect, the phenomena can rightly be subject to psychological, linguistic, sociological, anthropological, and other investigation, which can provide some understanding of the diverse manifestations of the Holy Spirit. But the spiritual aspect of charismatic phenomena ultimately escapes a purely scientific examination. While there is no essential conflict between science and faith, nevertheless, science has inherent limitations, particularly with regard to the dimensions of faith and spiritual experience.

36. A survey of the scientific literature on speaking in tongues was presented. Another presentation outlined a Jungian psychological evaluation of the phenomenology of the Holy Spirit. However neither of these topics was developed adequately in discussion and they await more extended consideration. This could be done in the context of a future treatment of the place of speaking in tongues as an essential factor in the Pentecostal experience.

37. The relationship between science and the exercise of spiritual gifts, including that of healing, was discussed. Classical Pentecostals, as well as other participants, believe that through the ministry of divine healing can come restoration to sound health. Full agreement was not reached in this matter in view of the importance of the therapeutic disciplines and the participants recommended further in-depth study.

DISCERNMENT OF SPIRITS

38. The New Testament witnesses to the charism of the discerning of spirits (1 Cor 12:10), and also to a form of discernment through the

testing of the spirits (1 John 4:1), and the proving of the will of God (Rom 12:2), each exercised in the power of the Spirit. There are different aspects of discernment of spirits which allow for human experience, wisdom, and reason as a consequence of growth in the Spirit, while other aspects imply an immediate communication of the Spirit for discernment in a specific situation.

39. Discernment is essential to authentic ministry. The Pentecostal tradition lays stress on the discerning of spirits in order to find "the mind of the Spirit" for ministry and public worship. It is also understood as a diagnostic gift, which leads to the further manifestation of other charismata for the edification of the body of Christ and the work of the gospel. The operation of this gift in dependence upon the Spirit develops both in the believer and community a growth in a mature sensitivity to the Spirit.

40. Normally, but not absolutely, expectancy is a requisite for the manifestations of the Spirit through human acts on the part of the believer and the community, that is, an openness which nevertheless respects the sovereignty of the Spirit in the distribution of his gifts. Because of human frailty, group pressure, and other factors, it is possible for the believer to be mistaken or misled in his awareness of the Spirit's intention and influence in the believer's acts. It is for this reason that criteria are essential to confirm and authenticate the genuine operation of the Spirit of truth (John 4:1–6). These criteria must be based upon the scriptural foundation of the incarnation, the lordship of Christ, and the building up of his church. The important element of community criteria involves the common wisdom of a group of believers, walking, and living in the Spirit, when, led by those exercising the ministry of discernment, a mature discipline results, and the group is capable of discerning the mind of God.

41. The Roman Catholic tradition understands such community discernment to be exercised by the whole church of which her leaders receive a special charism for this purpose. All traditions find a confirmatory individual criterion in the extent to which the believer is influenced in his daily life by the Spirit of Christ who produces love, joy, peace: the plenitude of the fruit of the Spirit (Gal 5:22).

PRAYER AND PRAISE

42. The relationship between the objective and the subjective aspect of Christian life was raised. Prayer has two main forms: praise and petition. Both have an objective and a subjective aspect.

In the prayer of praise, the essential aspect is worship itself, the adoration of the Father in the Spirit and in the truth of Christ (cf. John 4:23–24). One of the expressions of this prayer of praise is the gift of tongues, with joy, enthusiasm, etc.

In the prayer of petition, the believer has always to distinguish between God the giver, and the gift of God.

43. Also discussed was the relationship between the word of God and our experience of the Spirit. The Bible must always be a control and a guide in the Christian experience; but on the other hand, the spiritual experience itself constantly invites us to read the Bible spiritually, in order that it become living water in our Christian life.

44. We recognize multiple aspects of the total Christian experience, which embraces the presence of God (joy, enthusiasm, consolation, etc.), and also the experience of our own sin, and the experience of the absence of God, with Christ dying on the cross (Mark 15:34; Phil 3:10), desolation, aridity, and the acceptance of our personal death in Christ as an integral part of the authentic Christian life and also of the true praise of God.

TOPICS FOR FURTHER DISCUSSION

45. In the course of conversations, a number of areas were touched on that are recommended for further study. Among them were the following: a) speaking in tongues as a characteristic aspect of the experience in the Pentecostal movement; b) the subjective dispositions relative to the baptism in the Holy Spirit; c) the relationship between the faith of the individual and the faith of the community in terms of content; d) the relationship between faith and experience; e) the psychological dimension of charismatic experience; f) an examination of the charismata of healing and the casting out of demons; g) the relationship between the sacraments and conscious personal response of God; h) the nature of the sacramental event and, in this context, the nature of the church; i) the problem of interpreting Scripture; j) the

ministries and the ministry gifts: their purpose and operation; k) the social implications of spiritual renewal.

CHARACTER OF THE FINAL REPORT

46. The character of the final report compiled by the steering committee, which has served the dialogue does not represent the official position of the classical Pentecostal denominations, of the charismatic movement in the historic Protestant churches, or of the Roman Catholic Church. Rather it represents the content of the discussions. Though the conclusions are the result of serious study and dialogue by responsible persons, it does not commit any of the churches or traditions to the theological positions here expressed, but is submitted to them for suitable use and reaction.

It has been the consensus of all participants that the dialogue has been an occasion of mutual enrichment and understanding and offers the promise of a continuing relationship.

8

Final Report of the Dialogue between the Secretariat for Promoting Christian Unity of the Roman Catholic Church and Some Classical Pentecostals

1977–1982

INTRODUCTION[1]

1. The following is a report of conversations at the international level that represent a second five-year series, which had its beginnings in informal talks in 1969 and 1970 between the Vatican Secretariat for Promoting Christian Unity and some members of the classical Pentecostal churches. The co-chairmen of this quinquennium were the Rev. David du Plessis of Oakland, California, USA, and the Rev. Kilian McDonnell, OSB, of Collegeville, Minnesota, USA. The conversations took place according to the indications agreed to by the Secretariat for Promoting Christian Unity and the Pentecostal representatives in 1970.

2. This dialogue has its own specific quality. Growth in mutual understanding of classical Pentecostal and Roman Catholic theologies and spiritual practice rather than organic or structural unity is the special object of these bilateral conversations.

3. It is a concern of the dialogue to seek out those areas where classical Pentecostals and Roman Catholics represent divergent theological views and spiritual experiences, and in this way to foster mutual understanding in what distinguishes each partner, such as faith/experience and its role in the Christian life. Without minimizing these differences,

1. The report was published in *Pneuma: The Journal of the Society for Pentecostal Studies* 12.2 (1990) 97–115, and is printed here with kind permission

the dialogue also seeks common theological ground where "the truth of the gospel" is shared (Gal 2:14).

4. The Roman Catholic participants were officially appointed by the Secretariat for Promoting Christian Unity. There were various kinds of representation on the classical Pentecostal side. Some were appointed by their individual churches; a few were church officials; others were members who came with the approbation of their churches; in still other cases they came as members in good standing with their churches.

5. Besides the classical Pentecostals, there were in the first five year series (1972–1976) participants from the charismatic movement in various Protestant churches. These were members of Anglican or Protestant communions with whom the Roman Catholic Church was already in formal contact through bilateral dialogues. These Anglican and Protestant participants took part primarily because of their involvement in the charismatic renewal rather than as members of their own churches. The first five-year series of conversations extended from 1972 through 1976. In those meetings the following topics were discussed: "Baptism in the Holy Spirit" in the New Testament and its relation to repentance, sanctification, charism, rites of initiation; the historic background of the classical Pentecostal movement; the role of the Holy Spirit and the gifts of the Spirit in the mystical tradition; the theology of the rites of initiation, the nature of sacramental activity; infant and adult baptism; public worship, with special attention given to eucharistic worship; discernment of spirits; and the human dimension in the exercise of the spiritual gifts; prayer and praise.

6. In 1977, a second five year series was initiated. This second series, 1977–1982 (no session was held in 1978 because of the death of the Pope), had a different character than the first series. In order to more clearly focus the conversations, it was decided that this second series should be exclusively a conversation between the classical Pentecostals and the Roman Catholic Church. Therefore, participants in the charismatic renewal who were members of the Anglican and Protestant churches were not included in the dialogue in a systematic way.

7. At the first meeting of the second series of talks, held in Rome, Octo-ber 1977, the dialogue discussed speaking in tongues and the relation of experience to faith. The second meeting in Rome, October 1979, discussed the relation of Scripture and tradition, and the ministry of healing in the church. In Venice, October 1980, the meeting focused on

church as a worshiping community, and tradition and traditions. The meeting in Vienna in October, 1981, focused on the role of Mary. The last meeting of the series was held at Collegeville, Minnesota, in October 1982, where ministry was the area of concentration.

SPEAKING IN TONGUES

8. A personal relationship with Jesus Christ belongs to the definition of a Christian. Classical Pentecostals have never accepted the position or taught that this relationship must necessarily be expressed through speaking in tongues in the sense that one could not be a Christian without speaking in tongues.

9. The manifestation of tongues was never entirely absent in the history of the church, and is found in a notable way among Roman Catholics and other Christians involved in charismatic renewal, as well as among classical Pentecostals.

10. It was agreed that every discussion about Christian glossolalia should be founded on Scripture. That some New Testament authors saw tongues as playing a role in the Christian life is indicated in various books of the Bible. "And they were all filled with the Holy Spirit and began to speak in other tongues as the Spirit gave them utterance" (Acts 2:4; 10:46; 19:6; Mark 16:17; 1 Cor 12:4, 10, 18; 14:2, 5, 22; Rom 8:26).

11. The teaching of the classical Pentecostals on the charisms seeks to be faithful to the picture of the New Testament church as reflected in 1 Corinthians 12–14. Classical Pentecostals have rendered a service by encouraging the various communions to be open and receptive to those spiritual manifestations to which they claim to have been faithful.

FAITH AND EXPERIENCE

12. By experience the dialogue understands the process or event by which one comes to a personal awareness of God. The experience of God's "presence" or "absence" can be matter of conscious awareness. At the same time, and at a deeper level, there remains the constant abiding faith-conviction that God's loving presence is revealed in the person of his Son, through the Holy Spirit.

13. A Christian is one who experiences not only Easter and Pentecost, but also the cross. The experience of God's "absence" can lead a Christian to a sense of being abandoned, as Jesus himself experi-

enced on the cross. The death of Christ is to be found at the heart of our Christian experience, and therefore we too experience a death: "I have been crucified with Christ; it is no longer I who live, but Christ who lives in me" (Gal 2:20).

14. There was no unanimity whether non-Christians may receive the life of the Holy Spirit. According to contemporary Roman Catholic understanding, to which Vatican II gives an authoritative expression, "All must be converted to Jesus Christ as he is made known by the church's preaching" (*Ad gentes*, §7). "The church . . . is necessary for salvation" (*Lumen gentium* §14). But Vatican II also says that all without exception are called by God to faith in Christ, and to salvation (*Lumen gentium*, §1, 16; *Nostra aetate*, §1, 2). This is brought about "in an unseen way . . . known only to God" (*Gaudium et spes*, §22; *Ad gentes*, §7). This theology is seen as a legitimate development of the total New Testament teaching on God's saving love in Christ. The classical Pentecostal participants do not accept this development, but retain their interpretation of the Scripture that non-Christians are excluded from the life of the Spirit: "Truly, truly I say unto you, unless one is born anew, he cannot see the kingdom of God" (John 3:3).

15. In the Holy Spirit's manifestation in persons, he engages the natural faculties. In the exercise of the charisms, human faculties are not set aside, but used. The action of the Sprit is not identical with the forces inherent in nature.

16. Individual spiritual experience is seen as part of the communitarian dimension of the gospel. Persons live in community, and the church should be a lived-experience of community. There is rich history of community experience in the church.

17. No matter how vivid or powerful the individual's spiritual experience may be, it needs to be discerned and judged by the community. Love, which is the normative bond of community life, is the biblical criterion of all spiritual experience (cf. 1 Corinthians 13).

SCRIPTURE AND TRADITION

18. Both Pentecostals and Roman Catholics hold that the books of the Old Testament were accepted by the early church as inspired. The primitive church existed for a period without its own Christian Scriptures. Of the early Christian writings, a certain number were accepted by the church, in the light of the Holy Spirit, as inspired.

19. Roman Catholics believe that these Scriptures have been handed down through the centuries in a tradition of living faith, a tradition which has been experienced by the whole church, guided by church leaders, operative in all aspects of Christian life, and on occasion expressed in written form in creeds, councils, etc. This tradition is not a source of revelation separate from Scripture, but Scripture responded to and actualized in the living tradition of the church.

20. Pentecostals maintain that there are not two authorities (i.e., Scripture plus church tradition) but one authority, that of Scripture. However, Scripture must be read and understood with the illumination of the Holy Spirit. Pentecostals believe that the interpretation of Scripture can only be discerned through the Holy Spirit. In Pentecostal movements there is a broad consensus of what elements are fundamental to the Christian faith. But there is a reluctance to give this consensus a status of tradition, because of a fear that religious tradition operates against the gospel.

21. Pentecostals feel that further dialogue will be needed to discuss how the Roman Catholic Church can propose, as a matter of faith, doctrines such as the assumption of Mary, which go beyond the letter of Scripture, and which Pentecostals believe to be unacceptable tradition.

EXEGESIS

22. In contemporary Roman Catholic scholarship, the historical-critical method is the accepted framework within which exegesis is done. In this method emphasis is given to understanding an ancient author in his own idiom, cultural context, and religious background.

23. Pentecostals reject the philosophical and theological principles of form and redaction criticism as militating against the plenary inspiration of Scripture. They insist on the necessity of the light given by the Holy Spirit if the reader is to respond with faith and understanding to the Word of God. It was a consensus of the participants that this discussion a was valuable contribution to the dialogue.

24. Roman Catholics believe that the light of the Holy Spirit given in and through the church is the ultimate principle of interpretation of Scripture. They reject any exegetical method that would deny this. However, they believe that critical methods are compatible with a Spirit-inspired exegesis, and consider them necessary for a proper understanding of the text.

25. The Pentecostal form of exegesis, while having its roots in Evangelicalism, is not specifically defined. It is admittedly in a formative stage. Current exegesis would tend to be a pneumatic literal interpretation.

BIBLICAL INTERPRETATION

26. In the event of conflicting interpretation of Scripture texts, Roman Catholics accept the guidance of the Spirit as manifested in the living tradition. While the teaching of the church stands under the Word of God, this same teaching serves the authoritative and authentic communication of the Word of God to the people (*Dogmatic Constitution on Divine Revelation*, §10). While Catholics believe both Scripture and Tradition cohere in each other and, thus, transmit the Word of God, they do accord a priority to Scripture.

27. In the event of conflicting interpretation of Scripture texts, Pente-costals rely on the Holy Spirit's guidance, without the developed dogmatic structure found in the Roman Catholic Church. While there may be some danger or subjectivism, God is trusted to provide the guidance of the Spirit within the local body of believers (John 14:26; 15:26; 16:13; 2 John 2:27).

FAITH AND REASON

28. In the determination of the limits and validation of religious knowledge, it was agreed that faith and reason cannot be polarized. However, Pentecostals place a greater emphasis upon pneumatic inspiration and supernatural manifestations than on reason for determining the limits and validity of religious knowledge.

29. In spite of the differences mentioned above, it is seen that classical Pentecostals and Roman Catholics agree on the basic elements of the Christian faith, e.g., Trinity, incarnation, resurrection, inspiration of Scripture, the preaching of the gospel as an integral part of the ministry of the church, and the guidance of the Body of Christ by the Holy Spirit.

30. Still needing clarification in this dialogue is the relation between Scripture and tradition. In this relationship, Roman Catholics do grant a priority to Scripture. But according to Vatican Council II, Decree on Divine Revelation, *Dei verbum* (§10) "Sacred tradition and sacred Scripture make up a single sacred deposit of the Word of God. Hence

both Scripture and tradition must be accepted and honored with equal feelings of devotion and reverence." Also in need of further discussion is whether the various methods of exegesis, for example the form-critical method which Catholic exegetes use, are compatible with classical Pentecostal principles.

HEALING IN THE CHURCH

31. The ministry of healing in the church is practiced in both the Roman Catholic Church and the Pentecostal churches as part of their total ministry. Both Pentecostals and Roman Catholics agree that through prayerful petition they seek the healing of the whole person's physical, spiritual, and emotional needs. Catholics consider the "anointing of the sick" a sacrament. Pentecostals accept anointing with oil as a part of the commission to minister healing with the preaching of the gospel. (In the Roman Catholic Church, the sacrament of anointing of the sick was formerly named "extreme unction").

32. In the life of the Roman Catholic Church, there have been, and are, those who dedicate their lives to the care of and ministry to the sick. Pentecostals are becoming increasingly involved in this important aspect of ministry to the sick and suffering.

33. There are attitudinal differences with regard to healing. Roman Catholic practice regards healing of the body as one outcome of the ministry to the sick in the church. Pentecostals place more emphasis on the expectation of healing in the afflicted through preaching and praying. There is a basic difference in each approach to healing. Roman Catholics may seek healing in sacramental rites, in healing services, novenas, and similar forms of devotion. They also go on pilgrimage to shrines where healing may take place. At these places many seek and experience a deepening of faith and a spiritual healing. Pentecostals teach people to expect healing anywhere at any time.

34. Both, in their official teaching, recognize and accept that Jesus is the healer and that faith looks to Jesus for this grace. Pentecostals as well as Roman Catholics exercise reserve in making judgments about miraculous manifestations and healings.

35. There is a difference in expectation—that of Catholics being more passive while that of Pentecostals being more aggressive. There is admittedly a new awareness of the reality of the healing in the Roman Catholic Church, both within and outside the sacramental order. On the

other hand, the dialogue is aware of the existence of some popular religious expressions that may lack sufficient theological understanding.

36. The place of suffering in this life is looked upon by Roman Catholics and some Pentecostals as a means of grace, as a purifying of the soul, and as an instrument for opening one to God's spiritual strength which sustains one and causes one to rejoice in affliction. Both Roman Catholics and Pentecostals believe that suffering may lead one to understand and be conformed (Phil 3:10) to the redemptive suffering of Jesus. However, Pentecostals continue to expect healing unless there is a special revelation that God has some other purpose. Both Roman Catholics and Pentecostals accept that the will of God is preeminent in the whole matter of healing.

37. Although there appears to be some similarity in lay participation in the ministry of healing, the discussions revealed that there is still a wide gap between Catholics and Pentecostals. Catholics, singly and in community, pray for the sick and with the sick. However, only the priest may administer the "Anointing of the Sick" which is a sacrament. Pentecostals anoint with oil (James 5:14–15) but do not confine the anointing to the ordained ministry. The ministry to the sick, with the laying on of hands by all believers (Mark 16:17–18), is commonly practiced.

38. In contemporary Roman Catholic theology, the necessity for healing is applied to a broader spectrum of social ills. In this application of healing to problems of social injustice, Roman Catholics and classical Pentecostals have widely divergent views. Because of economic and cultural exploitation, many people live in sub-human economic disease. Roman Catholics and Pentecostals have different approaches to the mandate to heal the social conditions which hinder good health.

39. Classical Pentecostals are reluctant to apply divine healing to such a broad range of social injustices. Though they believe exploitative conditions should be rectified, they would emphasize the priority of direct evangelism as the best means of effecting social change.

40. There are a number of areas where there is agreement between Roman Catholics and Pentecostals: the necessity of the cross, healing as a sign of the kingdom, healing of the total person, the involvement of the laity in prayer for healing, the expectation of healing through the Eucharist/Lord's Supper, and Christ as the healer.

COMMUNITY, WORSHIP, AND COMMUNICATION

41. Pentecostals insist on a personal confession of faith in Jesus Christ as the basis of Christian community rather than on a sacramental and ecclesial approach to the mediating work of Christ. They hold that the believer experiences Christ in every aspect of the worshiping community: singing, praying, testimony, preaching, the ordinance of baptism, the celebration of holy communion, and also in daily living.

42. Roman Catholics insist on conversion to the living God by personal encounter with the living Christ. This conversation often takes place gradually. For Roman Catholics, the church, its ministry, and sacraments, are the normal instruments and manifestations of Christ's action and presence, and of the gift of His Spirit. The sacraments are acts of Christ which make present and active the saving power of the paschal mystery.

43. For membership in a Pentecostal church, individuals are expected to have experienced a personal confession of faith in Jesus Christ; and then participate in the life, follow the leadership, and be willing to accept responsibility in the church. In some Pentecostal churches, membership is concurrent with one's water baptism by immersion. Membership in the Roman Catholic Church requires baptism, profession of Roman Catholic faith, and active communion with the local community, the bishops, and the successor of St. Peter.

44. Both among Pentecostals and Roman Catholics, members may lose their fellowship in the community for serious deviation in doctrine or practice. This penalty of severance from the church is intended to be remedial, a reminder of one's guilt before God and the need for repentance.

45. Both Pentecostals and Roman Catholics celebrate the Lord's Supper/Eucharist with notable difference in doctrine and practice. Roman Catholics regard the Eucharist as a sacramental memorial of Christ's sacrifice on Calvary in the biblical sense of the word *anamnesis*. By God's power, in the eucharistic celebration, Jesus is present in his death and resurrection. This sacred rite is for Roman Catholics a privileged means of grace and the central act of worship. It is celebrated frequently, even daily. Among Pentecostals, the Lord's Supper does not hold an equally predominant place in their life of worship. Most Pentecostals celebrate the Lord's Supper as an ordinance in obedience to the command of the Lord. Other Pentecostal churches believe this

memorial to be more than a reminder of Jesus' death and resurrection, considering it a means of grace.

46. Generally, Pentecostals practice "open communion," that is, anyone may participate in the Lord's Supper provided they acknowledge the lordship of Christ and have examined their own dispositions (1 Cor 11:28). Except in certain cases of spiritual necessity determined by the church, the Roman church admits to communion only its own members provided they are free from serious sin. This is not meant to be a refusal of fellowship with other Christians, but rather expresses the Roman Catholic Church's understanding of the relationship between the church and the Eucharist.

47. The justification for this practice by Catholics was contested by Pentecostals. This was found to be painful on both sides, and the dialogue agrees that the subject with regard to admission to communion requires a great deal of further discussion.

48. Both Pentecostals and Roman Catholics agree that a common faith is the basis of communion in the body of Christ. For Roman Catholics, full communion means the collegial unity of the heads of the local churches; namely, the bishops, with the bishop of Rome who exercises the primacy. Pentecostals would not attach the same significance to structural bonds between churches. The Roman Catholic Church recognizes the mediation of Christ at work in churches, which are not in full communion with it, through the Word that is preached and believed, the sacraments that are celebrated, and the ministry that is exercised. If it considers that these gifts are not found in their fullness in a particular church, it does not thereby make any judgment on the actual holiness of the members of that church. The Roman Catholic Church describes the relationship of other Christians with Catholics as that of brothers and sisters in an incomplete communion (*Unitatis redintegratio*).

TRADITION AND TRADITIONS

49. Our views concerning the sacredness and importance of Holy Scripture allowed us to sense immediately that we had much more to affirm in one another than to question. Both sides of the dialogue agreed as to the inspired nature of both the Old Testament and the New Testament, thus giving Scripture a privileged place in both churches.

50. The canonicity of the New Testament is agreed upon in terms of selection and the process of its establishment by the church. Both

Pentecostals and Roman Catholics recognize the role of the church in the composition of the books of the New Testament and in the formation of the canon, and both acknowledge that the church preceded the written New Testament.

51. The Pentecostal representatives stress that the church itself was created by the calling (election) of Christ, and formed by the dominical sayings of Jesus, and the messianic interpretation of the Scriptures of Jesus himself (Luke 24:45ff.). In this sense, according to Pentecostals, the church itself was formed by the Word of God. The church's role in the formation of the New Testament is then essentially that of one who transmits, interprets, and applies the salvific message of Jesus Christ. Roman Catholics emphasize more the role of the church as having an authority recognizing and enunciating the truth of the gospel in doctrinal pronouncement.

52. Both sides recognize that Scripture is of necessity linked to interpretation. Both agree that scriptural content itself includes interpretation; that it requires interpretation, and thus an authoritative interpreter. There is significant divergence as to the degree of interpretation within Scripture and the kind of interpretation by the church necessary in order to understand Scripture accurately. Disagreement centers around what or who is an authoritative interpreter. To the Pentecostal it is the right interpretation under the illumination of the Holy Spirit leading to consensus. To the Roman Catholic, it is the church interpreting Scripture as understood by the people of God and discerned by the teaching office of the church. Both Pentecostals and Roman Catholics see interpretative authority as an expression of the activity of the Spirit in the church.

53. Both Catholics and Pentecostals recognize the existence of a process of theological discernment in the on-going life of the church. The Roman Catholics affirm the ministry of discernment by the teaching office of the church and also recognize that a ministry of discernment may exist outside the Roman Catholic Church. The sharpest disagreement arose concerning the irreformable character of some of these discernments. Roman Catholics hold that the faithful will not be led into error when the authority of the church is fully engaged in enunciating the faith. Pentecostals make no such claim.

54. Pentecostals recognize the strength of the Roman Catholic understanding of corporate and collegial interpretation of Scripture. However, Pentecostals would like to share with Roman Catholics their

characteristic experience of direct dependence upon the Holy Spirit for illumination and interpretation of Scripture.

55. A major difference was encountered in the understanding of the role of tradition. Roman Catholics in the dialogue explain tradition in a twofold sense, each sense related to the other. Tradition, here spelled with a capital T, stands for everything that is being and has been handed down; the once for all revelation made by God in Jesus Christ, the Word of God proclaimed in written and oral form, and the whole of the Spirit-filled community response to the truth of the gospel. As such, Tradition contains both an active element of handing down by the church, and a passive one of the material handed down. Within Tradition in this sense, the Word of God as Scripture has a kind of primacy. In this understanding Tradition is a continuous process.

56. Tradition in this sense is not to be confused with traditions. These are various ways of practice and teaching whereby Tradition is transmitted. These traditions become binding only when they are made the object of a special decision of church authority.

57. Classical Pentecostals would not place the same value upon Tradition (or tradition) as Roman Catholics, unless grounded in the express witness of Scripture. The Pentecostals, while acknowledging the accumulation of traditions in their own history, would say that these traditions, apart from Scripture, have little authority in the church.

PERSPECTIVES ON MARY

58. Since Catholic doctrine concerning Mary was perceived as a point of divergence, it was important to classical Pentecostals to discuss this topic. Considerable time was needed to treat the various issues: the doctrine itself, the method by which the doctrine is justified, and the practical consequences at the popular level. The time devoted to the issues is reflected in the space given this topic in the report.

59. Both classical Pentecostals and Roman Catholics agree that the various biblical texts, which mention Mary, witness to the importance of Mary in the New Testament. The point of divergence was the doctrinal development, which took place on the basis of these texts. Classical Pentecostals insist that they cannot go beyond the clear meaning of the text, which is normative for any and all later doctrinal development. But they further hold that the church, praying, and preaching the Scriptures,

can, through the guidance of the Holy Spirit, who leads into all truth, find in the biblical texts, and in complete fidelity to them, a meaning which goes beyond the classical Pentecostals' interpretation.

60. Behind the differences between classical Pentecostals and Roman Catholics in interpretation of specific Marian texts in the Scriptures lie doctrinal differences, often implicit and unexpressed. Possibly the most important of these are in the area of Mary's relationship to the church and her role in the communion of saints.

61. Both classical Pentecostals and Roman Catholics were surprised that they had entertained unreal perceptions of the others' views on Mary. Classical Pentecostals were pleased to learn of the concern of authorities in the Roman Catholic Church to be prudent in appraising Marian doctrinal development, which claims a biblical basis. Classical Pentecostals, while recognizing that doctrinal development that is clearly based on scriptural evidence is not entirely absent from Pentecostal history, admit no doctrinal development with regard to Mary.

THE MOTHERHOOD OF MARY

62. Both Roman Catholics and Pentecostals agree that Mary is the mother of Jesus Christ who is the Son of God, and as such she occupies a unique place. Both Roman Catholics and classical Pente-costals recognize the historical origins of the title "mother of God" (*theotokos*), arising from the christological disputes at the Council of Ephesus (AD 431). In order to preserve the unity of the one person, having two natures, to which the Virgin gave birth, the council approved the title "*theotokos*" ("God-bearer" or "Mother of God"). This was not a Marian definition, concerned to give Mary a new title, but a christological definition concerned with the identity of Jesus Christ. It is only at the moment of the incarnation that she becomes the Mother of God. She is not the mother of God in his eternal triune existence, but the mother of God the Son in his incarnation.

THE VENERATION OF MARY

63. Roman Catholics and classical Pentecostals concur in the special respect due to Mary as the mother of Jesus. Both view her as the outstanding example or model of faith, humility and virtue. Both Roman Catholics and Pentecostals share a concern for the necessity of a correct

perspective on Mary. However, there are significant differences in the understanding of the veneration to be given to Mary.

64. Pentecostals expressed concern about what they consider to be excesses in contemporary veneration of Mary. For Pentecostals, certain Roman Catholic practices of Marian veneration appear to be superstitious and idolatrous. For Roman Catholics, there is an apparent failure among Pentecostals to take account of the place of Mary in God's design as indicated in Holy Scripture.

65. Roman Catholics, while admitting the occurrence of certain excesses in the practice of veneration of Mary, were careful to point out that proper veneration of Mary is always christological. In addition, Roman Catholics gave evidence that practical steps are being taken to correct excesses where they occur, in line with the norms of the Second Vatican Council, *Lumen gentium*, §8, and Pope Paul VI in his encyclical, *Marialis cultus* (1974), §§24–36.

THE INTERCESSION OF MARY

66. Both Pentecostals and Roman Catholics teach that Mary in no way substitutes for, or replaces, the one savior and mediator Jesus Christ. Both believe in direct, immediate contact between the believer and God. Both pray to God the Father, through the Son, in the Holy Spirit. Catholics believe that intercessory prayers directed to Mary do not end in Mary but in God himself. Pentecostals would not invoke the intercession of Mary or other saints in heaven because they do not consider it a valid biblical practice.

CATHOLIC DOCTRINE ON THE GRACES GIVEN TO MARY

67. Roman Catholics believe that Mary always remained a virgin, that she was conceived free from all stain of sin, and that at the end of her life she was assumed body and soul into heaven. Pentecostals reject these beliefs.

68. Roman Catholics claim that belief about these graces given to Mary belongs to the tradition of the church in which the Word of God is unfolded. Pentecostals can find no warrant for these beliefs in Scripture. As well as questioning the value of tradition as a basis for the doctrines of faith, Pentecostals would suggest that these traditions about perpetual

virginity, immaculate conception, and assumption are without Scriptural basis.

69. In the "hierarchy of truths" of faith held by the Roman Catholics, these three doctrines are placed among the truths that are integral to the Roman Catholic faith. Roman Catholics do not believe that those outside the Roman Catholic Church who do not hold these truths are, on that account, excluded from salvation.

THE VIRGINITY OF MARY

70. Both Pentecostals and Roman Catholics agree that Mary was a virgin in the conception of Jesus and see in the texts which state it an important affirmation of the divine Sonship of Christ. Roman Catholics believe that Mary remained a virgin after the birth of Jesus and did not have other offspring. Pentecostals commonly maintain that Scripture records she had other offspring and lived as the wife of Joseph in the full sense.

71. Roman Catholics take the evidence of Scripture as being open to the developments concerning the virginity of Mary that they find expressed in the earliest Fathers of the church. They found in Tradition (understood in the total experience and response of the church as she prays and preaches the Word of God) evidence of Mary's virginity.

THE IMMACULATE CONCEPTION OF MARY

72. Roman Catholics hold the doctrine of the immaculate conception to be founded on the church's reflection on the Bible, both the Old and New Testaments. This doctrine is seen to follow upon texts which present her as the perfect fulfillment of Old Testament types, e.g., "the virgin daughter of Sion" (Luke 1:26–38; cf. Zeph 3:14–20; Zech 2:10; 9:9), the "woman" (John 2:1–11; 19:25–27; cf. Gen 3:15). These texts form a biblical theology of Mary, which provides a basis for the development of the doctrine of the immaculate conception. The explicit development of the doctrine in the life of the church led to its definition by Pope Pius IX in 1854.

73. Pentecostals acknowledge Catholic assurances that the special grace claimed for Mary is a redeeming grace that comes from Jesus. She stands among the redeemed and is a member of the church. However, Pentecostals cannot find any basis for the doctrine of Mary's immaculate

conception in Scripture. Furthermore, Pentecostals do not see any value for salvation in this doctrine. Roman Catholics see in the Pentecostal attitude a failure to appreciate fully the implications of the incarnation and the power of Christ's saving and sanctifying grace.

74. Further clarification of issues arising from this doctrine would entail a wider discussion by us of pneumatology, christology, and ecclesiology. Roman Catholics believe a basic distortion takes place when this doctrine is considered in isolation.

THE ASSUMPTION OF MARY

75. Roman Catholics see the doctrine of the assumption, which was explicitly affirmed in the Fathers of the church as early as the sixth century, to be in accordance with basic biblical doctrines. The risen Christ is the beginning of the new creation, which is born from above in the death and resurrection of Christ. In Mary, because of her unique relationship with Christ, this new creation by the Spirit was achieved to the point that the life of the Spirit triumphed fully in her. Consequently she is already with her body in the glory of God, with her risen Son.

76. The Pentecostal difficulty rests in the absence of biblical evidence. There is a generally accepted view that Mary, as one of the faithful, awaits the day of resurrection when she, along with all Christians, will be united bodily with her Son in glory. Pentecostals see a parallel between Mary's "assumption" and the Pentecostal understanding of the "bodily resurrection" or the "rapture of the church" (1 Thess 4:13–18, cf. esp. v. 17), but differ as to when this will take place for Mary.

MINISTRY IN THE CHURCH

77. While it is recognized that the word "ministry" in the New Testament covers many activities, the focus of the dialogue bears upon how ministry in the church continues the ministry of the apostles.

78. Such ministry includes all that pertains to the preaching and proclamation of God's Word on which the churches are founded, and all that is required for the building up of the church in Christ.

79. For Roman Catholics, all ministries contribute to these ends, but particular importance is attached to the ministry of bishops, and to that of the presbyters and deacons who collaborate with them. Classical Pentecostals find an exercise of apostolic ministry wherever through

the preaching of God's Word churches are founded, persons and communities are converted to Jesus Christ, and manifestations of the Holy Spirit are in evidence. Within the variety of polity found in Pentecostal circles, biblical terms such as elder, deacon, bishop, and pastors are used to designate a variety of offices and ministries, and are not always given the same meaning.

80. It is agreed by both sides of the dialogue that order and structure are necessary to the exercise of ministry.

81. In the development and structuring of ministry, there is no single New Testament pattern. The Spirit has many times led churches to adapt their ministries to the needs of place and time.

82. Roman Catholics see evidence of ministerial office in the New Testament and find in such office part of God's design for the early church, but find in the gradual emergence of the threefold ministry of bishop, presbyter, and deacon the way in which God's design is fulfilled and structural and ministerial needs are met in the church.

83. The position of Classical Pentecostals are more varied. Although there is reluctance in some Pentecostal circles to speak of the ministries of apostle and prophet because of the historical abuse sometimes associated with these ministries, they are recognized as existing and important to the life of the church. Even though there is no uniformity in the way that the New Testament depicts ministry, it is the desire of Pentecostals to seek guidelines for ministry and office in the New Testament.

84. Pentecostals appeal primarily to the priesthood of all believers, which connotes access to God and a participation in ministry on the part of all believers. Pentecostals point to a problem of over-institutionalization of ministry. They believe that they find evidence of this in the history and practice of the Roman Catholic Church.

85. Roman Catholics place emphasis on the need for the institution of ecclesial offices as part of the divine plan for the church. They also see such institutions and ministries as related to and aiding the priesthood and ministry of all within the one body.

ORDINATION

86. Pentecostals see ordination as a recognition of spiritual gifts already imparted. For Pentecostals, ministry is always initiated by a divine call and attended by evidence of reception of necessary gifts and graces. Ordination of one who has received appropriate gifts provides denomi-

national authority for his continuing function in the ministry to which he has been called.

87. For Roman Catholics, the ministry of ecclesial office is given by God who calls a candidate and pours out his Spirit upon him and gives him a special share in the priesthood of Christ. This gift must be discerned by the church, in the form laid down by church discipline. Ordination is considered a sacrament, which imparts grace, gifts and authority for the ministry of the word, sacrament and pastoral office.

APOSTOLIC SUCCESSION

88. Both Roman Catholics and Pentecostals believe that the church lives in continuity with the New Testament apostles and their proclamation, and with the apostolic church. A primary manifestation of this is to be found in fidelity to the apostolic teaching.

89. For Roman Catholics, the succession of bishops in an orderly transmission of ministry through history is both guarantee and manifestation of this fidelity.

90. For Pentecostals, the current dynamic of the Spirit is regarded as a more valid endorsement of apostolic faith and ministry than an unbroken line of episcopal succession. They look to apostolic life and to the power of preaching, which leads to conversions to Jesus Christ as an authentication of apostolic ministry. They question Roman Catholics as to whether in their insistence on episcopal succession they have at times ignored the requirements of apostolic life. Roman Catholics held the necessity of apostolic life for an effective ministry. However, they maintain that the sovereignty of God's act in the transmission of the Word and the ministry of sacrament is not nullified by the personal infidelity of the minister.

91. Both partners to the dialogue strongly assert that holiness of life is essential to an effective ministry and recognize that the quality of apostolic life of the minister has an effect on the quality of his ministry. Both, by their respective discipline and practice, seek to provide seriously for the holiness of ministers. Both recognize that, at times, the power and sovereignty of God is operative in the ministry of a weak and sinful minister, although the discipline of both classical Pentecostals and Roman Catholics provides for the removal from office of anyone who is plainly unworthy.

RECOGNITION OF MINISTRIES

92. Each partner to the dialogue recognizes that God is at work through the ministry of the other and recognizes that the body of Christ is being built up through it (*Unitatis redintegratio*, §3 and §22). The issue of recognition depends on ecclesiological questions that still need elucidation. However, serious disagreements still remain.

TOPICS FOR FURTHER DISCUSSION

93. During our conversations, we touched on a number of topics which could not be discussed adequately and would have to be taken up at a later date. Among them were the following: a) the personal moment of faith, b) the communion of saints in relation to Mariology and the intercession of the saints, c) the development of doctrine in its relation to Scripture and Tradition, d) the inadequacy and limitation in doctrinal formulations marked with the stamp of a certain historical moment, e) the binding force of the Marian doctrines, which have been defined as they relate to salvation, within the Roman Catholic Church.

CHARACTER OF THE FINAL REPORT

94. This international dialogue with representatives of classical Pente-costals and Roman Catholics has been characterized by the seriousness of the exchange as participants seek to reflect in all fidelity the doctrine of their church and at the same time to learn from their opposite partners in dialogue what their true faith stance is. These responsibilities have been exercised with candor and earnestness and have resulted in this final report. Clearly, the report does not commit any church or tradition to any theological position but is offered to them for their reflection and evaluation.

CONCLUSION

95. The members of the dialogue have experienced mutual respect and acceptance, hoping that the major points of difference will provide an occasion for continuing dialogue to our mutual enrichment.

96. It is the consensus of the participants that the dialogue should continue in this same spirit. Every effort will be made to encourage opportunities for similar bi-lateral theological conversation at the local level.

97. To that end, the dialogue enters into a period of assimilation to digest the results of the first two phases of exchange and to give broader exposure to mutual efforts undertaken to promote better understanding.

98. Finally, the participants wish to affirm the dialogue as an ongoing instrument of communication between the two traditions.

9

Perspectives on *Koinonia*. Final Report of the Dialogue between the Roman Catholic Church and Some Classical Pentecostal Churches and Leaders

1985–1989

INTRODUCTION[1]

1. This is a report of conversations held on the international level between the Pontifical Council for Promoting Christian Unity[2] and some classical Pentecostal churches and leaders. It contains the results of the third phase of dialogue held 1985–1989.

2. Contacts for the dialogue were initiated in 1969 and 1970. Among the topics discussed during the first quinquennium (1972–1976) were baptism in the Holy Spirit, Christian initiation and the charisms, Scripture and tradition, and the human person and the gifts. In the second quinquennium (1977–1982), consideration was given to faith and religious experience, speaking in tongues, and Mary. The co-chairpersons during this third quinquennium, 1985–1989, were the Rev. Kilian McDonnell, OSB, Collegeville, Minnesota, USA, and the Rev. Justus T. du Plessis of the Apostolic Faith Mission of South Africa. The conversations dealt with the subject of the church as *koinonia*.

3. The Rev. David J. du Plessis chaired the Pentecostal delegation during the first two phases of the dialogue. Indeed, the origin of the international Pentecostal-Roman Catholic dialogue, almost twenty years

1. The report was published in *Pneuma: The Journal of the Society for Pentecostal Studies* 12.2 (1990) 117–42, and is printed here with kind permission.

2. Until 1989 the Pontifical Council was known as the Secretariat for Promoting Christian Unity.

ago, owes much to initiatives he took during and after the Second Vatican Council. David du Plessis continued to take part in the third phase of the dialogue, providing important insights to our deliberations, until his death in 1987. The dialogue commission acknowledges, with gratitude to God, David du Plessis' important contribution to the origin and continuation of our work.

4. This particular series of discussions has been noted for the growing acceptance of the dialogue by the worldwide Pentecostal community. For the first time, several Pentecostal churches authorized the participation of officially appointed representatives to the dialogue. These churches include: the Apostolic Church of Mexico (1986); the Apostolic Faith Mission of South Africa (1985–1989); the Church of God (Cleveland, Tennessee, USA) (1985–1988); the Church of God of Prophecy, USA (1986–1988); the Independent Assemblies of God International, USA (1987); the International Church of the Foursquare Gospel, USA (1985–1989); the International Communion of Charismatic Churches, USA (1986).

5. Although the unity of the church is a concern of Pentecostals and Roman Catholics alike, the dialogue has not had as its goal or its subject, either organic or structural union. These discussions were meant to develop a climate of mutual understanding in matters of faith and practice; to find points of genuine agreement as well as to indicate areas in which further dialogue is required. We hope that further theological convergence will appear as we continue to explore issues together.

6. Building upon the groundwork laid in the previous two series of discussions, this phase of dialogue focused upon the theme of *koinonia*. At its 1985 meeting in Riano, Italy, discussion was directed to the subject of the communion of the saints. In Sierra Madre, California, USA, during 1986, the subject was the Holy Spirit and the New Testament vision of *koinonia*. Discussion was directed toward the relationship of sacraments to *koinonia*, in 1987 and 1988. At the meeting in Venice, Italy, in 1987, the dialogue focused upon *koinonia*, church, and sacraments emphasizing the place of the Eucharist, while in its 1988 meeting at Emmetten, Switzerland, the discussion was on *koinonia* and baptism. During the 1989 meeting in Rome we summarized our findings in this report. The presentation of the findings in this report follows a more systematic order than the chronological sequence in which the topics were discussed.

7. The theme of *koinonia* was chosen for several reasons. First, the subject of communion of saints emerged from the portions of the discussions in the second phase of dialogue which had centered on Mary. Participants in the second phase believed that the topic of communion was pregnant with possibilities. Second, they also realized that the larger worldwide ecumenical dialogue was viewing the topic of communion with interest and expectation.

8. *Koinonia* has been an important topic for discussion in a number of international dialogues, for example, in the Orthodox-Roman Catholic dialogue; the second phase of the Anglican-Roman Catholic international dialogue; the Methodist-Roman Catholic dialogue; the Lutheran-Roman Catholic dialogue; the Baptist-Roman Catholic dialogue; and the Disciples of Christ-Roman Catholic dialogue.

9. The theme of *koinonia* is proving fruitful in the reflection about ecclesiological self-understanding in many Christian churches and communions, as for example in the Anglican Communion and the Lutheran World Federation.[3]

10. During the Second Vatican Council, the Roman Catholic Church emphasized the ecclesiology of communion. The Extraordinary Synod of Bishops, which met in 1985 to celebrate the twentieth anniversary of the closing of the Second Vatican Council, recognized the importance given to the notion of communion by the Council. In Pentecostal teaching, *koinonia* is understood as an essential aspect of church life, as it relates to the church's ministry to the world and to the relationships of Christians to one another. Both the Roman Catholics and Pentecostals, therefore, have come to appreciate the biblical importance of *koinonia* as portrayed in Acts 2:42: "they [Christians] devoted themselves to the apostles' teaching and fellowship [*koinonia*], to the breaking of bread and the prayers."[4]

11. One of the difficulties we faced in our discussions was the historical difference between the development of the doctrine of the church in Roman Catholicism and in the various Pentecostal traditions. Roman Catholics have a centuries-long tradition of ecclesiological reflection; the

3. At its Eighth General Assembly in February, 1990, the Lutheran World Federation voted to change its constitution. It now describes itself as a "communion of churches."

4. Scripture quotations in this publication are from the Revised Standard Version of the Bible, copyrighted 1946, 1957, 1971, 1973 by the Division of Christian Education of the National Council of the churches of Christ in the USA.

Pentecostal movement is less than a century old and has had little opportunity to engage in sustained theological reflection on ecclesiology. Although Pentecostals do not possess a developed ecclesiology, they do embrace a variety of ecclesiological polities, and they hold strongly to certain basic ecclesiological convictions (e.g., the importance of the local congregation). These convictions have been brought to bear on the various issues discussed.

12. While all dialogue participants have sought to represent their church's positions faithfully, the views expressed in this document are those of the joint commission, which now offers its work to the sponsoring bodies.

I. KOINONIA AND THE WORD OF GOD

13. Though the focus of our dialogue was church as *koinonia*, the question of Scripture and Tradition kept surfacing in all our discussions. We found that much of the agreement and also the disagreement stemmed from the similarities and differences in our understandings of the ultimate bases on which doctrine and practice of the church should rest. Even though we discussed the topic of Scripture and Tradition more extensively in previous phases of the dialogue,[5] we offer the following brief summary of our respective views on Scripture and Tradition because of its link to the topic of this particular dialogue.

A) Jesus Christ the Perfect Word of God

14. After speaking in many places and in a variety of ways through the prophets, God has now "in these last days . . . spoken to us by a Son" (Heb 1:1–2). He sent his Son, the Eternal Word of God, who became flesh (cf. John 1:14).

15. Together we believe that our Lord Jesus Christ revealed God in a perfect way through his whole ministry: through his words and deeds,

5. Final Report (1972–1976) nos. 28–30; Final Report (1977–1982) nos. 18–21; 49–57. These reports are published in *Information Service*. Secretariat For Promoting Christian Unity Vatican City, No. 32 (1976/111) pp. 32–37, and No. 55 (1984/11–111) pp. 72–80. The 1977–1982 reports are also published in Kilian McDonnell, ed. *Presence, Power, Praise*, vol. 3 (Collegeville, MN: Liturgical Press, 1980) 373–95, and in Arnold Bittlinger, *Papst und Pfingstler*, Frankfurt: Lang, 1978. For the report of the 1977–1982 discussions, see Jerry L. Sandidge, *Roman Catholic Pentecostal Dialogue (1977–1982): A Study in Developing Ecumenism* (Frankfurt: Lang, 1987).

his signs and wonders, but especially through his death and glorious resurrection from the dead, and finally by sending the Spirit of truth (cf. John 15:26; 16:7,12).

16. Jesus Christ is the ultimate and permanent Word of God. The Chris-tian dispensation, as the new and definitive covenant, will never pass away, and we now await no further revelation before the glorious manifestation of our Lord Jesus Christ (1 Tim 6:14; Titus 2:13).

B) The Written Word of God

17. We believe together that the books of both the Old and New Testaments have been written, in their entirety, under the inspiration of the Holy Spirit (cf. John 20:31, 2 Tim 3:16; 2 Pet 1:19, 21; 3:15–16). Scripture is the Word of God written in human words in history.

18. Without suppressing the humanity of the biblical writers, God used them to express God's perfect will to God's people. The Scripture teaches faithfully and without error that truth which God wanted put into the sacred writings for our salvation (cf. 2 Tim 3:16).

19. We disagree on the limits of the canon of Scriptures. Roman Catholics and Orthodox have the same canon. Pentecostals agree with the Reformation churches in their view of the canon as limited to the sixty-six books of the Old and New Testaments. While Pentecostals do not deny that the books which Roman Catholics treat as deutero-canonical are valuable for the edification of God's people, they do not consider them as normative for faith and practice.

20. Catholics argue that it is significant that the church precedes chronologically the writings of the New Testament. These writings collectively bring together the message transmitted orally by the early apostolic Christian community, filled with the Holy Spirit, and constitute also the witness and response of the people of God to the truth of the gospel.

21. The Roman Catholic Church sees in the texts of the New Testament—whose authors were inspired—the normative expression of revelation which closed with the death of the last apostle. The writings of the New Testament thus express, in a normative fashion, the apostolic tradition. The determination of the canon of Scripture by the church is also an act of that Tradition. The proper interpretation of Scripture has to be made in the communion of the believers, within the living Tradition which is guided by the Holy Spirit. The same Spirit, who inspired the

Scriptures, also opens the sense of the Scripture to the people of God, so that it nourishes their faith.

22. Both Roman Catholics and Pentecostals recognize that the chosen vessels of God, who wrote the New Testament, belonged to the church, and they stress that the New Testament biblical authors had a unique place in the history of revelation. Since the church inherited the Scripture from the Old Testament people of God, Israel, and from Jesus himself, and since the church rose out of the proclamation of Christ's chosen apostles, it must be considered the creation of the Word of God. The church can live in accordance with the will of God only as it submits itself to the prophetic and apostolic testimony contained in the Scriptures. By accepting the books of the New Testament into the canon of Scriptures, the church recognized the New Testament writings as the Word of God addressed to humanity.

23. Pentecostals believe that some traditions express correctly the saving truth to which Scripture testifies (e.g., Apostles' and Nicene creeds), but they seek to evaluate all traditions in the light of the Word of God in Scripture, the ultimate norm of faith and practice in the church.

24. Both Pentecostals and Roman Catholics agree that Scripture, inspired by the Spirit, can be properly interpreted only with the help of the Holy Spirit. "So also no one comprehends the thoughts of God except the Spirit of God" because spiritual things "are spiritually discerned" (1 Cor 2:11,14).

25. There is, however, a significant divergence as to the nature of interpretation which is necessary to understand Scripture accurately. In Roman Catholicism, the interpretation of the Scripture goes on daily in the lives of the faithful at many levels, such as in the family, in the pulpit, and in the classroom. The whole body of the faithful, who have an anointing that comes from the Holy One, cannot err in matters of belief (cf. 1 John 2:20, 27). This characteristic is shown in the supernatural appreciation of the faith (*sensus fidei*) of the whole people, when "from the bishops to the last of the faithful" they manifest a universal consent in matters of faith and morals" (Second Vatican Council, *Lumen gentium*, §12).[6] Roman Catholics hold that the teaching office of the church "is not above the Word of God, but serves it, teaching only what has

6. All quotations from the Second Vatican Council are from Walter M. Abbott, ed. *The Documents of Vatican II* (New York: Guild Press, America Press, Association Press, 1966).

been handed on, listening to it devoutly, guarding it scrupulously, and explaining it faithfully by divine commission and with the help of the Holy Spirit" (*Dei verbum*, §10).

26. Pentecostals appreciate the work of interpretation of Scripture going on in the Catholic church; however they look with skepticism on any claim that the whole body of faithful cannot err in matters of belief. Pentecostals also believe that God has given special gifts of teaching to the believing community (1 Cor 12:28; Eph 4:12). But, because Pentecostals hold that Scripture is clear in all essential points, they believe that each Christian can interpret Scripture under the guidance of the Spirit and with the help of the discerning Christian community. Thus, Christians can make responsible judgments for themselves in matters of faith and practice through their use of Scripture.

27. Roman Catholics encourage Pentecostals to develop greater contact with the wider Christian community's historical interpretation and biblical hermeneutics. Both Roman Catholics and Pentecostals are together growing in respect for the exegetical endeavor and its enriching findings.

28. Since the beginning of this century, Roman Catholics have been according a greater place to Scripture in preaching, liturgy, personal reading, and prayer. Pentecostals in recent years have come to appreciate the importance of the faithful teachers of the Word of God through church history. The aspiration of all parties in the dialogue is that, under the guidance of the one Holy Spirit, there will be an increasingly common insight into the meaning of Scripture, which would help overcome the divisions between Christians.

II. THE HOLY SPIRIT AND THE NEW TESTAMENT VISION OF *KOINONIA*

A) Koinonia with the Triune God

29. Both Pentecostals and Roman Catholics believe that the *koinonia* between Christians is rooted in the life of Father, Son, and Holy Spirit.[7] Furthermore, they believe that this trinitarian life is the highest

7. A segment of Pentecostals known as "Oneness" or "Jesus Name" Pentecostals are opposed to the trinitarian formulation of the faith. Their view of God tends toward modalism and the baptismal formula which they pronounce is "in the name of Jesus Christ" (Acts 2:38) instead of the traditional trinitarian appeal to Matthew 28:19. Most

expression of the unity to which we together aspire: "that which we have seen and heard we proclaim also to you, so that you may have fellowship with us; and our fellowship is with the Father and with his Son Jesus Christ" (1 John 1:3).

30. Both Roman Catholics and Pentecostals agree that the Holy Spirit is the source of *koinonia* or communion. The church has been gathered in the Holy Spirit (cf. 2 Cor 13:13). They differ, however, in their points of departure and in their emphases.

31. Roman Catholics, on the one hand, stress the God-givenness of the *koinonia* and its trinitarian character. Their point of departure is the baptismal initiation into the trinitarian *koinonia* by faith, through Christ in his Spirit. Their emphasis is also on the Spirit-given means to sustain this *koinonia* (e.g., Word, ministry, sacraments, charisms).

32. Pentecostals, on the other hand, stress that the Holy Spirit convicts people of sin, bringing them through repentance and personal faith into fellowship with Christ and one another (cf. 1 Cor 1:9). As believers continue to be filled with the Spirit (cf. Eph 5:18), they should be led to seek greater unity in the faith with other Christians. The Holy Spirit is the Spirit of unity (cf. Acts 2:1ff.). Just as the Spirit fell on Gentiles and showed the church to be a universal community, made of both Jews and Gentiles (cf. Acts 10), so also today God is bestowing his Spirit everywhere on Christians from different churches, promoting unity around our common Lord. The common experience of the Holy Spirit challenges us to strive for greater visible unity as we reflect on the shape God wants this unity to take.

33. Our dialogue has helped both partners to discover and appreciate each other's specific emphases. On the one hand, by listening to the Roman Catholic participants, Pentecostals have been reminded of the importance of the communitarian dimension of the New Testament understanding of *koinonia*. Roman Catholics, on the other hand, have been reminded of the importance of the personal dimension of the same *koinonia* with God that comes from the Holy Spirit, who convicts persons of sin and brings them to faith in Jesus Christ. We believe that these two emphases are not mutually exclusive, but rather that they are complementary.

Pentecostals, however, strongly disagree with this position.

B) Oneness of the Church

34. Roman Catholics and Pentecostals believe that there is only "one holy catholic apostolic church" made of all believers (cf. Eph 4:4–6). They differ, however, in their understanding of that one church and of the way one belongs to it. Roman Catholics consider the establishment of denominations which result from the lack of love and/or divergence in matters of faith as departures away from the unity of the one church, which in fulfillment of the command of the Lord always remains visibly one and subsists in the Roman Catholic Church (*Lumen gentium*, §8). Pentecostals tend to view denominations as more or less legitimate manifestations of the one, universal church. Their legitimacy depends on the degree of their faithfulness to the fundamental doctrines of the Scripture. We both agree that the Holy Spirit is the Spirit of unity in diversity (cf. 1 Cor 12:13ff.) and not the Spirit of division.

35. By appealing to Jesus' teaching on the wheat and tares (Matt 13:24–30), some Christians distinguish between an invisible church (which is one) and a visible church (which may be divided). While this distinction can be of use in distinguishing between sincere and insincere members of the church, it can cause misunderstanding, since both Pentecostals and Roman Catholics affirm that the church is both a visible and an invisible reality. Neither should the distinction between visible and invisible dimensions of the church be used to justify and reinforce separation between Christians.

36. The essential unity of the church neither implies nor mandates uniformity. "For just as the body is one and has many members, and all the members of the body, though many, are one body, so it is with Christ" (1 Cor 12:12). The diversity is due to the Spirit. "Now there are varieties of gifts, but the same Spirit; and there are varieties of service, but the same Lord; and there are varieties of working, but it is the same God who inspires them all in every one. To each is given the manifestation of the Spirit for the common good" (1 Cor 12:4–7). The unity, which the Spirit forges, is resplendent with diversity. The basis of this unity is the lordship of Jesus Christ. No one can confess this lordship except in the Holy Spirit (cf. 1 Cor 12:3). The unity, which the Spirit gives, must not be identified simply with likemindedness, sociological compatibility, or the felt need for togetherness.

C) Koinonia and Gospel Witness

37. The present state of visible separation in Christianity is a contradiction of the unity into which we are called by Christ. Fidelity to the concept of *koinonia* places upon all Christians the obligation of striving to overcome our divisions, especially through dialogue. We need to discern alertly, and in an on-going way, the character and shape of the visible unity demanded by *koinonia*.

38. Roman Catholics and Pentecostals lament the scandal of disunity between Christians. The lack of agreement on how *koinonia* should be lived out in the church, and our resulting divisions cloud the world's perception of God's work of reconciliation. Insofar as *koinonia* is obscured, the effectiveness of the witness is impaired. For the sake of giving an effective gospel witness, the issue of Christian unity must be kept before us. For our Lord has prayed for his disciples "that they may all be one; even as thou Father, art in me, and I in thee, that they also may be in us, so that the world may believe that thou has sent me" (John 17:21; cf. John 13:34).

III. KOINONIA AND BAPTISM[8]

A) The Meaning of Baptism

39. Pentecostals and Roman Catholics agree that baptism is prefigured in Old Testament symbolism, e.g., in the salvation of Noah and his family (cf. 1 Pet 3:20–21); the Exodus through the Red Sea (cf. 1 Cor 10:1–5); washing as a symbol of the cleansing power of the Holy Spirit (cf. Ezek 36:25).

40. They further agree that baptism was instituted by Christ, and that he commanded his disciples to go "and make disciples of all nations, baptizing them in the name of the Father and of the Son and of the Holy Spirit" (Matt 8:19). In accordance with the Lord's commission, his disciples baptized those who were added to the fellowship of believers (cf. Acts 2:41).

41. Pentecostals and Roman Catholics differ in that Roman Catholics understand baptism to be a sacrament, while most Pentecostals understand it in terms of an ordinance (i.e., a rite that the Lord has commanded his church to perform). Some Pentecostals, however, do use

8. We devote a special section to baptism because of the difficulty which baptism and the practice of baptism have in our dialogue.

the term sacrament to describe baptism. These differences illustrate the need for further discussion between Roman Catholics and Pentecostals on the meaning of the terms "sacrament" and "ordinance."

42. Most Pentecostals hold that believers' baptism is clearly taught in Scripture (cf. Mark 16:16; Acts 2:38; 8:12, 36–39; 10:34–38) and, therefore, believe that baptism of infants should not be practiced. Roman Catholics admit that there is no incontrovertible evidence for baptism of infants in the New Testament, although some texts (notably the so-called household baptism texts, e.g., Acts 16:15 and 16:31–33) are understood as having a reference in that direction. Roman Catholics note, however, that through a process of discernment during the early centuries of the church, a development took place in which infant baptism became widely practiced within the church; was seen as being of apostolic origin; was approved by many of the Fathers of the church; and was received by the church as authentic.

B) Faith and Baptism

43. Pentecostals and Roman Catholics agree that faith precedes and is a precondition of baptism (cf. Mark 16:16), and that faith is necessary for baptism to be authentic. They also agree that the faith of the believing community, its prayer, its instruction, nurture the faith of the candidate.

44. Roman Catholics believe that the faith of an infant is a covenant gift of God given in the grace of baptism, cleansing the child from original sin, and introducing it to new life in the body of Christ. Infant baptism is the beginning of a process towards full maturity of faith in the life of the Spirit, which is nurtured by the believing community.

45. The majority of Pentecostals practice believers' baptism exclusively, rather than infant baptism. They affirm that faith is the gift of God (cf. Eph 2:8), but at the same time stress that it is essentially a personal response of an individual. The Scripture says: "if you confess with your lips that Jesus is Lord and believe in your heart that God raised him from the dead, you will be saved" (Rom 10:9). Because they believe that faith must be personally expressed, Pentecostals maintain that an infant cannot receive the impartation of faith unto salvation (Eph 2:8), or the Holy Spirit. And because they believe that a conscious faith response to the proclamation of the gospel on the part of the candidate is a necessary precondition for baptism, they do not baptize infants.

46. The general refusal of the Pentecostals to practice infant baptism notwithstanding, Roman Catholics and Pentecostals affirm that the grace of God is operative in the life of an infant. It is God who takes initiative for our salvation, and God does so not only in the life of adults but also in the life of infants. Scripture tells us, for instance, that John the Baptist was filled with the Holy Spirit from his mother's womb (cf. Luke 1:15; cf. also Jer 1:5).

47. Pentecostals and Roman Catholics differ over when one "comes to Christ" and about the significance of baptism itself. For all Pentecostals, there is no coming to Christ apart from a person's turning away from sin in repentance and toward God in faith (cf. 1 Thess 1:9), through which they become a part of the believing community. Baptism is withheld until after a person's conscious conversion. Most Pentecostals regard the act of baptism as a visible symbol of regeneration. Other Pentecostals have a sacramental understanding of baptism.

48. Roman Catholics describe conversion as a process incorporating the individual in the church by baptism. Even in infant baptism, a later personal appropriation, or acceptance, of one's baptism is an absolute necessity.

49. Roman Catholics and Pentecostals agree that a deep personal relationship to Christ is essential to Christian life. They also see how conversion is not only a personal or individual act, but an act that presupposes a proclaiming community before conversion and requires a nurturing community for growth after conversion. Further discussion is needed, however, on the nature of faith, the sense in which faith precedes baptism, and the meaning of corporate faith in Roman Catholic teaching. What is the nature of the gift of faith given to the infant born into the covenant community by baptism?

50. In the Roman Catholic understanding, one is incorporated into the death and resurrection of Christ through baptism, thereby also entering into the *koinonia* of those saved by Christ. Pentecostals affirm a relationship between baptism and incorporation into the death and resurrection of Christ (Rom 6:3ff). Even if Pentecostals do not consider baptism, which makes possible incorporation into the *koinonia*, as a sacrament, most of them would not see baptism as an empty church ritual. It serves to strengthen the faith of those who have repented and believed in Christ through the Holy Spirit. Often, a person will have a deep spiritual experience at baptism (manifested, sometimes, for instance by speaking

in tongues). Provided that the person who is being baptized has experienced conversion, some Pentecostals would even speak of baptism as a "means of grace." Without denying the salvation of the unbaptized, all Pentecostals would consider baptism to be an integral part of the whole experience of becoming Christian.

51. Roman Catholics and Pentecostals agree that faith is indispensable to salvation. Pentecostals disagree with the Roman Catholic teaching that baptism is a constitutive means of salvation accomplished by the life, death, and resurrection of Christ. Nevertheless, Pentecostals do feel the need to investigate further the relationship between baptism and salvation in light of specific passages which appear to make a direct link between baptism and salvation (e.g., John 3:5; Mark 16:16; Acts 22:16; 1 Pet 3:21). Further discussion is also needed on the effect of baptism.

C) Baptism and the Church

52. For Roman Catholics, baptism is the sacrament of entry into the church, the *koinonia* of those saved in Christ and incorporated into his death and resurrection. For Pentecostals. baptism publicly demonstrates their personal identification with the death and resurrection of Christ (cf. Rom 6:3ff.) and their incorporation into the Body of Christ. In keeping with the long tradition of the catechumenate, some Pentecostals believe that baptism is a precondition for full church membership to the extent that unbaptized converts are not, strictly speaking, called "brothers and sisters in Christ" but "friends."

53. For both Roman Catholics and Pentecostals, the believing community is important in the preparation for baptism, in the celebration of baptism, and in nurturing the faith of the one baptized. It is essential for the newly baptized believer to continue to grow in faith and love and to participate in the full life of the church.

54. For the Roman Catholic Church, the basis of ecumenical dialogue with Pentecostals, properly speaking, is found in the Catholic recognition of the baptism performed by Pentecostals in the name of the Father, Son, and Holy Spirit. This implies a common faith in the Lord Jesus Christ. This recognition by Roman Catholics of Pentecostal baptism means, in consequence, that Roman Catholics believe that they share with Pentecostals a certain, though imperfect *koinonia* (cf. *Unitatis redintegratio*, §3). The unity of baptism constitutes and requires the unity

of the baptized (cf. *Unitatis redintegratio*, §22). Our agreement on the trinitarian basis of baptism draws and impels us to unity.

55. Pentecostals do not see the unity between Christians as being based in a common water baptism, mainly because they believe that the New Testament does not base it in baptism. Instead, the foundation of unity is a common faith and experience of Jesus Christ as lord and savior through the Holy Spirit. This implies that, to the extent that Pentecostals recognize that Roman Catholics have this common faith in and experience of Jesus as Lord, they share a real though imperfect *koinonia* with them. "For just as the body is one and has many members, and all the members of the body, though many, are one body, so it is with Christ. For by one Spirit we were all baptized into one body—Jews or Greeks, slaves or free and all were made to drink of one Spirit" (1 Cor 12:12–13—a passage Pentecostals tend to interpret as not referring to water baptism). Insofar as baptism is related to this experience of Christ through the Spirit, it is also significant for the question of unity between Christians.

D) Baptismal Practice

56. Roman Catholics and most Pentecostals agree that a person is to be baptized in water in the name of the Father, Son, and Holy Spirit. Roman Catholics and most Pentecostals disagree with those Pentecostals who do not baptize according to the trinitarian formula, especially if in baptizing only in Jesus name (e.g., Acts 2:38) they deny the orthodox understanding of the Trinity.[9]

57. Baptism by immersion is the most effective visible sign to convey the meaning of baptism. Most Pentecostals hold that immersion in water is the only biblical way to baptize. Roman Catholics permit immersion and pouring as legitimate modes of baptism.

58. Pentecostals and Roman Catholics agree that baptism, when it is discerned as properly administered, is not to be repeated.

59. In addition to theological difficulties, Pentecostals perceive certain pastoral difficulties with the practice of infant baptism. These difficulties, commonly associated with the practice of infant baptism, are significant enough for Pentecostals to suggest that Roman Catholics continue to examine this practice.

9. See note 6.

60. Roman Catholics freely acknowledge the possible pastoral difficulties (e.g., creation of a body of baptized but unchurched people) inherent in the misuse of the practice of infant baptism. But infant baptism often provides a pastoral opportunity to help those parents weak in faith and practice, and is the beginning of a whole process of Christian life for the child. "Conversion" in this sense becomes a series of grace-events throughout life, resulting in a commitment equally as firm as that stemming from a sudden conversion in adulthood.

61. Roman Catholics point out that there is a new emphasis upon adult initiation among Roman Catholics in the post-Vatican II rites, without denying the value of infant baptism. Indeed, because adult baptism is now expressed as the primary theological model, the theology and practice of infant baptism is itself enriched. Not only is faith given to the infant through the sacrament, but the parents themselves are fortified as the ones responsible for the infant's future growth, and so are caught up in the grace-giving event, frequently having their own faith strengthened.

62. Roman Catholics and Pentecostals agree that instruction in the faith necessarily follows upon baptism in order that the life of grace may come to fruition. In this connection, a pastor should delay or refuse to baptize an infant if the parents (or guardians) clearly have no intention of bringing up the infant in the practice of faith. To baptize under those circumstances would be to act in manner contrary to the canon law of the Roman Catholic Church.

63. There are some parallels between the Roman Catholic practice of infant baptism and the common practice of infant dedication in Pentecostal churches in terms of the activity of grace and the role of the Christian community in the life of an infant. In infant dedication, as in infant baptism, the parents of the infant and the believing community publicly covenant together with God to bring the infant up so that he or she will come into a personal relationship with Christ. Though Pentecostals do not believe that dedication mediates salvation to an infant or makes him/her a member of the Christian church, they do believe that because of the prayer and the faith of the believing community, a blessing of God rests upon the dedicated infant. Both practices acknowledge in their own way the presence of the grace of God in the infant and are concerned with creating an atmosphere in which the child may grow in the grace and knowledge of the Lord Jesus Christ.

E) Baptism and the Experience of the Spirit

64. Roman Catholics and Pentecostals agree that all of those who belong to Christ "were made to drink of one Spirit" (1 Cor 12:13). We agree that God intends that each follower of Jesus enjoy the indwelling of the Holy Spirit (Rom 8:9). This indwelling of the Spirit is not the fruit or product of human works but is due to the unmerited, efficacious action of grace by which each person responds to the special initiative of God.

65. We acknowledge that Roman Catholics and Pentecostals have different understandings of the role of the Spirit in Christian initiation and life, but may nonetheless enjoy a similar experience of the Spirit. Our experience of the Holy Spirit, furthermore, heightens our mutual awareness of the need for unity.

66. We agree that the experience of the Holy Spirit belongs to the life of the church. Wherever the Spirit is genuinely present in the Christian community, its fruit will also become evident (cf. Gal 5:22–23). Genuine charismata mentioned in Scripture (e.g., 1 Cor 12:8–10, 28–30; Rom 12:6–8; etc.) also indicate the presence of the Spirit. All such manifestations, however, call for discernment by the community (cf. 1 Thess 5:19–22; 1 Cor 14; 1 John 4).

67. Generally, Roman Catholics have tended to be cautious about accepting the more spectacular manifestations of the Spirit, such as speaking in tongues and prophecy, although the charismatic renewal has helped them to rediscover ways in which such gifts are rooted in their oldest tradition.

68. Roman Catholics fear that Pentecostals limit the Spirit to specific manifestations. Pentecostals fear that Roman Catholics confine the Spirit's workings to sacraments and church order. Therefore, we share a mutual concern not to confine or to limit the Holy Spirit whom Jesus described by the imagery of the freely blowing wind (cf. John 3:8). Each of us seems more worried about the other limiting the Spirit than ourselves. Still, we have learned through our discussions together that there is greater freedom for the Holy Spirit in both of our traditions than we expected to find, and our fears once shared, have made us more aware of our shortcomings in this regard.

69. Our discussions, too, have made us more aware about the ways in which we use language related to the Holy Spirit. We agree that such

ideas as what it means to be "baptized in the Spirit" or "filled with the Spirit" would be fruitful fields for mutual exploration.

IV. KOINONIA IN THE LIFE OF THE CHURCH

A) Koinonia in the Life of God

70. Both Pentecostals and Roman Catholics recognize that believers have a share in the eternal life which is *koinonia* with the Father and with his Son Jesus Christ (cf. 1 John 1:2–3), and a communion in the Holy Spirit whom God's Son, Jesus Christ, has given to them (cf. 1 John 3:24; 2 Cor 13:14). This, the deepest meaning of the *koinonia*, is actualized at various levels. Those who believe and have been baptized into Christ's death (cf. Mark 16:16; Rom 6:3–4) have *koinonia* in his sufferings and become like him in his death and resurrection (cf. Phil 3:10). The next step is the Eucharist or the Lord's Supper. "The cup of blessing which we bless, is it not a participation [*koinonia*] in the blood of Christ? The bread which we break, is it not a participation [*koinonia*] in the body of Christ?" (1 Cor 10:16) All believers, furthermore, who have *koinonia* in the eternal life of Father, Son, and Holy Spirit, and who have *koinonia* in Christ's death and resurrection, are bound together in a *koinonia* too deep for words. We look forward to the day, when we will also have *koinonia* in his body and blood (1 Cor 10:16).

71. While both Roman Catholics and Pentecostals teach the indwelling of the Father, Son, and the Holy Spirit in the believer (cf. John 17:21; Rom 8:9), the emphasis on the indwelling of the Trinity in believers is more explicitly articulated in the Roman Catholic faith than in that of the Pentecostals. The nature of the language used to describe it is in need of further exploration together.

72. Together with Roman Catholics, most Pentecostals have a strong commitment to the trinitarian understanding of God. They believe, for instance, that at baptism the trinitarian formula should be used because of Jesus' mandate: "Go therefore and make disciples of all nations, baptizing them in the name of the Father, and of the Son and of the Holy Spirit" (Matt 28:19).[10] The Pentecostals do, however, feel challenged by Roman Catholics to develop all the implications for faith and piety which their full trinitarian commitment implies.

10. See note 6.

B) Church as Koinonia

73. The importance of an active response to the gifts of God in the service of *koinonia* requires mutuality in its many dimensions. Some of these dimensions are the assumption and sharing of responsibility, and a fuller participation in the life of the local congregation. When church members of whatever rank act arbitrarily, without taking into account this sharing, their actions obscure the expressions of communion. For Roman Catholics and Pentecostals, *koinonia* in the church is a dynamic concept implying a dialogical structure of both God-givenness and human response. Mutuality has to exist on every level of the church, its source being the continuing presence of the Holy Spirit.

74. Roman Catholics must often confess to a lack of mutuality at the local and universal levels, even though mutuality is recognized as a criterion for fellowship. Difficulties surrounding lay participation in decision making processes and the lack of sufficient involvement of women in leadership were examples cited by participants in this dialogue. Roman Catholics, however, would insist that order and hierarchy do not in themselves imply such a defect in mutuality.

75. At the same time, Pentecostals acknowledge both the reluctance that many of their members have in submitting to ecclesial authority and the difficulty which their charismatic leaders have in working through existing ecclesial institutional channels which could protect them from acting irresponsibly or in an authoritarian manner.

76. The difficulties of some Pentecostals with their ecclesial institutions stem in part from frequent emphasis on their direct relation to the Spirit. They forget that the Spirit is given not only to individual Christians but also to the whole community. An individual Christian is not the only "temple of the Holy Spirit" (1 Cor 6:19). Roman Catholics have rightly challenged Pentecostals to think of the whole community, too, as a "temple of God" in which the Spirit dwells (1 Cor 3:16). If Pentecostals were to take the indwelling of the Spirit in the community more seriously, they would be less inclined to follow the personal "leadings of the Spirit" in disregard of the community. Rather they would strive to imitate the apostles who, at the first church council, justified their decision with the following words: ". . . it has seemed good to the Holy Spirit and to us . . ." (Acts 15:28).

77. In their theology, both Pentecostals and Roman Catholics see themselves standing in a dependent relationship to the Spirit. They ac-

knowledge the need to invoke the Holy Spirit. In accordance with this invocation, they believe in the presence of God whenever two or three are gathered in Christ's name (cf. Matt 18:20).

78. Pentecostals recognize that while there is an emphasis on holiness in the Roman Catholic Church, they observe that it seems possible for some Roman Catholics to live continuously in a state of sin, and yet be considered members in the church. This seems to the Pentecostals to undermine the concept of Christian discipleship. Though they are mindful of John's words that if "we say we have not sinned, we make him (God) a liar" (1 John 1:10), Pentecostals want to take seriously the warning of the same apostle concerning the unrepentant sinner, namely that "no one who sins has either seen him [the Father] or known him" (1 John 3:6).

79. Roman Catholics wonder how Pentecostals deal with the sins of their own members. Do they have an adequate tradition of bringing those who have fallen into sin into a process of repentance and a sense of God's forgiveness? Without such a tradition, how can they avoid harshness when a sinner fails to live up to the congregation's ideal of holiness?

80. Both bodies would do well to recall the scriptural warnings that we must try to see the log in our own eye rather than the speck in our brother's or sister's eye (cf. Matt 7:4). We should reflect, too, on the Lord's caution against trying to have a wheat field from which all tares have been removed (cf. Matt 13:24ff.).

C) Koinonia, Sacraments, and Church Order

81. Roman Catholics hold that a basic aspect of *koinonia* between local churches is expressed in the celebration of the sacraments of initiation, namely, by the same baptism, the same confirmation, the same Eucharist. Moreover, the celebration of these sacraments requires ordained ministers to preside,[11] ordination being also a sacrament, i.e., an act of Christ in the Spirit celebrated in the communion and for the

11. This relationship between church order and ordained ministry presiding over a community is well illustrated in the celebration of water baptism, although in cases of necessity every Christian is requested to baptize. Until 1923 even the deacons were not allowed to be the ordinary ministers of baptism. Presently bishops retain for themselves the baptism of adults and parish priests must have their bishop's permission to perform such a baptism.

communion of the church. Furthermore, according to the Catholic tradition, only ordained ministers, principally the bishop, can preside over a local church or diocese.

82. According to Catholic understanding, *koinonia* is rooted in the bonds of faith and sacramental life shared by congregations united in dioceses pastored by bishops. Through their bishops, the local churches are in communion with one another by reason of the common faith, the common sacramental life, and the common episcopacy. Among the fellowship of bishops, the bishop of Rome is recognized as the successor of Peter and presides over the whole Catholic communion. Through their day to day teaching, and more specifically through local and universal councils, bishops have responsibility to articulate clearly the faith and discipline of the church. Church order is thus grounded in the *koinonia* of faith and the sacraments; church order is at the same time an active expression of *koinonia*.

83. Roman Catholics hold that some existing ecclesiastical structures (such as the office of a bishop) are "God-given" and that they belong to the very essence of church order rather than serving only its well-being.

84. While Pentecostals disagree among themselves concerning how the church should best be ordered (the views range from congregational to episcopal), they accept the full ecclesial status of the churches ordered in various ways. Observing the diversity of the church structures in the New Testament, they believe that the contemporary church should not be narrower in its understanding of the church order than the sacred Scriptures themselves.

85. Although Pentecostals do not limit celebration of the sacraments and leadership in the church to the ordained ministers, they do recognize the need for and the value of ordination for the life of the church. Pentecostals do not consider ordination to be a sacrament. Ordinarily, Pentecostals recognize that a charism of teacher/pastor is recognized or can be given to a person at the laying on of hands, but they do not consider that at ordination the power of the Holy Spirit is bestowed to the person being ordained. Instead, ordination is a public acknowledgment of a God-given charism which a person has received prior to the act of ordination.

86. Some Pentecostals observe what appears to be a "mechanical" or "magical" understanding of the sacraments, especially among Roman

Catholic laity, and do not accept the grace-conveying role of the sacraments distinct from their function as a visible Word of God. Roman Catholic theology, however, maintains that the sacraments are not "mechanical" or "magical" since they require openness and faith on the part of the recipient. In Catholic understanding, the grace of the sacraments is not bestowed automatically or unconditionally, irrespective of the dispositions of the recipient. What Paul says in 1 Cor 11:27 ("profaning the body and blood of the Lord") is common teaching in the Roman Catholic Church. Sacramental actions can produce "shriveled fruit," as Augustine describes it, when the recipients are not in right relation to the Lord.[12] Furthermore, the efficacy of the sacraments is not dependent upon the personal piety of those who minister them, but rather, is ultimately dependent upon the grace of God.

87. Pentecostals believe that church order demanded by *koinonia* is not satisfactorily expressed in some important aspects of Roman Catholic ecclesiology. Even within the context of collegiality, examples which seem to bear this out include those passages where it is stated that "the episcopal order is the subject of the supreme and full power over the universal church," and even more importantly, when it is stated that "the Roman Pontiff has full, supreme, and universal power over the church" which "he can always exercise . . . freely" (*Lumen gentium*, §22). On the whole, Pentecostals propose that presbyteral and/or congregational ecclesial models express better the mutuality or reciprocity demanded by *koinonia*.

88. Roman Catholics are more inclined to see the Spirit operating through certain ecclesial structures, although Pentecostals, too, recognize that the Spirit may work through ecclesial structures and processes.

89. Both Roman Catholics and Pentecostals are troubled by the discrepancy between the theology and the practice of their own parishes or congregations.

D) The Church and Salvation

90. According to Roman Catholic ecclesiology, the church can be considered both a *sign* and an *instrument* of God's work in the world. This formulation from the nineteenth century is still very useful for understanding the role of the church in the world.

12. The later distinction made between "fruitful" and "unfruitful" sacraments is another way by which the Roman Catholic teaching asserts the same understanding.

91. The church is a sign of the presence of God's saving power in the world. It is also a sign of the eschatological unity to which all peoples are called by God. It is to be this sign both through its individual members and its gathered communities. Insofar as Christians are divided from one another, they are a counter sign, a sign of contradiction to God's reconciling purpose in the world.

92. The church is also an instrument of God for announcing the saving news of grace and the coming of God's kingdom. The church is God's instrument in making disciples of all nations by preaching the good news of Jesus' life, death, and resurrection, and baptizing them (cf. Matt 28:19).

93. In recent years, Roman Catholics have come to describe the church as "a kind of a sacrament" (*Lumen gentium*, §1). This new insight is consistent with its past understanding of the sacraments as signs and instruments of God's saving power.

94. Though Pentecostals do not accept the Roman Catholic understanding of sacraments and the Roman Catholic view of the church as "a kind of sacrament," in their own way they do affirm that the church is both a sign and an instrument of salvation. As the new people of God, the church is called both to reflect the reality of God's eschatological kingdom in history and to announce its coming into the world, insofar as people open their lives to the in-breaking of the Holy Spirit. In Pentecostal understanding, the church as a community is an instrument of salvation in the same sense in which each one of its members is both a sign and instrument of salvation. In their own way, both the community as a whole and the individual members that comprise it give witness to God's redeeming grace.

V. KOINONIA AND THE COMMUNION OF THE SAINTS

A) The Church as Communio Sanctorum

95. God calls us into communion with himself (*communio* with the Holy One), into communion in the body and blood of Christ (*communio in sanctis*), and into communion between Christians (fellowship of the saints: *communio sanctorum*). In the Nicene Creed, the phrase *communio sanctorum* has eschatological significance: the saints on earth and those in heaven, marked by the same Spirit, are a single body.

96. In terms of the sharing in holy things (*communio in sanctis*), for Roman Catholics, participation in baptism, confirmation, and Eucharist is constitutive of the church. For Pentecostals, the central element of worship is the preaching of the Word. As persons respond to the proclamation of the Word, the Spirit gives them a new birth, which is a pre-sacramental experience, thereby making them Christians and in this sense creating the church. Of secondary importance are participation in baptism and the Lord's Supper, spontaneous exercise of the charismata, and the sharing of personal testimonies.

97. Pentecostals would like Catholics to share more among themselves the private devotional reading of the Scriptures. Pentecostals ask Roman Catholics whether they could not deepen the experiential dimension of *koinonia* through spontaneous exercise of the gifts and the sharing of personal testimonies. Convinced that Word and sacrament cannot be separated in worship, Catholics ask Pentecostal to re-examine the dynamic relationship between these two in the celebration of baptism and the Lord's Supper.

98. The relation between *koinonia*, sacraments, and church order (see above, nos. 81–89) explains why both the sharing in the same eucharistic faith and also in full communion are normal prerequisites for receiving the Eucharist in the Roman Catholic Church. Since for Catholics the Eucharist is essential and central in the life of the church, participation in the eucharist means and requires unity of faith. Catholics would like to see Pentecostals express clearly what is required for full communion in their churches.

99. According to the Roman Catholic view, the *communio sanctorum* includes a relationship to all the holy ones of God, the saints on earth and also the saints in heaven. Members of the church are given *koinonia* in the very holiness of God. As a result, they form "a great cloud of witnesses" (Heb 12:1), a "great multitude which no man could number, from every nation, from all tribes and peoples and tongues" (Rev 7:9).

100. In Roman Catholic faith and practice, God alone is the object of worship (*latria*). However, veneration (*doulia*) is given to saints who have "run the race," "finished the course," and have received "a crown of life." It is also important to realize that no Catholic has an obligation *jure divino* of venerating either relics, icons, or saints. While this kind of devotion is not necessary for salvation, the church recognizes the usefulness of such forms of devotion, recommends them to its members, and

resists any condemnation or contempt of such practices (cf. Council of Trent, session 25).

101. Pentecostals find reassuring the stress in Roman Catholic theology that worship belongs only to God. It is, however, the Pentecostal teaching that the unique mediatorial role of Christ positively excludes veneration of relics, icons, and saints. Pentecostals do, however, affirm that in their worship the earthly saints join in worship with saints in heaven and with them comprise the one holy catholic and apostolic church. As the Scripture says: "we are surrounded by so great a cloud of witnesses" (Heb 12:1), who have lived in history from the beginning of God's dealing with the human race.

B) Holiness, Repentance, and Ministry in History

102. All the baptized are called to be "saints," and indeed, according to Scripture, they called themselves such in the early church (e.g., Acts 9:13; 26:10; Rom 15:25–26; 2 Cor 8:4; 9:1. etc.).

103. We agree that because of sin, the church is always in need of repentance. It is at once holy and in need of purification. The church is a "holy penitent," and is ever in need of renewal, both in its persons and in its structures. Both Catholics and Pentecostals recognize the fact that their respective theologies of *koinonia* are all too seldom reflected in the empirical reality of the life in their respective communities.

104. Both sides of this dialogue agree on the fundamental demands for holiness in the minister and agree that the unworthiness of a minister does not invalidate the work of the Holy Spirit. For Roman Catholics, God's acts in the sacraments are effective because they are based on God's faithfulness. They believe that the Holy Spirit works with consistency in ministering to those who come in faith. The church gives serious attention to church discipline, because human weakness and sin can become obstacles to the effectiveness of ministry. Pentecostals, too, believe that God can work through the ministers of the Word of God in spite of their grave failures and sin in their lives. "Some indeed preach Christ from envy and rivalry, but others from good will . . . What then? Only that in every way, whether in pretense or in truth, Christ is proclaimed: in that I rejoice" (Phil 1:15, 18). Pentecostals also believe that the ordinances administered by an unworthy minister are valid (in the sense that, for instance, baptism need not be repeated). Together we believe, however, that the unworthiness of ministers is often a stumbling block which pre-

vents non-believers from coming to faith in a true and living God, and it frequently hinders the work of the Spirit in the believing community.

105. Although Pentecostals stress the freedom of the Spirit to act in the community and emphasize the need for active participation of all members of the church, they do acknowledge the necessity of church order. They affirm church order (which can legitimately take different forms) as the will of the Lord for his church, since they observe from the New Testament that the earliest church has not "been without persons holding specific authority and responsibility" (BEM, Ministry, 9) (cf. Acts 14:23; 20:17; Phil 1:1). Since Pentecostals do not reject ecclesial institutions, they recognize that the Spirit operates not only through charismatic individuals but also through the permanent ministries of the church.

106. There is agreement that the offices and structures of the church, as indeed every aspect of the church, are in a continual need of renewal insofar as they are institutions of men and women here on earth. This presumes that the Spirit can breathe new life into the church's offices and structures when these become "dry bones" (Ezek 37). This on-going effort at renewal has important ecumenical implications. This is an essential dynamism of "the movement toward unity" of the People of God (*Unitatis redintegratio*, §6).

107. Pentecostals and Roman Catholics appear to view the history of the church quite differently. The members of this dialogue believe that the differences in these perspectives deserve further mutual exploration. Both Pentecostals and Roman Catholics recognize that continuity in history by itself is no guarantee of spiritual maturity or of doctrinal soundness. Increasingly, both traditions are coming to share a genuine appreciation for the value, which church history reveals to them today.

108. Roman Catholics believe that the contemporary church is in continuity with the church in the New Testament. Pentecostals, influenced by restorationist perspectives, have claimed continuity with the church in the New Testament by arguing for discontinuity with much of the historical church. By adopting these two positions, one of continuity, the other of discontinuity, each tradition has attempted to demonstrate its faithfulness to the apostolic faith "once for all delivered to the saints" (Jude 3). The significance of this for the welfare of the whole church urges upon us the need of further common theological reflection on the history of the church.

CONCLUSION

109. It is hoped that this dialogue might inspire dialogues on national or local levels between Roman Catholics and classical Pentecostals. The participants recommend to their parent bodies that the dialogue continue into a fourth round of discussions.

110. The members of the dialogue, during this quinquennium, visited worship services representing both traditions. Learning was not confined only to the dialogue table but also took place in local Catholic parishes and Pentecostal congregations visited during this series of discussions and at informal conversations between sessions.

111. We have explored the subject of *koinonia* and have been richly rewarded as together we affirmed the Lordship of Jesus. We felt his pain as we understood our part in the on-going brokenness of this body. Nonetheless, that we could spend day after day together sharing in great detail and depth our most dearly held Christian convictions, and come away closer to our risen Lord and to each other, we understand is possible only by the grace and mercy of God.

112. The prayer of Jesus, "That they all may be one" (John 17:21), has become increasingly important to us and the cause for much prayer and repentance still. Nevertheless, we are heartened by the realization that fresh winds of the Spirit are blowing in the church universal, and we are waiting expectantly to see what in the providence of God is yet to come. Our prayer continues to be "Come, Holy Spirit!"

10

Evangelization, Proselytism, and Common Witness. Final Report of the Dialogue between the Roman Catholic Church and Some Classical Pentecostal Churches and Leaders

1990–1997

INTRODUCTION[1]

1. This is a report from the participants of the fourth phase of the international dialogue (1990–1997) between the Pontifical Council for Promoting Christian Unity and some classical Pentecostal denominations and leaders. The dialogue began in 1972. The co-chairpersons in the fourth phase were the Rev. Kilian McDonnell, OSB, of Collegeville, Minnesota, USA, and the Rev Justus du Plessis, of Faerie Glen, South Africa, who was succeeded in 1992 by the Rev. Cecil M. Robeck, Jr., of Pasadena, California, USA.[2]

1. The report was published in *Pneuma: The Journal of the Society for Pentecostal Studies* 21.1 (1999) 11–51, and is printed here with kind permission.

2. The failing health of the Rev Justus du Plessis caused him to withdraw from active participation in the Dialogue in 1993. The Rev. Jerry Sandidge, who had served as co-secretary on the Pentecostal team, died in 1992 after a lengthy illness with which he had bravely struggled for years. The participants note with great appreciation their very significant work in promoting this Dialogue and other relationships between our communities. We also remember with great appreciation the work of Msgr. Heinz-Albert Raem who joined us in 1990 as co-secretary for the Catholic side. He applied his excellent organizational and theological skills in service to this fourth phase for seven years, but he never lived to see its completion because he died in March, 1997. Their absence was deeply felt by all members of the Dialogue, both Catholic and Pentecostal.

2. The unity of the church is a concern for Pentecostals and Catholics alike. The particular purpose of these discussions is to develop a climate of mutual respect and understanding in matters of faith and practice, to find points of genuine agreement as well as indicate areas in which further dialogue is required. The goal is not structural unity, but rather the fostering of this respect and mutual understanding between the Catholic Church and classical Pentecostal groups.

3. As we, the participants, have come to the task before us, we have done so as peers. Nevertheless, we have recognized that there is at least one important difference between the Catholic and the Pentecostal teams that bears mention. The Roman Catholic Church possesses that which may be described as official teaching on some of these topics, teaching that has been expressed in various authoritative texts, such as the conciliar documents of the Second Vatican Council and in papal encyclicals. The Pentecostals possess no comparable body of teaching, which may serve as a resource for their position. The diversity of the Pentecostal movement mitigates against a single position on certain topics. When the Pentecostal participants speak as a single voice throughout this document, then, they do so by gathering together what they believe to be the common consensus, held by the vast majority of Pentecostals worldwide.

4. We, the participants, have sought to represent faithfully the positions held by our churches. However, we have made no decisions for the churches, since we have no authority to make such decisions. The churches are free to accept or reject the report either in whole or in part. Yet, as responsible persons, representing our traditions either officially or in some other way, we have come together over a period of years to study the issues of evangelization, proselytism, and common witness. In accordance with our understanding of the gospel, we are making proposals to our churches. We, the participants, hereby submit our findings to our respective churches for review, evaluation, correction, and reception.

5. Since many Christians have seen the last decade of the second millennium as one in which to emphasize evangelization, and since significant tensions exist between Pentecostals and Catholics on this issue, it appeared appropriate to concentrate on this topic. The previous three phases focused on (1) the baptism in the Holy Spirit, Christian initiation, and the charisms, Scripture and Tradition, and the human person

and the gifts (1972–1976), (2) faith and religious experience, speaking in tongues, and the role of Mary (1977–1982), and (3) *koinonia* (Christian communion and fellowship) (1985–1989).

6. Specific themes, which helped us reach our conclusions in this phase of the dialogue included: *The Meaning of Mission and Evangelization* (1990, Emmetten, Switzerland); *The Biblical and Systematic Foun-dation of Evangelization* (1991, Venice, Italy); *Evangelization and Culture* (1992, Rocca di Papa, Italy); *Evangelization and Social Justice* (1993, Paris, Frante); *Evangelization/Evangelism, Common Witness, and Proselytism* (1994, Kappel am Albis, Switzerland), and *Common Witness* (1995, Brixen/Bressanone, Italy). The dialogue members convened once again in Brixen/Bressanone, Italy, in 1996 to examine a first draft of the report of this dialogue. They continued their drafting in Rome, Italy, in June 1997. The steering committee was then authorized to make the final editorial decisions in keeping with the mind of the participants. This they did in Geneva, Switzerland, in November, 1997.

7. The procedure used throughout this phase included the discussion of papers presented by members of each side. Each team then asked the other to respond to a limited number of questions, which arose from the discussions of the paper. These questions were designed to challenge participants to think creatively and substantively about the emerging issues. The substance of these discussions were recorded in most years in an "agreed account," which took note of areas of agreement or disagreement, areas of possible convergence, and topics which might need further study. These materials, together with continuing conversations, provided the basis for the final report.

8. Both Pentecostals and Catholics recognize as an essential part of the mission of the church the call to evangelize. As the two teams explored the topic together, they were encouraged by new perspectives, and they gained clarity on problematic issues. They hope that their work together points toward possibilities of cooperation in mission for the sake of the gospel.

9. Both the Catholic and the Pentecostal participants of the dialogue have become increasingly aware of the scandal of a divided witness. It is a scandal when unbelievers are more aware of those things which separate these churches than those things they hold in common. It is a scandal, too, when Catholics and Pentecostals demonstrate a lack of love or trust by speaking negatively about one another or acting in

ways that antagonize or exclude one another. Because of their divisions, Catholics and Pentecostals are unable to participate together at the table of the Lord. Furthermore, they make evident their division insofar as they proclaim the Lord's death in isolation from one another.

10. Touched by this divided witness, the participants of this dialogue have experienced and expressed to one another their sorrow over this state of affairs. It is a sorrow which has, in part, moved them to search for ways in which these divisions might be resolved, following the Pauline exhortation to "make every effort to maintain the unity of the Spirit in the bond of peace" (Eph 4:3).

I. MISSION AND EVANGELIZATION[3]

11. Both Pentecostals and Catholics believe that God has charged all Christians to announce the gospel to all people, in obedience to the great commission given by Christ (cf. Matt 28:18–20). Proclaiming God's reconciliation of the world through Christ is central to the church's faith, life and witness (cf. 2 Cor 5:18–19).

12. The mission and the task of evangelization—proclaiming "the name, teaching, life, promise, the kingdom and the mystery of Jesus of Nazareth, the Son of God" (*Evangelization in the Modern World* [1975], 22)—lies at the heart of the Catholic faith. Mission has been part of the life of the Church throughout the ages. Catholic women and men, especially those in religious orders, have gone to the ends of the earth proclaiming the good news of Jesus Christ. The Second Vatican Council's *Decree on the Church's Missionary Activity* [1965], 2, taught that "the church on earth is by its very nature missionary since, according to the plan of the Father, it has its origin in the mission of the Son and the Holy Spirit." Following in the path of the council, both Paul VI and John Paul II in their teaching insist on the need to pursue a "new evangelization."

13. Pentecostals place special emphasis on the proclamation of Jesus as savior and lord, resulting in a personal, conscious acceptance and conversion of an individual; a "new birth" as in John 3:3. Pentecostals

3. Papers were delivered on this topic by Karl Müller, SVD, of St. Augustin, Germany ("A Catholic Perspective of Evangelization: *Evangelii nuntiandi*"), and by Dr. Gary B. McGee, of the Assemblies of God Theological Seminary, Springfield, MO, USA ("Apostolic Power for End-Times Evangelism: A Historical Review of Pentecostal Mission Theology").

are also concerned to evangelize the world in these "last days" before Christ returns (cf. Acts 2:14–17; Joel 2:28–32), making disciples as Jesus instructed in the great commission.

14. Both Pentecostals and Catholics agree that "evangelization will . . . always contain—as the center and at the same time the summit of its dynamism—a clear proclamation that, in Jesus Christ, the Son of God made man, who died and rose from the dead, salvation is offered to all humankind, as a gift of God's grace and mercy" (*Evangelization in the Modern World*, 27; cf. Eph 2:8; Rom 1:16). From this divine initiative arises the church as an eschatological community, a *koinonia*. To the extent that Christians participate in this *koinonia*, they share deep bonds of unity in the Spirit even now, despite divisions which continue. The eschatological nature of this *koinonia*, which fosters unity in diversity, serves as a prophetic sign toward divided humankind (cf. John 17:21).

15. While Catholics and Pentecostals agree on the essential core of the gospel, namely that "in Christ God was reconciling the world to Himself" (2 Cor 5:19), on occasion they differ in practice and language concerning the emphasis they give to certain aspects of evangelization.

Catholics tend to use the term to indicate proclamation of the gospel toward the conversion of persons to Christ. They also acknowledge that evangelization is a complex process made up of various elements, including "the renewal of humanity, witness, explicit proclamation, inner adherence, entry into the community, acceptance of signs, apostolic initiative" (*Evangelization in the Modern World*, 24). Pentecostals have used the terms evangelization and evangelism interchangeably to focus on the proclamation of the gospel toward converting individuals to Christ, followed by their discipling to be effective witnesses for Christ among unbelievers and in society. In short, Pentecostals make a sharper distinction than Catholics between the proclamation of the gospel to those they consider "unsaved" and the discipling of believers or promotion of Christian values in society. Today, there is growing convergence between Catholics and Pentecostals in that both see the task as leading individuals to conversion, but also as the transformation of the cultures, and the reconciliation of the nations.

16. Catholics and Pentecostals are motivated to evangelize by love for Christ, obedience to the great commission, and the desire that unbelievers may receive the blessings of eternal life now and in the future.

While Catholics and Pentecostals teach the second coming of Christ as the blessed hope of the church, Pentecostals stress the urgency of proclamation because many believe in the imminence of that event. Furthermore, Pentecostals view the "baptism in the Spirit" as essential for every believer to receive empowerment for Christian witness (Acts 1:8). While Catholics and Pentecostals express a genuine desire to see the Lord add to the church those who are being saved (cf. Acts 2:47), they also express concern over attitudes expressed by Christian evangelizers which are inconsistent with the central message of the gospel, the great commission (Matt 28:19–20), the great commandment (Matt 22:37–39), and the nature of the church. For example, they are troubled when people are dealt with as though they were impersonal objects, instead of being respected as individuals, who have been created with dignity in the image of God. They are also troubled when evangelization proceeds exclusively by strategies that aim at limiting the composition of congregations to one race, class, ethnic group, or other social groupings resulting in an intended and lasting segregation, which does harm to the nature of Christ's church (cf. Rev 7:9; 14:1–7). Continued growth, both qualitative and quantitative, will demand more self-criticism and openness to the questions and insights of others in the body of Christ.

17. All Catholics are called to witness to the good news. In practice, over the part few centuries, Catholic evangelization in non-Christian countries has often depended almost exclusively on clergy and religious orders. Most of them received a theological and spiritual formation, which prepared them for this mission. In recent years, the Catholic church has also encouraged lay participation in evangelization with the recognition that a proper preparation is necessary for this task (cf. *Decree on the Apostolate of Lay People*, 28–32).

18. While in recent years, Pentecostals have begun to place more attention on the formal training of lay people and clergy for ministry, Pentecostals have always emphasized that all believers should evangelize, whether formally trained or not, especially by sharing their personal testimony.

19. Both sides understand evangelization as encompassing missionary proclamation to non-Christians, as well as outreach to those who once claimed to have accepted the gospel, but who apparently live a life totally indifferent to the faith they have professed. We need to recog-

nize the delicacy of making judgements as to whether other persons are in fact living indifferently or not.

20. Catholics and Pentecostals both agree that the Holy Spirit prepares individuals and peoples for the reception of the gospel, despite the fallen condition of humankind. While they believe that "ever since the creation of the world, the visible existence of God and his everlasting power have been clearly seen by the mind's understanding of created things" (Rom 1:20; cf. Psalm 19:1–4), their perspectives diverge over the existence and/or meaning of salvific elements found in non-Christian religions. Catholics and Pentecostals agree that those who are saved have been saved without exception through the death of Jesus Christ. Catholics do not deny that the Spirit may be at work in other religions "preparing the way for the gospel" (cf. *Evangelization in the Modern World*, 53). Catholics also say, "Those who, through no fault of their own, do not know the gospel of Christ or his church, but who nevertheless seek God with a sincere heart, and, moved by grace, try in their actions to do his will as they know it through the dictates of their conscience—those too may achieve eternal salvation" (*Dogmatic Constitution on the Church*, 16).

21. Many Pentecostals, on the other hand, like many of the early Christians, tend to point out the demonic elements in other religions. While Pentecostals acknowledge the work of the Holy Spirit in the world, convincing people of sin, righteousness, and judgment (cf. John 16:8–11), they generally do not acknowledge the presence of salvific elements in non-Christian religions. Some Pentecostals would see a convergence towards the Catholic position above in that the Holy Spirit is at work in non-Christian religions, preparing individual hearts for an eventual exposure to the gospel of Jesus Christ. Pentecostals and Catholics, however, together believe that there is only one name whereby we can be saved (cf. Acts 4:12). Both believe in the necessity of responding to the divine invitation to seek him and to find him (cf. Acts 17:27).

II. THE BIBLICAL AND SYSTEMATIC FOUNDATION OF EVANGELIZATION[4]

22. Catholics and Pentecostals both point to the biblical foundation of evangelization of all people. From the very beginning, it was promised

4. Papers were delivered on this topic by Rev. William Menzies, President and Pro-

to Abraham that through him all generations would be blessed (cf. Gen 17:1–8). God's covenant with Abraham has a global significance (cf. Gen 22:18). The prophets show that Israel's election also has importance for all peoples in that they expected the gathering of all peoples at Mount Sion at the coming of the messiah (cf. Is 23; 49:6–8; Joel 3:1–5). Jesus' ministry in his earthly life was focused on Israel, not excluding others in special cases (cf. Matt 15:21–28), but he came for the salvation of the whole world (cf. John 3:15–17; Matt 26:28). Paul emphasizes the universal and cosmic dimensions of Jesus' death and resurrection (cf. 2 Cor 5:19; Rom 8:21). Then, receiving the Spirit from the Father, Jesus pours out that same Spirit as the agent through whom the work of redemption is being carried out throughout the whole world until the end of time (cf. Acts 2:33). Therefore, the biblical mandate for mission is grounded in the redemptive purpose of God.

23. The content of the message of salvation is Jesus Christ himself, the way to reconciliation with the Father; he is the good news (cf. Gal 1:16), which he entrusted to his disciples (cf. Matt 28:19f). The Holy Spirit, poured out on all people (cf. Acts 2:17; Joel 3:1), is to be understood as giving the inner dynamism of the process of evangelization and salvation. The transmission of the Christian faith consists in proclaiming Jesus Christ in order to lead others to faith in him. From the beginning, the first disciples burned with the desire to proclaim Christ: "we cannot but speak of what we have seen and heard" (Acts 4:20). And they invite people of every era to enter into the joy of their communion with Christ and the Father which is the basis of fellowship among Christians (cf. 1 John 1:1–4).

24. Catholics and Pentecostals agree that the proclamation of Jesus Christ is necessary for the liberation of humanity from sin and the attainment of salvation, because all are subject to "the fall," all are "lost." This condition results in alienation from God and also in alienation from others. Deliverance from oppression and domination of "the principalities and powers," including exorcism in certain cases is an important part of gospel proclamation.

---

fessor of Theology at Asia Pacific Theological Seminary, Baguio City, Philippines (*The Biblical Basis for Mission and Evangelism: An Evangelical, Pentecostal Perspective*) and Rev. Karl Müller, SVD, St. Augustin, Germany (*The Biblical and Systematic Foundation of Evangelization*).

25. In the process of salvation, God always takes the initiative through grace, which frees human hearts to respond (Acts 2:37). He acts through the Word and through the exercise of "signs and wonders" according to his sovereign will (cf. 1 Cor 2:4; Rom 15:18f). The only role humans have in reconciliation with God is to respond positively and constantly in the power of the Holy Spirit to God's initiatives through Jesus Christ, who is the only mediator (1 Tim 2:5) and the head of the church (Col 1:18).

26. The ordinary context in which salvation is worked out is the church, the community of believers. *Koinonia* is to be lived out for the mutual enrichment of the members of the body (1 Cor 12:26), which in turn makes it possible for the church to become a servant, gift, and sign to the world. Acknowledging this, and acting accordingly, would counteract individualism and total independence of individual communities, on the one hand, and the tendency toward sterile formalism in personal and institutional life, on the other.[5]

27. The life of *koinonia* is empowered by the Holy Spirit; in recent times many have experienced that power through "the baptism in the Holy Spirit."[6] This presence of the Spirit has been shown in a fresh activity of biblical charisms, or gifts, (cf. 1 Cor 12:8–11), reminding all Christians to be open to charisms as the Spirit gives to everyone individually, whether these gifts are more or less noticeable. Some of the charisms are given more for personal edification (cf. 1 Cor 14:4a), while some provide service to others, and some especially are given to confirm evangelization (cf. Mark 16:15–20). All of them are intended to help build up the *koinonia*.

III. EVANGELIZATION AND CULTURE

28. Both Catholics and Pentecostals recognize the complexity of the relationship between church and culture. The faith community evangelizes through its proclamation and through its common life: this means that our proclamation and our Christian lifestyle are always embodied in a specific culture. We accept that there is considerable good in cultures, notwithstanding the fact of humanity's fall from grace. Pentecostals em-

5. For a more complete discussion of *koinonia* please refer to "Perspectives on *Koinonia*: Report from the Dialogue between the Roman Catholic Church and some Classical Pentecostal churches and Leaders, 1985–1989."

6. Discussion on this issue took place in the first phase of the dialogue.

phasize the changing of individuals who, when formed into a body of believers, bring change into the culture from within. Catholics emphasize that culture itself in its human institutions and enterprises can also be transformed by the gospel.

29. Pentecostals and Catholics agree that when the gospel is introduced into a dominant non-Christian culture, a twofold attitude is required. On the one hand, we have to respect, affirm and support the positive elements in it, elements which will have prepared the people in advance for the reception of the gospel or which are good in themselves. On the other hand, we may have to try to transform this non-Christian culture from within. To do this the local people may be in a better position than foreign missionaries, who may be tempted to impose their own culture as a substitute for the gospel.

30. Pentecostals and Catholics also agree that both evangelizers and evangelized need to realize that neither operate in a cultural vacuum. Evangelizers act unjustly toward peoples and cultures if they import political, economic, or social ideologies alongside the gospel. The evangelized, too, must be aware of their own culture and religious history and discern how their response to evangelizers is faithful to the gospel as embodied in their own religious history and culture.

31. Pentecostals point out that, in recent years, an intentional and concentrated focus on "unreached peoples" has arisen. Some Evangelical Christian and Pentecostal movements have targeted the parts of the globe roughly fitting with the longitude/latitude configuration (the 10/40 window) for a significant emphasis of missionary personnel and finances. The 10/40 window includes regions in which the gospel has never historically made significant inroads and shows Pentecostal consciousness that the so-called "unreached people" have been neglected.

32. Pentecostals in this dialogue wish to observe that in some cultural contexts, such as in Africa, or Asia, or even Latin America, Pentecostals have actively and successfully engaged in mission without the benefit of any formal training on issues related to the inculturation of the gospel. They have actually communicated their Christian spirituality, worship, and forms of evangelization through their local cultures. Pentecostals believe that this process has been facilitated by their emphasis upon the freedom of the Holy Spirit, with their consequent openness to the diversity of forms of expression in the worship and praise of God (e.g., their recognition of dance as a genuine form of spiritual

worship). Their missionary work has been effective because they have a missionary model based on the recognition that all members of the community have been given the gifts or charisms of the Spirit necessary to share the full message of the gospel.

33. Catholics not only see the need to evangelize persons, but also see the need to evangelize cultures, for example through educational institutions. Furthermore, they have often evangelized through aesthetics embodying religious values. However, the ultimate focus of evangelization is the person. Catholics acknowledge instances of shortcomings in their evangelization, for instance, by insufficient Christian initiation and discipleship formation and by not always bringing parishioners to a personal faith commitment. Shortcomings, however, can often be better understood if concrete conditions, such as poverty, illiteracy, a shortage of ministers, and the structures of oppression are known.

34. Both Catholics and Pentecostals recognize that the great social changes in Western society result in secularization processes and consequently a decline in religious practice. We deplore and condemn this secularization process, especially when these attitudes become part of a political agenda, which promotes a value-free society in the name of tolerance and liberalism. To deplore and condemn are not enough. More positively, as Christians, we have to understand these new challenges and help our people to find new ways and insights to face them in light of Christian values. The fact is that many people face new challenges without guidelines in the fields of religion and ethics.

35. For example, over the past thirty years, technological and scientific innovations have radically changed the concrete conditions in which human beings are born and die in the "Western world." Progress in medicine far more than philosophical ideology has influenced our way of seeing the beginning and end of human life. In former times, procreation and the birth of a child depended much more on "chance," and consequently parents placed their trust in divine providence in this matter. Today, an increasing ability to regulate birth allows a child to be "planned." Well before birth, through the pictures we see, we know whether the child is a boy or a girl. Further, the birth of a child takes place in a medical environment, far from the family home.

36. In the same way, at the other end of existence, no society before has ever seen such longevity, such a high proportion of elderly people. And none has taken death away from the family environment to such

an extent: some 70% of all people in western societies die in a hospital, in a medical, and technical environment. Such far-reaching changes require that we actively engage in these challenges and learn as a Christian community how to respond to them in our preaching, our liturgy, and our service. In a way, we have to reformulate the everlasting message of salvation in a convincing way for contemporary men and women and not simply repeat it in antiquated language.

IV. EVANGELIZATION AND SOCIAL JUSTICE[7]

37. Since our traditions have approached the linkages between these two subjects in such different ways, we have decided to have each side elaborate the connection in its own way before we show our convergences and differences.

1. Pentecostal Reflections on Evangelization and Social Justice

38. Pentecostal churches believe that they have been called by God in the "last days" (Acts 2:17) to be Christ-like witnesses in the power of the Spirit. One of the major contributions of Pentecostals to other Christian communities is an understanding of the church as a Spirit-filled missionary movement, which not only founds communities but also cultivates them, while the Holy Spirit empowers them with the charisms.

39. Pentecostals have sometimes been accused of emphasizing evangelization to the exclusion of helping people in their practical needs. The sense of urgency, which Pentecostals have concerning witness and salvation of the lost, like that of the early church, is not inconsistent with love and care for one another and for others. There are many examples of their sacrificial care throughout the world. The hope in the imminent coming of the Lord has sustained Pentecostals during persecution, harassment, imprisonment, and martyrdom during this century. They have consistently taught that the church must be ready for the coming of the Lord by means of faithful witness and holy living. They have taught

7. The papers done for this section were by John C. Haughey, sj of Loyola University, Chicago (*Evangelization and Social Justice: An Inquiry Into Their Relationship*), and by Murl O. Dirkson, PhD and Karen Carroll Mundy, PhD, (Church of God) of Lee University, Cleveland, Tennessee, USA (*Evangelization and Social Justice: A Pentecostal Perspective*).

that all will have to give account to the righteous judge for those things, which have been done or left undone.

40. Pentecostals have a great concern for the eternal salvation of the soul but also for the present welfare of the body, as is readily apparent on the high priority they give to the doctrine of divine healing. In addition, they have had a real concern for the social as well as for the spiritual welfare of their members, especially in the third world. Theologically, the rebirth of a person by the Spirit is the anticipation of the transformation of the cosmos (cf. 2 Cor 5:17; Rom 8:21). This is why conversion and incorporation into the community of faith cannot be seen apart from the transformation of society. The person filled by the Spirit of God is impelled by that same Spirit to cooperate with God in the work of evangelism and social action in the anticipation of the new creation.

41. With their increasing numerical strength and upward social mobility, Pentecostal communities are now confronted by greater challenges for the kinds of social justice and human-rights concerns, which the Catholic dialogue partners rightfully voice. Pentecostals continue to believe that intense hope has been and will continue to be necessary for endurance, healing, and engagement of the forces—both social and spiritual—which oppress and violate people.

42. If it seems to Catholics that Pentecostals have reflected too little on problems related to social structures, Pentecostals suggest that social conditions under which they existed during early stages of their corporate experience be kept in mind. They had no access to structures of power by which they could influence public policy directly. This has meant that:

A. Most Pentecostals do not give priority to systematic reflection on problems related to social structures. They place more attention on the ways people experience those problems in their own lives and communities.

B. Pentecostalism, for the most part, has not existed until recently among "well educated" people who are able to reflect more systematically on structural dimensions of social justice.

C. Pentecostals do not read the New Testament as placing high priority on structural change; rather they read it as emphasizing personal conversion and commitment to the communities of faith, and through that process they effect social change.

43. The perceived lack of stress on structural change does not, however, imply a lack of interest in social issues. Pentecostal conversion, while being personal, is not simply an individual experience, but also a communal one. In the life of the community, Pentecostals have found a new sense of dignity and purpose in life. Their solidarity creates affective ties, giving them a sense of equality. These communities have functioned as social alternatives that protest against the oppressive structures of the society at large. Along with some social critics, Pentecostals have discovered that effective social change often takes place at the communal and micro-structural level, not at the macro-structural level.

44. Pentecostals have continued to speak and act on behalf of those victimized by abortion, pornography, violence, oppression, etc. They have been concerned with feeding the hungry, clothing the naked, and providing emergency disaster relief. They have expanded their educational efforts and have begun to address issues of social-structural evil more explicitly. They are discovering their responsibility for those structures and their ability to influence them for good. This awareness was particularly fostered in situations of political and economic oppression.

45. From their earliest existence, Pentecostals have been active in missionary endeavors in the so-called "two-thirds" world. The churches established there have opposed social evils from the pulpit and on an interpersonal level in the oral fashion typical of the non-literary culture of Pentecostals. This concerns evils, such as the Caste-system in India, polygamy in Africa and the Pacific, and genital mutilation in some African countries. Here exists a difficulty of perception. For older, more literary publics, only what is written and documented is perceived as having real existence. Pentecostals have begun to document work being done on these kinds of social issues in which they may have participated for many years.

46. In recent years and in various parts of the world, there have been a number of attempts to formulate Pentecostal social ethics which address the issues of structural change. Some Pentecostals have used the category of the new creation/Kingdom of God with its characteristics of justice and peace to develop criteria for structural change. This has been connected with passages such as Luke 4:16–18 which demands the liberation of the oppressed in the power of the Spirit. Other Pentecostals speak more in terms of principalities and powers, of demonic forces, which are present in the structures of the oppressive systems (cf. Eph

6:12; Col 2:13–15) that need to be fought with prayer and prophetic denunciation.

47. But even prior to these efforts, Pentecostals, sometimes consciously, but usually unconsciously, have long used a number of significant theological criteria for taking social responsibility. More specifically, the ongoing narrative or story of Pentecostal communities has functioned to move people from their experience of the biblical witness to serious and often successful attempts to solve social problems. Likewise, ethical concerns about matters of justice and peace have developed in Pentecostal communities as they have correlated specific biblical injunctions with the reading of the Bible as a whole.

48. In summary, the emphasis Pentecostals place on personal evangelism and incorporation into Christian communities as a means of cultivating, pursuing, and even propagating social structures may differ in method or emphasis from other Christian communities. Certainly as these relatively young churches continue to grow and mature, they will need to grow also in their capacity to address social issues on the societal level from their own perspective and identity. Nevertheless, up to this point, these emphases in Pentecostal ministry have not been without impact and not just in terms of generating and supporting acts of mercy. All this being said, however, we would anticipate that the Pentecostal style of engaging in justice will continue to differ from that of other Christian traditions.

2. *Catholic Reflections on Evangelization and Social Justice*

49. Catholics tend to view the questions of societal change, church and state relationships, and human rights, from the perspective of a complex and rich Catholic social teaching, which is more than a century old in its development. It has its roots in the Scriptures, reached its highpoint at Vatican II, and continues on in the pontificate of John Paul II. For example, two of these documents from Vatican II, the *Pastoral Constitution on the Church in the Modern World* and the *Decree on Religious Liberty*, put the Catholic Church on record as representing legitimate pluralism, religious liberty, and the rights of people to be politically and civilly self-determining. It furthermore holds that they have socio-economic rights. It sees the human person as the inviolable subject of these rights, which include religious liberty. Human freedom

is the condition not only of civil liberty, but is fundamental to accepting the gospel in the first place.

50. The synod of bishops of 1971, which focused on the question of justice, spoke of the way in which the quest for justice is an important part of the mission of the church in these words: "Action on behalf of justice and the transformation of society is integral to the mission of the church and the preaching of the gospel, or, in other words, of the church's mission for the redemption of the human race and its liberation from every oppressive situation" (*Justice in the World*, introduction).

51. All believers are called by God to engage in works of charity and to strive for social justice. According to the *Decree on the Apostolate of Lay People* of Vatican II, the laity, within the church as a whole, led by the light of the gospel and according to the mind of Christ, are called to renew the temporal order as their own special obligation (*Decree on the Apostolate of Lay People*, 7). The Decree points to the need to change unjust structures, stating that "the demands of justice should first be satisfied. . . . Not only the effects but also the causes of various ills must be removed. Help should be given in such a way that recipients may gradually be freed from dependence on others and become self-sufficient" (*Decree on the Apostolate of Lay People*, 8).

52. The transforming power of the gospel on individuals, communities, and society is the grace of God, especially as mediated through Word and sacraments. It is in the prayer of the church (i.e., in the Eucharist, in the other sacraments, as well as in the daily prayer of the people) that we are united to the transforming prayer of Christ. He taught us to pray for the coming of the kingdom (Matt 6:10), which by its very nature is God's gift and work. We do not construct the kingdom but rather ask for it, welcome it, and rejoice in its growth within us. Prayer empowers us, in fact, demands that we strive for just and loving relationships among people, in family, in community, and in society. These are all included in Christ's redemptive work.

53. Any account of modern Catholicism's efforts in these matters of evangelization, education, and social justice would be incomplete if it did not mention men's and women's religious communities. Many of these religious congregations view their doing works of justice and faith as intrinsic to their particular calling. Many of their members live out this vision at great sacrifice—even of their lives.

54. To speak of the "kingdom of God" is to speak of the ultimate will of God for the whole of creation. The symbol of the kingdom conveys not only what we hope for but also a sense of urgency about our present responsibilities to be about the work of justice and the ministry of reconciliation between individuals, social classes, and racial and ethnic groups. It also furnishes criteria for promoting social well-being on personal, communal, and structural levels.

3. Our Common Views Regarding Faith and Justice

55. Pentecostals and Catholics agree that the Word of God is the foundation of both evangelization and social justice.

56. In the Old Testament there is a strong insistence that the people whom God has freed should live justly (e.g., Jer 21:12 and 22:3; Amos 5:7–12; 8:4–6; Mic 6:12). One OT passage about justice, in particular (namely, Isa 61:1–3), is quoted by Jesus to characterize his own proclamation (Luke 4:18–21). The fact that we find in the gospel both the great commission to evangelize the nations (Matt 28:16–20; Mark 16:15–18) and the great commandment to love God and one's neighbor (Matt 22:34–40; Mark 12:28–34; Luke 10:27–28) suggests that there is a continuum between the two.

57. *Koinonia* as lived by the early Christians (Acts 2:42–47; 4:32–37) had social implications. Their communities did not act from a concept of social justice. The concern they showed for the poor, widows, and strangers was not seen as an entirely separate activity but rather as an extension of their worship.

58. We agree that:

- evangelization and love for one's neighbor are intrinsically connected and that basic to this love is active work toward social justice;
- even as we engage in evangelization, we need to give due attention to the social welfare of our neighbor;
- both Pentecostals and Catholics need to resist reductionism, anthropocentrism, and politicization of Christ or the gospel, and the privatization of the kingdom and individualization of society. Here we see a point of strong convergence.

59. Clearly, any striving for social justice in which our faith communities engage needs to be rooted in the life of God—Father, Son, and Holy Spirit. God the Father, who blessed the creation and called it good, commands us to look for justice for our neighbor, particularly orphans, widows, and foreigners (Jer 22:3–5).

God the Son, the redeemer, who accomplished the work of salvation for the whole world, calls us to imitate his compassionate ministry of preaching the good news of the kingdom, healing the sick, and feeding the hungry (Luke 4:16–21). In fact, he identifies himself with them (Matt 25:31–46).

God the Spirit, who gives life, empowers us to witness to the world—in word and deed (Acts 1:8). Life in the Holy Spirit energizes Christians to engage in evangelization and to work for justice in society. Transformed people are compelled by the Spirit, the creator and sanctifier, to transform the world in the light of the in-breaking kingdom of God.

4. Things We Have Learned Together Perceptions and Convergences

60. Pentecostals and Catholics exhibit strengths and weaknesses in their understanding and practice of evangelization and social justice. Pentecostals believe that Catholics do not appreciate the social impact of Pentecostal ministry. Though Pentecostals may lack a formal social doctrine, Pentecostal evangelization has arguably a powerful social impact on individuals, on family life, and the whole community.

61. We have come to realize that Pentecostals and Catholics have much to bring to one another with regard to social justice. While Catholics believe in the importance of personal faith, they also put great emphasis on the power of the gospel to change societal structures. Pentecostals, on the other hand, have traditionally pursued social change at the individual and communal levels. Catholics wonder whether the Pentecostal theology of evangelization leaves them ill-equipped for engaging in social justice. Pentecostals believe that Catholics should take more seriously the importance of personal and communal transformation for promoting societal change.

62. Catholics realize that, in some predominantly Catholic regions of the world, there are places where the gospel does not always appear to be effectively proclaimed and/or lived out in daily life.

63. Pentecostals believe that Catholics tend to minimize the impact of the power of the Holy Spirit when it brings concrete changes on the level of the individual, family, and community. Pentecostals realize that, in the past, they were often not sufficiently aware of the implications of the gospel for social systems.

64. Pentecostals and Catholics agree that the regrettable division among Christians is a counter-witness to the credibility of the gospel and a hindrance to the effectiveness of promoting justice in the world. Some non-Christians have used this division as a sign of God's favoring of their own particular faith.

65. In the work of evangelization and social justice, we believe, as we have said above, that our communities are currently undergoing a form of convergence. While the Catholic church is in a process of renewal in evangelization and pastoral formation, Pentecostals are growing in an awareness of their responsibilities in the matter of structures and social systems.

66. Pentecostals and Catholics believe Jesus Christ to be the lord of the kingdom he came to proclaim, and in our preaching and understanding, the kingdom of God and social justice should not be separated. Churches should strive to be faithful to the demands of the kingdom of God. Scandal is given when the churches, in their social and historical existence, grow slack in pursuing the divine purposes of the kingdom.

67. We differ in our emphases on the sources of evil, specifically, as to what extent they are human, natural, and/or supernatural origin. We also differ in the ways in which to recognize and deal with them. This is an area in which both traditions have much to learn from one another. We see the need to explore together the theological nature of power and its appropriate or inappropriate meditations. We need to ask how our spiritualities, explicitly or implicitly, empower people to bear witness in evangelization and social justice.

V. PROSELYTISM[8]

1. Moving Towards a Common Position on Proselytism

68. Since 1972, members of this dialogue have committed themselves to address the issue of proselytism. That this discussion has at

8. Papers were presented by Rev. Karl Müller, svd of St. Augustin, Germany

last begun is a sign of the growing trust and maturation of Pentecostal-Catholic relations. Both teams in this international Roman Catholic-Pentecostal dialogue entered into a conversation on this topic with a number of misgivings. It is difficult enough to address this subject as an abstract object of study. But Catholic-Pentecostal relationships in many parts of the world have been troubled at times with accusations of insensitivity to the presence of long-standing Christian communities, charges of proselytism, and counter charges of persecution. Some people, in both traditions, have made it clear that they do not want Catholics and Pentecostals to speak to one another. Others have made it clear that they did not even want the topic of proselytism itself addressed. Both the Catholic and the Pentecostal teams debated within themselves, and then together, the wisdom of undertaking such a discussion in the light of possible repercussions on our mutual and growing relationship. Indeed, even the dialogue itself could suffer, we feared. In spite of these significant concerns, we decided that the urgency of the situation and the need to proclaim the gospel in a credible manner demanded a beginning to this discussion.

69. The members of the dialogue observed that proselytism exists, in large part, because Pentecostals and Catholics do not have a common understanding of the church. To give one illustration, they do not agree on the relationship between the church, on one hand, and baptism as an expression of living faith, on the other.

Nonetheless, in our previous discussions, we have expressed the ways in which we perceive the bonds between us that already exist. Catholics, for example, hold that everyone who believes in the name of the Lord Jesus and is properly baptized (cf. *Perspectives on Koinonia*, 54) is joined in a certain true manner to the body of Christ, which is the church. For Pentecostals, "the foundation of unity is a common faith and experience of Jesus Christ as lord and savior through the Holy Spirit. This implies that to the extent that Pentecostals recognize that Roman Catholics have this common faith in and experience of Jesus as lord, they share a real though imperfect *koinonia* with them" (*Perspectives on Koinonia*, 55). This is true even though each has different understandings of the church.

(*Proselytism, Common Witness and Evangelization*) and by Dr. Cecil M. Robeck Jr. (Assemblies of God), Fuller Theological Seminary, Pasadena, CA, USA (*Evangelization, Proselytizing and Common Witness: A Pentecostal Perspective*).

70. Still, members of the dialogue think that Pentecostals and Catholics already agree on critical points of faith. Recognition of this fact makes it possible for each of our communities to act in ways that do not impede the growth of the other. Lack of mutual recognition, however, has led at times to dismissive charges and countercharges (e.g., "sects," "unbelievers," "syncretists," etc.), and actions and counteractions (e.g., unilateral decisions for the good of one community, often at the expense of the other community), by members of both communities. These charges and actions have detracted from the ability of Catholics and Pentecostals to witness credibly before the world to the reconciling power of God through Jesus Christ.

71. A primary example of such a conflict may be found in the tensions which exist between Christians, who are not in fellowship with one another. It is not our purpose in this document to give priority to the interests of one particular church over those of another. While in the example given in the following paragraphs, the Catholic Church is described as the long-established church and the Pentecostals as the newcomers, such as may be the case in any given European country, there are instances, such as in the case of Northeast Zimbabwe, in which Pentecostals may be described as the long-established church and the Catholics as newcomers. In the use of our example, our concern is merely to illustrate, in concrete terms, the tensions which may arise with respect to mission in a given region between two such churches.

72. Catholics, for instance, may have preached the gospel and established churches in a region centuries ago. Through the centuries, these churches have played an important role in the lives of the people of that region. The role, which the church has played, has extended far beyond the walls of the congregation, permeating every aspect of the culture of the people from art to music, to social institutions, to festivals and other public celebrations. The lives of the people flow easily between church and the wider culture, because the church has impacted the culture in a major way.

73. However, there is another side to this. Often, the earlier Christianization of a given culture by Catholicism takes for granted that it remains permeated by faith. As with an individual, so also with a culture, critique by the Word and on-going transformation are necessary.

74. The time and investment in the church by devout Catholics have been significant in many cultures. Sometimes, their attempt to live

the life of faith has come at a great price--persecution, even martyrdom. Actively embracing the challenges of living and transforming the society to which the gospel has been brought is no small feat. The faithful have struggled to maintain the gospel, even at times when the society has not wanted to hear it. The local church has rejoiced when the gospel has taken root, and sorrowed when it has failed to do so. In other words, evangelization is an on-going need for any culture.

75. Conflict erupts, when another community of Christians enters into the life of an already religiously impacted community and begins to evangelize without due consideration of the price that has been paid for witness to the gospel by believers who have preceded them. Difficulties arise, when there is no acknowledgment of the significant role which the church plays in all aspects of the lives of those who are citizens of this region. This conflict comes about, because the two Christian communities are separated and have not recognized the legitimacy of one another as members of the one body of Christ. They have been separated from one another. They have not spoken with one another. Certain assumptions have been made by each about the other. Judgments have taken place without proper consultation between them.

76. Even if the motives of newcomers are irreproachable with respect to the welfare of the people in this region, including a genuine concern to see that the citizens of the region have really heard the gospel, their method of entry into the region often contributes to misunderstanding and conflict, and perhaps even to a violent response. Courtesy would seem to call for some communication with the leaders of the older church by the new evangelizers. Without this, the older church and culture are easily violated. The people and church leaders in some of these areas have often been offended by what they see as disrespect or disregard of pastoral activities that have been exercised for a long time. It is easy to see why serious tensions might arise.

77. The conflicts, which have occurred between us, demonstrate clearly the problem which disunity creates even for well-intentioned Chris-tians. Disunity isolates us from one another. It leads to suspicion between us. It contributes to a lack of mutual understanding, even to an unwillingness for us to try to understand each other. And all of these things have resulted in a general state of hostility between us in which we even question the Christian authenticity of each other. Our different readings of the gospel, reached in our isolated states, have led to doctri-

nal differences which have only further contributed to the question of whether or not the other truly proclaims the gospel.

78. If each perceives the other through the lens of this disunity, the result is all too often that one sees the other as an adversary to its own mission and may, therefore, feel the need to place impediments in the way of the other. There may be public denunciations, even persecution, of one another. Both sides have suffered, Pentecostals in particular, since they have usually been the minority. But the main tragedy, and on this both the Catholic and Pentecostal teams agree, is that the conflict resulting from the disunity of Christians always "scandalizes the world, and damages that most holy cause, the preaching of the gospel to every creature" (*Decree on Ecumenism*, 1). What needs to be faced honestly, and examined with great care, are the reasons behind these conflicts. What we both desire is the pure preaching of the gospel. Most of our conflicts would diminish if we agreed that this is what evangelization is all about.

79. Instead of conflict, can we not converse with one another, pray with one another, try to cooperate with one another, instead of clashing with one another? In effect, we need to look for ways in which Christians can seek the unity to which Christ calls his disciples (cf. John 17:21) starting with basic respect for one another, learning to love one another.

2. *Replacing Dissatisfaction with Hope*

80. By the fourth century, church and state were deeply involved in the life of each other. Since then, both have occasionally resorted to coercion to assure political-religious homogeneity in society. This has been expressed in the repression of heresy (inquisition) and of other religions (the expulsion of Jews and Muslims from various European countries). The same concern shaped the principle, *cuius regio, eius religio* ("all citizens must accept the religion of their ruler"), which was enforced in Europe, especially during the sixteenth and seventeenth centuries. The process by which churches and states moved, first, to religious toleration and, then, to religious freedom, only began in the late eighteenth century and did not become more or less universal in the West until the mid-twentieth century.

81. In this historical context, Catholics are well aware that attempts at Christianization have often been attached to political and economic expansion (e.g., Latin America), and that sometimes pressure and vio-

lence have been used. They also acknowledge that, prior to Vatican II, Catholic doctrine has been reluctant to support full religious freedom in civil law.

82. Today, Catholics and Pentecostals condemn coercive and violent methods. Nevertheless, all too often, aggressiveness still characterizes our interaction. Words have become the new weapons. Catholics are affronted when some Pentecostals assume that they are not even Christians, when they speak disrespectfully of the Catholic Church and its leaders, or when Pentecostals lead Catholic members into newly established Pentecostal fellowships. Pentecostals are affronted when some Catholics in some parts of the world view them as "rapacious wolves," when they are ridiculed as "*panderetas o aleluyas*" ("tambourines or alleluias"), or when they are indiscriminately classified as "sects."

83. Further proof of the fact that neither Catholics nor Pentecostals are satisfied with the state of division, which exists between them, can be seen in their own discussions of proselytism. An initial working definition of proselytism is that it is a disrespectful, insensitive, and uncharitable effort to transfer the allegiance of a Christian from one ecclesial body to another. Actions have already been taken by several traditions, which reveal that they believe that "proselytism" is something to be condemned.[9]

84. Pentecostals did not participate directly in the development of those documents, but Pentecostals have also demonstrated their concern over proselytism, on a more limited scale. They have enacted various bylaws, adopted statements on ministerial ethics, and developed other guidelines, which provide leadership to their ministers on issues, such as how close together congregations can be planted, what permissions need to be obtained from other pastors in the area in which a new

9. On the Catholic side, the theme has been addressed in several international bilateral dialogues in which the Roman Catholic Church has been involved, namely with Evangelicals (*The Evangelical-Roman Catholic Dialogue on Mission, 1977–1984: A Report*, Information Service [IS] 60 (1986/I–II) 71–97; with Baptists (*Summons To Witness to Christ in Today's World: A Report of the Baptist-Roman Catholic International Conversations, 1984–1988*, IS 72 (1990/I) 5–14); with the Orthodox (*Uniatism: Method of Union of the Past, and the Present Search for Full Communion, 1993*, IS 83 (1993/II) 96–99). On the multilateral level, the Joint Working Group between the Roman Catholic Church and the World Council of churches has recently published a study document entitled *The Challenge of Proselytism and the Calling to Common Witness*, 1996, IS 91 (1996/I–II) 77–83. In so doing, Catholics, like many Protestant and Orthodox groups, have expressed the desire to condemn all proselytism.

work is being planted, and what type of relationship a minister must maintain when working within the parish of another minister of the same denomination, or within a district that is not his or her own. These bylaws, codes of ethics, and other guidelines have been developed to resist any temptation, which one minister might have to proselytize (cf. 2 Cor 10:16). These guidelines work, because there is mutual recognition between those who are subject to them.

85. The early writings of Pentecostals reveal a number of rich and fertile visions of unity among Christians, even if at times they were triumphalistic. Among them was the vision of Charles F. Parham who viewed himself as called by the Holy Spirit to serve as an "apostle of unity." Another was repeatedly published by the African-American pastor William J. Seymour of the famous Azusa Street Mission, in *the Apostolic Faith*, that the movement stood for. ". . . Christian unity everywhere." The ministers of the Assemblies of God, in their organizational meeting of April 1914, went so far as to state that they opposed the establishment of "unscriptural lines of fellowship or dis-fellowship," since such lines stood counter to Jesus' desire for unity as expressed in John 17:21. A number of other early Pentecostal leaders shared these sentiments also, and read this impulse toward unity as one which was birthed by the Holy Spirit.

86. While some Pentecostal bodies, especially some indigenous groups in Latin America and Africa, have retained their original visions for unity, most Pentecostals around the world have chosen to pursue more limited visions of unity. This has happened due to a number of factors. Fundamentalists outside Pentecostalism publicly criticized existing Pentecostal cooperation with many other Christians as inconsistent with biblical teaching. The adoption by some Pentecostals of certain eschatological interpretations, popular among fundamentalists and Evangelicals, led to growing suspicion of the modern movements toward unity among Protestants. Peer pressure, which suggested that Pentecostals would be granted acceptance as full members of the Evangelical community if they would cut existing ties with certain other Christians, further compromised the original visions of unity.[10]

10. Cecil M. Robeck, Jr., "The Assemblies of God and Ecumenical Cooperation, 1920–1965," in Wonsuk Ma and Robert P. Menzies, eds. *Pentecostalism in Context: Essays in Honor of William W. Menzies*, JPT Supplement Series 11 (Sheffield: Sheffield Academic Press, 1997) 107–50.

Many Pentecostals also withdrew their support of larger movements toward unity, when they believed that their own priorities were not being taken seriously. Vestiges of these original visions of unity are still to be found among the published statements, which outline the *raison d'être* of many Pentecostal organizations including the *Pentecostal World Conference*.[11]

87. The Pentecostal members of this dialogue lament the impact of the factors which have led to the loss of the original visions of unity. They would like to challenge Pentecostals to look once again at their roots, that they might rediscover the richness of their earliest call to facilitate unity between all Christians by internalizing anew the role the Holy Spirit has presumably played in the birth of these deep yearnings.

88. All members of this dialogue also wish to encourage Pentecostals to share their visions of greater Christian unity with other Christians. In turn, we urge the latter to bring their own visions of unity to the discussion. In this way, we believe that together we can "discover the unfathomable riches of the truth," thereby deepening our own understanding of what we believe the Holy Spirit has caused to emerge within us. We are all called to be stewards of this precious gift of unity, which we already enjoy and to which we yet aspire in the bond of peace (cf. Eph 4:3).

89. In the light of these realities, which have contributed to our own coming together for dialogue, the members of both teams felt keenly the need to acknowledge that neither Catholics nor Pentecostals have fulfilled sufficiently the demands of the gospel to love one another. While the past cannot be undone and is not even wholly retrievable, we must make every effort to know and express it as accurately as possible.

11. In its May 21-29, 1949 meeting in Paris, the Executive Committee of the *World Pentecostal Conference* (now called *Pentecostal World Conference*) unanimously adopted a two-page "Manifesto and Declaration" in which it outlined its "common purpose and objective." Included as point 6b was the following: "To demonstrate to the world the essential unity of Spirit—baptized believers fulfilling the prayer of the Lord Jesus Christ: 'That all may be one' *John* 17:21." This action was subsequently announced by the conference secretary, David J. du Plessis, in a report titled "World Pentecost holds its Third International Conference," which appeared in H. W. Greenway, ed., *World Pentecostal Conference 1952* (n.p.: The British Pentecostal Fellowship, 1952) 6. A copy of the original "Manifesto and Declaration" is on file in the Archives of David du Plessis Center for Christian Spirituality at Fuller Theological Seminary, Pasadena, CA 91182, USA.

3. *Defining the Challenge*

90. The term "proselytism" is not found in the Bible, but the term "proselyte" is. It is originally derived from the Old Testament vocabulary relating to those strangers and sojourners who moved into Israel, believed in Yahweh, and accepted the entire Torah (e.g., Ex 12:48–49). This term carried a positive meaning, i.e., to become a convert to Judaism. In the New Testament, proselytes were present in Jerusalem on the day of Pentecost (cf. Acts 2:11), and at least one of them was chosen to serve the widows (cf. Acts 6:5). But in recent times, "proselytism," as used within Christian circles, has come to carry a negative meaning associated with an illicit form of "evangelism."

91. An issue between Catholics and Pentecostals that relates to the problem of proselytism concerns the way a living faith is perceived in the life of an individual Christian or in a community. Through dialogue, we have learned that Pentecostals and Catholics may have different ideas about who is "unchurched," different understandings of how living in a deeply Christian culture can root the Christian faith in someone's life. They may have different ideas of how to assess whether, or in what way, pastoral needs are being met in a Christian community or in a person's life. They may have different ways of interpreting whether or not a person can be considered an evangelized Christian.

92. The dialogue has taught us that, because of these differences, there is a continual need to learn from one another so as to deepen mutual knowledge and understanding of each others' doctrinal traditions, pastoral practices, and convictions. We need to learn to respect the integrity and rights of the other, so as to avoid judgments that create unnecessary conflict in regard to evangelization and obstacles to the spreading of the gospel, in addition to those already caused by our divisions.

93. Attempts to define proselytism reveal a broad range of activities and actions that are not easily interpreted. These tend to be identified and evaluated differently by the parties involved. In spite of these difficulties, we have concluded that, both for Catholics and for Pentecostals, proselytism is an unethical activity that comes in many forms. Some of these would be:

- all ways of promoting our own community of faith that are intellectually dishonest, such as contrasting an ideal presentation of our own community with the weaknesses of another Christian community;

- all intellectual laziness and culpable ignorance that neglect readily accessible knowledge of the other's tradition;
- every wilful misrepresentation of the beliefs and practices of other Christian communities;
- every form of force, coercion, compulsion, mockery or intimidation of a personal, psychological, physical, moral, social, economic, religious or political nature;
- every form of cajolery or manipulation, including the exaggeration of biblical promises, because these distortions do not respect the dignity of persons and their freedom to make their own choices;
- every abuse of mass media in a way that is disrespectful of another faith and manipulative of the audience;
- all unwarranted judgments or acts, which raise suspicions about the sincerity of others;
- all competitive evangelization focused against other Christian bodies (cf. Rom 15:20).

94. All Christians have the right to bear witness to the gospel before all people, including other Christians. Such witness may legitimately involve the persuasive proclamation of the gospel in such a way as to bring people to faith in Jesus Christ or to commit themselves more deeply to him within the context of their own church. The legitimate proclamation of the gospel will bear the marks of Christian love (cf. 1 Corinthians 13). It will never seek its own selfish ends by using the opportunity to speak against or in any way denigrate another Christian community, or to suggest or encourage a change in someone's Christian affiliation. Both the Pentecostal and Catholic members of this dialogue view as proselytism such selfish actions as an illegitimate use of persuasive power. Proselytism must be sharply distinguished from the legitimate act of persuasively presenting the gospel. Proselytism must be avoided.

95. At the same time, we acknowledge that if a Christian, after hearing a legitimate presentation of the gospel, freely chooses to join a different Christian community, it should not automatically be concluded that such a transfer is the result of proselytism.

96. For the most part, people hear the preaching of the gospel within their own particular church, where their own spiritual needs are also met. It may also happen, on a given occasion, that members of different Christian communities help to organize an evangelistic campaign, in which they also participate. The primary aim of such an evangelistic campaign should always be the proclamation of the gospel. We believe that the Reverend Billy Graham has provided an important model in this regard. Respecting the ecclesial affiliation of the participants, he organizes such campaigns only after he has sought the support and agreement of the churches in the area, including Catholics and Pentecostals. When those, who are already part of a Christian community, respond to his call to commit themselves more deeply to Christ, the pastoral resources from their own church are immediately made available to help them in their renewed commitment. Thus, proselytism is avoided. The churches involved receive the respect and regard they deserve, illustrating the results of communication and cooperation, demonstrating a measure of real, visible unity.

97. Confusion has resulted when the terms "proselytism" and "evangelism" have been used as though they were synonyms. This confusion has impacted the civil realm. Some countries, for instance, have passed so-called "anti-proselytism" laws which prohibit or greatly restrict any kind of Christian evangelism or missionary activity. We deplore this.

4. *Promoting Religious Freedom*

98. Mention of these anti-proselytism laws introduces us to the complex matter of religious freedom. There is general agreement that religious liberty is a civil right. For Christians there is also the religious freedom they are to accord to one another as brothers and sisters in Christ, and to all human beings, since they are made in the image and likeness of God.

99. Religious freedom is promoted by both secular society, for example, in statements from the United Nations (cf. *United Nations Declaration on Human Rights*, 1948; *UN Declaration on the Elimination of all Forms of Intolerance and Discrimination Based on Religious Belief*, 25 November 1981, Art. 1.1) and by the church (e.g., *Declaration on Religious Liberty*, Vatican II [1965]). Pentecostals and Catholics are in full agreement in the support of religious freedom, whether it is seen as a

civil right or as one of the principles that should guide their relationships with each other.

100. Religious freedom as a civil right is very complex in the way it is pursued and resisted in the endlessly varied political situations that have church related to state and state to church. Catholics and Pentecostals need to stand as one in respecting and promoting this civil right for all peoples and for one another.

101. Historically, Pentecostals have not enacted broadly representative resolutions on the subject of religious freedom largely because of their minority status in the societies where they have functioned. They have recently, however, joined with other Christians when issues of religious freedom have been at stake. They have also led efforts to end persecution or to promote legislation towards religious freedom, especially in countries where in the past the rights of their Pentecostal sisters and brothers have been violated (e.g., Italy, and a number of Latin American countries). It is clear, therefore, that they believe that the state has a legitimate role in guaranteeing religious freedom.

102. Because of these convictions, members of the dialogue reject:

- all violations of religious freedom and all forms of religious intolerance as well as every attempt to impose belief and practices on others or to manipulate or coerce others in the name of religion;
- inequality in civil treatment of religious bodies, although, we affirm, as Vatican II affirmed, that in exercising their rights, individuals and social groups "are bound by the moral law to have regard to the rights of others, to their own duties toward others and for the common good of all" (*Declaration on Religious Liberty*, 7).

103. Catholics believe that the state is obliged to give effective protection to the religious liberty of all citizens by just laws and other suitable means, and to ensure favorable conditions for fostering religious life (cf. *Declaration on Religious Liberty*, 6).

104. Religious freedom has also been the subject of significant ecumenical dialogue (e.g., *Summons to Witness to Christ in Today's World: A Report on the Baptist-Roman Catholic International Conversations*, 1984–1988).[12] A statement that is even more comprehensive in scope is that of the Joint Working Group between the Catholic Church and the World Council of Churches. With them we agree that "religious freedom

12. See note 9.

affirms the right of all persons to pursue the truth and witness to the truth according to their conscience. It includes the freedom to acknowledge Jesus Christ as Lord and Savior and the freedom of Christians to witness to their faith in him by word and deed" (Joint Working Group, *The Challenge of Proselytism and the Calling to Common Witness* [1996], 15). Religious freedom includes the freedom to embrace a religion or to change one's religion without any coercion which would impair such freedom (cf. ibid.).

5. *Resolving Conflicts in the Quest for Unity*

105. Conflicts among Christian groups are not unusual. Difficulties experienced by Protestant missionary movements of the nineteenth and twentieth centuries highlighted the need to resolve tensions among denominations. It became obvious that divisions were obstacles to the preaching of the gospel. These concerns led to the first World Missionary Conference at Edinburgh, Scotland, in 1910, at which an international body of Protestants and Anglicans assembled to discuss ways to cooperate rather than compete in mission. This conference led to other movements for Christian cooperation. As we approach the end of the century, virtually all major Christian families, Anglican, Catholic, Orthodox, Pentecostal, and Protestant, are now involved in efforts to find ways to work together, to overcome misunderstandings, and to resolve doctrinal differences, so that these will no longer be obstacles to the proclaiming of the gospel of Jesus Christ.

106. These concerns have implications for Pentecostals and Catholics, where conflict arises from mission activities. Two points need to be kept in mind. On the one hand, we affirm that the principles of religious freedom are basic for evangelization. On the other hand, divided Christians have real responsibilities for one another, because of the bonds of *koinonia* they already share (cf. *Perspectives on Koinonia*, 54–55). In facing conflicts, the right to religious freedom must be seen in relationship to the responsibility to respond to Christ's call for the unity of his disciples. Christ calls Christians to live their freedom. At the same time, he calls Christians to unity "so that the world may believe" (John 17:21).

107. The call of the Lord of the church cannot be ignored. It is reinforced by the apostle Paul, who exhorted the Ephesians to make "every effort to maintain the unity of the Spirit in the bond of peace" (Eph 4:3)

for "there is one body, and one spirit . . . one Lord, one faith, one baptism, one God and Father of all" (Eph 4:4–5). Christians, who have been reconciled to God and entrusted with the ministry of reconciliation (cf. 2 Cor 5:18), need to be reconciled with each other in order to carry out their ministry effectively. Ongoing division jeopardizes the impact of the gospel.

108. We realize that some of our readers will think that our conclusions are idealistic. We do not agree. We recognize that not everyone has had the same experience and the same opportunity that we have had to work together, to pray together, and to learn from one another. We have come to recognize, in a fresh way, that with God all things are possible to those who believe (cf. Mark 9:23). The Scriptures teach us that Christ calls us and the apostle invites us to unity (cf. John 17:21; Eph 4:3). The patterns of our relationships in the past have not reflected this call. We engaged in this dialogue because of what we understand is the will of Christ, which our past relationships have not reflected. Our efforts are intended as a contribution to re-thinking the lack of conformity between Pentecostal-Catholic relationships and the call of Christ. We commend our findings to our readers recognizing that some will find them to be a real challenge.

109. We look forward to the day, when leaders within our two communities will be able to pray together, develop mutual trust, and deal with tensions which arise. Through our theological dialogue, now 25 years old, we have gained a deeper understanding of the meaning of faith in Christ and a mutual respect for one another. We covet for our leaders these same gifts and believe such relationships might yield greater sensitivity on issues of mutual concern. The relationship might even yield a code of ecclesial etiquette to help prevent difficulties from arising.

All of this seems possible and desirable. Are we not, as believers, being prepared for a future in which we will be judges not only of the world but also of the angels (cf. 1 Cor 6:2–3)? Would it not be a sign of contradiction if we had to hand over our present disputes to the judgement of the world? But this is what is happening when we arrive at impasses. "Can it be," Paul asks, "that there is no one among you wise enough to decide between one believer and another" (1 Cor 6:5)?

6. Affirming Principles for Mutual Understanding

110. The discussion on the nature of proselytism leads very quickly into practical matters. Even if Pentecostals and Catholics explicitly or implicitly denounce proselytism, many people may need practical guidance on how to live up to this commitment. The members of the dialogue have agreed upon the following principles, which seek to express the spirit of Christian love as it is portrayed in Scripture (cf. 1 Corinthians 13). They submit these principles for consideration by their respective churches.

111. The deep and true source of any Christian witness is the commandment, "You shall love the Lord your God with all your heart, and with all your soul, and with all your mind and you shall love your neighbor as yourself" (Matt 22:37 and 39; cf. Lev 19:18; Deut 6:5). Christian witness brings glory to God. It is nourished by the conviction that it is the Holy Spirit whose grace and light brings about the response of faith. It respects the free will and dignity of those to whom it is given, whether or not they wish to accept.

112. Pentecostals and Catholics affirm the presence and power of the gospel in Christian communities outside of their own traditions. Pentecostals believe that all Christians of whatever denomination can have a living personal relationship with Jesus as lord and savior. Catholics believe that only in their own visible communion "the fullness of the means of salvation can be attained." But they also believe that "some, even very many, of the significant elements and endowments which together go to build up and give life to the church itself, can exist outside the visible boundaries of the Catholic Church" (*Decree on Ecumenism*, 3). It is the responsibility of all Christians to proclaim the gospel to all who have not repented, believed, and submitted their lives to the lordship of Christ. It is imperative for every Christian to speak "the truth in love" (Eph 4:15) about all Christian communities. We affirm the obligation to portray the beliefs and practices of other Christian communities accurately, honestly, and charitably, and wherever possible, in cooperative efforts with them. We pray and work "for building up the body of Christ, until all of us come to the unity of the faith and of the knowledge of the Son of God, to maturity, to the measure of the full stature of Christ" (Eph 4:12b–13).

113. Individual Christians have the right and responsibility to proclaim the gospel boldly (Acts 4:13, 29; Eph 6:19) and persuasively

(cf. Acts 17:3; Rom 1:14). All people have the right to hear the gospel preached in their own "language" in a culturally sensitive fashion. The good news of Jesus Christ addresses the whole person, including his or her behavioral, cognitive, and experiential dimensions. We also affirm responsible use of modern technology as a legitimate means to communicate the gospel.

114. In the light of these issues, we offer the following proposals to our communities:

- to incorporate these principles in our own daily lives and ministries;
- to pursue contacts with Christian leaders for consideration of these issues;
- to conduct our preaching, teaching, and pastoral ministry in the light of these principles;
- to invite scholarly and professional societies at all levels to discuss this document;
- to incorporate these insights into the various programs for educators, ministerial students, and other church workers;
- to encourage the development of relationships of mutual understanding and respect, which will enable us to work together on these issues.

115. We encourage prayer for and with each other. Above all, we pray that Pentecostals and Catholics will be open to the Holy Spirit, who will convince the hearts of all Christians of the urgency, and the biblical imperative of these concerns.

116. Without a doubt, proselytism is a sensitive issue among Pentecostals and Catholics, but we believe that through open and honest dialogue and docility to the Spirit, we can respond to the challenge before us. This may not always be easy, but the love of Christ compels us to deal with "a humility and gentleness, with patience, bearing with one another in love, making every effort to maintain the unity of the Spirit in the bond of peace" (Eph 4:3). It is only then that we will give credible witness to Christ in a world which urgently needs to hear the good news.

VI. COMMON WITNESS[13]

117. Jesus Christ is the unique witness to the Father, and the Spirit comes from the Father to witness to Jesus Christ. Therefore, witness which belongs to the nature of the Christian life is an imperative of the great commission and is an ideal for which we strive. In different ways, both Pentecostals and Catholics base their witness on Matthew 28. Both consider the Pentecost event as central to their Christian faith. In the biblical sense, witness is the unique testimony of the apostles and disciples to what they have seen and heard (1 John 1:1–4). Witness is rooted in the apostles' experience of Jesus, who is the image of the Father sent in the power of the Spirit to return all to the source, the Father. Disciples are empowered by the Holy Spirit to proclaim the gospel (Acts 1:8; 4:20).

118. Common witness means standing together and sharing together in witness to our common faith. Common witness can be experienced through joint participation in worship, in prayer, in the performance of good works in Jesus' name, and especially in evangelization. True common witness is not engaged in for any narrow, strategic denominational benefit of a particular community. Rather, it is concerned solely for the glory of God, for the good of the whole church, and the good of humankind.

119. Common witness requires personal inward conversion, a renewal of heart and mind. This enables all to hear the Word of God anew and to listen again to what the Spirit is saying to the churches. Purification of our own hearts and minds and the renewal of our respec-

13. Papers were delivered on this topic by Kilian McDonnell, OSB, of Collegeville, Minnesota, USA (*Can Classical Pentecostals and Roman Catholics Engage in Common Witness?*) and by Prof. Walter J. Hollenweger (Swiss Reformed), Krattigen, Switzerland (*Common Witness*). The Pentecostal team invited participation from Prof. Hollenweger for three reasons. He was formerly a Pentecostal pastor. He was formerly on staff of the Office of Mission and Evangelism of the World Council of Churches. He was formerly a professor in the field of mission and evangelism at the University of Birmingham, England for many years, where his study of global Pentecostalism was a life long passion. Other dialogue documents which have dealt with Common witness are: "The Challenge of Proselytism and the Calling to Common Witness: A Study Document of the Joint Working Group", *The Ecumenical Review* 48.2 (1996) 212–21; the ERCDOM report *The Evangelical-Roman Catholic Dialogue on Mission, 1977–1984* (Grand Rapids/Exeter: Eerdmans/Paternoster, 1986 and IS 60 (1986/I–II) 71–97) and *Summons to Witness to Christ in Today's World: A Report of the Baptist-Roman Catholic International Conversations, 1984–1988* (see note 9).

tive communities help make common witness a possibility. One sign that this purification has taken place is that in the process of growing mutual understanding and trust, our stereotypes of one another diminish. In other words, we change, but the change is not compromise.

120. Once mutual trust as persons and reciprocal respect for each others' traditions has been established, then some limited measure of common witness is possible. Are there any precedents? There are innumerable precedents from all over the world. For example, when a Pentecostal leader was murdered, in Iran, in 1995 the eulogy was preached by a Catholic priest. In Berlin, the classical Pentecostals are members of the association of churches and cooperate in its activities. In Munich, a Benedictine monastery provided a Pentecostal pastor just starting his ecumenical ministry with meeting rooms in the center of the city. In the United States, a Pentecostal invited a Catholic priest to give a retreat for ministers. A Pentecostal leader was invited to preach in the Catholic Cathedral in Los Angeles. The revivals of Billy Graham have long enjoyed both Pentecostal and Catholic participation. In Chile, some Pentecostal leaders participate together with Catholics, Orthodox, and other Protestants in the *Fraternidad Ecumenica*. Pentecostals and Catholic charismatics have for some time now participated together in many ways, including planning such significant international conferences as those held in Jerusalem, Singapore, Bern, Brighton, Port Dickson (Malaysia), Kansas City, New Orleans, Indianapolis, and Orlando.

121. Pentecostals and Catholics are still at the beginnings of their relationship and their search for mutual understanding. Some are only now exploring ways of giving common witness. Others do not want to give common witness. As members of the dialogue, we believe that a limited common witness is already possible, because in many ways a vital spiritual unity exists between us, a real though imperfect communion (*Perspectives on Koinonia*, 54–55). We already have communion in the grace of Jesus Christ. We both believe in the centrality of Scripture. We proclaim together that there is no evangelization unless the name, teaching, and life of Jesus Christ, the Son of God, is proclaimed (cf. *Evangelization in the Modern World*). We share a common belief in the fatherhood of God; the lordship of Jesus Christ, messiah, savior, and coming lord; the power of the Spirit for witness; the enduring nature of Pentecost; the love of God poured out through the Spirit. We both acknowledge the unique character of salvation, the belief that anyone

without exception, who is saved, attains salvation through Jesus Christ; the forgiveness of sins, the promise of eternal life, the significant role of the charisms, the ten commandments, and the beatitudes. Common witness shows the bonds of communion (*koinonia*) between divided churches.

122. No one is called to compromise. Common witness is not a call to indifference or to uniformity. In fact, though division and separation are contrary to the will of God, the diversity within the unity of the one body of Christ is a precious and indispensable gift which is to be recognized, valued, and embraced. Common witness prevents neither individuals nor communities from witnessing to their heritage. This can even include our witnessing separately on things over which we seriously disagree. However, this can be done without being contentious, with mutual love and respect.

123. At a deeper level, common witness and forgiveness are intrinsically related to one another. Forgiveness also leads to a more credible common witness. Praying together is a case in point. In fact, mutual forgiveness is itself an act of common witness. Here, equity in the recognition of guilt is not the goal. One side may have offended more than the other. That determination is left to God. Rather, as Jesus himself has given us an example, each side takes on the sins of the other. In Christian forgiveness, it is not a question of who threw the first stone (John 8:7), of who did what to whom first; rather it is the willingness to make the first step. Both sides should take the initiative according to gospel norms: Pentecostals should take the initiative for reconciliation because they feel themselves the most aggrieved; Catholics should take the initiative because they are the elder in inter-church relations. In both cases, if asked for our coat, we give also our cloak; if asked to go one mile, we go two (Matt 5:41).

124. We need to be aware of the dark side of our histories, with full recognition of all the circumstances which gave rise to the distrust. Forgiveness is based on the truth established by both sides. The truth shared by the followers of Christ is not established by judicial procedure (cf. 1 Cor 6:4–7). There is another way of resolving difficulties, more appropriate for those who are profoundly related to one another in the unity of the Spirit. The offended should not have to prove their position to the last detail. The model here is a more relational one. Once mutual forgiveness has been expressed, reconciliation should be effected. In our

cases this reconciliation should be expressed publicly in a form acceptable to both groups.

125. Both should have acquaintance with the other's history and theological positions. Otherwise we will not escape our histories of mutual distrust. Common witness gives Pentecostals and Catholics the opportunity to work together in the writing of our common and separate histories, without excluding different interpretations of the facts. Once Pentecostal and Catholic students have a firm grounding in their own tradition, sharing in institutes of higher learning is possible, especially in disciplines such as intellectual history, philosophy, government, law, sociology, and medicine. This activity could include not only students but mature scholars. We already share in scholarly biblical research and we participate together in learned societies, such as the *Society of Pentecostal Studies.*

126. We often underestimate the degree of common witness, which already exists among Pentecostal and Catholic relatives and neighbors, who pray together, and cooperate in many ways, including visiting the sick and caring for others. Is it possible that the people in our local congregations and parishes are perhaps more involved in common witness than their pastors and church leaders realize?

127. In our Pentecostal-Catholic dialogue, we have discovered two useful principles:

- we cannot do what conscience forbids;
- we can do together what conscience permits in the area of common witness.

The first principle, "we cannot do what conscience forbids," emphasizes that our witness must be prudent, honest, and humble. We recognize today that there are limits as to what we can do together. Both Pentecostals and Catholics have diverse pastoral and worship understandings, as well as doctrinal points, which they do not fully share with one another. While we build on those things that unite us, our common witness should also acknowledge our divergences. The present inability of Catholics and Pentecostals to share together at the table of the Lord is a striking example of our divisions and the lack of common witness in this respect (cf. 1 Cor 11:26). All of us experience this as deeply troubling.

The second principle raises the provocative question: Why do we not do together what we can do together? While recognizing that relations between Pentecostals and Catholics are a matter of a growth progress, what is possible at a later stage of growth may not be possible at an earlier stage. Many Pentecostals and Catholics may not see some of our suggestions as options for today. But both need to know what doors can be opened, if not today, perhaps in the future. Above all, no one wants to close off either the present or future inspiration of the Holy Spirit.

128. Some measure of common prayer seems indispensable for common witness. How can we witness together, if we have not prayed together? To pray together is already common witness. The *Week of Prayer for Christian Unity*, which is generally celebrated in January or before Pentecost, is a possibility where Pentecostals and Catholic charismatics already share profound experiences in prayer together. There could be exchange of pulpits related to non-eucharistic worship services. We can exchange films, videos, and printed materials, which explain the faith but betray no denominational animus.

129. We believe that Pentecostals and Catholics can together be proactive in promoting values and positive actions in human society. In the spirit of Matt 25:31–46, we can stand together against sin in promoting human dignity and social justice. Though with changing times other issues will present themselves, currently there are many examples of the kinds of issues on which we can work together. We can cooperate in such works as the quest for disarmament and peace, providing emergency relief for refugees, for victims of natural disasters, feeding the hungry, setting up educational opportunities for the illiterate, establishing drug rehabilitation programs, and rescuing young women and men from prostitution. We can work together to eliminate racial and gender discrimination, working for the rights and dignity of women, opposing offensively permissive legislation (such as abortion and euthanasia), promoting urban and rural development and housing for the poor, denouncing violations of the environment and the irresponsible use of both renewable and unrenewable natural resources. In some parts of the world, Pentecostals already collaborate with Catholics on many of these issues and others, yet there are still many more opportunities for cooperation, especially in North America. Why do we do apart what we can do together?

130. This document comes out of our experience of dialogue with one another over twenty-five years on a variety of topics, with years of focused discussions on evangelization, proselytism, and common witness. Strong bonds of affection and trust between Pentecostals and Catholics in the dialogue have created an atmosphere in which differences have been faced with candor, even when those differences seem to be irreconcilable. We hope that the text conveys something of the frustrating and rewarding moments that have been part of our experience over the years. We also hope that the text will help readers to re-experience what we ourselves experienced, namely, the joy of discovering together astonishing areas of agreement. But the text would lack integrity if it did not also offer to the reader the opportunity to re-experience with us the shocks of the gaps between our positions. Still, we hold dear the unity in diversity which exists among us and look forward to the day when we may work more closely together despite our differences. In reality, what unites us is far greater than what divides us. Though the road to that future is not entirely clear to us, we are firm in our conviction that the Spirit is calling us to move beyond our present divisions. We invite our readers to travel this road with us.

11

Word and Spirit, Church and World. Final Report of the International Dialogue between Representatives of the World Alliance of Reformed Churches and Some Classical Pentecostal Churches and Leaders

1996–2000

INTRODUCTION[1]

1. This is a report from the participants of an international dialogue (1996–2000) between the World Alliance of Reformed Churches (WARC) and leaders from some classical Pentecostal churches. It had its beginnings in the 22nd WARC General Council in Seoul, Korea, which proposed exploration of the possibility of organizing an international dialogue with Pentecostal churches. This was made possible through the contacts made in 1993 between the General Secretary of the World Alliance of Reformed Churches, Milan Opočenský, and Professor of Church History and Ecumenics at Fuller Theological Seminary, Cecil M. Robeck Jr., a Pentecostal minister. Over the next two years, they exchanged correspondence and talked with one another about the possibility that such a dialogue might be held. They attempted to discern both the need for such a conversation, and the potential outcomes that might result. Finally, they agreed to bring together a small group of scholars, who could explore the potential for such a dialogue with them.

2. In 1995, Dr. Opočenský received encouragement from the executive committee of the WARC to pursue an exploratory meeting with the

1. The report was published in *Pneuma: The Journal of the Society for Pentecostal Studies* 23.1 (2001) 9–43, and is printed here with kind permission.

Pentecostals. Dr. Opočenský appointed Dr. Henry Wilson of the WARC staff to facilitate the discussion from the WARC side. Dr. Robeck acted in that capacity for the Pentecostals. They convened a small exploratory committee at Mattersey Hall in Mattersey, England, July 8–9, 1995.[2] The committee determined that a dialogue between the WARC and Pentecostals might serve several useful purposes. They noted that those who are disciples of Jesus Christ are all members of the one church. They were concerned, however, that this reality receive attention not merely at an abstract theological or ideological level, but that it receive some attention at the practical level, where the churches of the Reformed tradition and the churches of the Pentecostal movement touch the lives of one another directly.

3. The committee noted that in many places around the world, members of the Pentecostal and Reformed communities are uncomfortable with one another. Sometimes they are openly antagonistic toward one another. In a few places, such as South Korea, Brazil, and South Africa, tensions between the Reformed and Pentecostal communities were clearly evident and often painful for both parties. The committee was concerned that there was no identifiable, formal way for these communities to relate to each other. These facts seemed to indicate that conversation between the various parties involved was not only advisable; it was essential.

4. The exploratory committee believed that some of these tensions were the result of the state of ignorance that these communities often manifested towards one another. Other tensions seemed to emerge as a direct result of honest theological disagreement. Some of these issues were rooted deeply in the history of one group or the other, while other issues were the result of more recent claims. Still other tensions could be attributed to certain contemporary practices in which one group or the other was engaged. In some places in the world, these practices yielded public charges of unfair competition, proselytism, fanaticism, or dead religion. The committee believed that this state of affairs was not only unhealthy for Christians to endure, but that it communicated the wrong message to the world. If the gospel of reconciliation seemed to lack the power necessary to help Christians to resolve differences between them-

2. Those present at the Mattersey conference included Hugh Davidson, Margaret M. McKay, Salvatore Ricciardi, and Henry Wilson for the Reformed churches, and Richard Israel, Frank Macchia, Jean-Daniel Pluss, and Cecil M. Robeck Jr., for the Pentecostals.

selves, how could it be trusted to bring reconciliation between human beings and their God?

5. As a result of these considerations, the committee concluded that an international dialogue between representatives of these traditions would go far to help both groups gain a greater understanding of one another, to explore their common concerns, and to confront their differences. They established three limited goals by which the dialogue could begin. First, they hoped that such a dialogue would increase mutual understanding and respect between the churches of the Reformed and Pentecostal traditions. Second, they asked that the dialogue seek ways to identify areas of theological agreement, disagreement, and convergence so that both communities might be mutually strengthened. Third, they suggested that those who would engage in the dialogue would help these two communities by exploring various possibilities for common witness. They also hoped that, by entering into the life of these local communities, the dialogue might be an encouragement to Christians who were embattled, or who were looking for new ways to validate their message of reconciliation before the world.

6. The next step was more difficult. Since members of the Pentecostal community and members of the Reformed community did not already have close relations, the exploratory committee looked for ways by which to enter such a dialogue. There is no international Pente-costal group that is equivalent to the World Alliance of Reformed Churches. Thus, there was no formal organizational source willing or able to provide support or direction for the Pentecostal participants. While this fact held the potential for some inequity in the process, the committee believed that it was better to begin the conversation than not. This would be a new experience for many of the participants. The committee struggled with what topics should be addressed and with what methodologies of exploration they would recommend.

7. The committee recommended that the dialogue begin with a tentative discussion of contemporary understandings of spirituality as it is viewed and practiced in these respective communities. To aid the dialogue in understanding spirituality, not only theologically, but also as experienced practically, the committee recommended that the dialogue be hosted in alternate years by each of the traditions. They further recommended that the dialogue include, as part of its ongoing life together, opportunities for worship in each of the traditions. It was agreed that

the members of the subsequent dialogue teams would engage in acts of common prayer and Bible study on a daily basis, but further, that they would enter into the parish life of the local community of the team that acted as host. This tradition of common worship and witness has proven to be one of the most significant tools for helping both teams understand one another.

8. The first official meetings of the international Reformed-Pentecostal dialogue was finally convened May 15–20, 1996, in Torre Pellice, Italy. The Waldensian Church served as the dialogue's host. Abival Pires da Silveira and Cecil M. Robeck, Jr., were asked to serve as co-chairs. The dialogue included delegates from the Pentecostal and Reformed traditions that literally came from throughout the world. The theme for the opening discussion was "Spirituality and the Challenges of Today." Papers were offered by members of both teams in the following three areas, "Spirituality and Interpretation of Scripture," "Spirituality and Justice," and "Spirituality and Ecumenism."[3] Each of these papers provided insight into the similarities and differences between the traditions, but as the members of the dialogue felt their way into the lives of each other, they began to recognize two things. First, it was too much to ask for the members of the dialogue to do justice to all the material that was presented in these papers in the time allotted. Second, various members of the teams lacked an adequate understanding of the other tradition and, therefore, often lacked a language by which the two could communicate. They decided that they would seek fewer papers at their next meeting and spend more time exploring the ideas that were presented.

9. The dialogue held its second meeting in Chicago, Illinois, USA, May 11–15, 1997. While the Pentecostal team hosted this meeting,

3. The presentations made in 1996 included Aldo Comba, "Spirituality and Ecumenism: Reformed," Abival Pires da Silveira, "Spirituality and Justice," and Henry Wilson, "Spirituality and Interpretation of Scripture," for the Reformed team, and Daniel Albrecht, "Spirituality and Ecumenism: Pentecostal," Anthea Butler, "Facets of Pentecostal Spirituality and Justice," and Richard Israel "Pentecostal Spirituality and the Use of Scripture," for the Pentecostals. Edited versions of the papers by Anthea D. Butler and Richard D. Israel have since been published in Hubert van Beek, ed. *Consultation with Pentecostals in the Americas: San Jose, Costa Rica, 4–8 June 1996* (Geneva, Switzerland: World Council of Churches, 1996) 28–55. Daniel Albrecht's paper was published under the title "Pentecostal Spirituality: Ecumenical Potential and Challenge," in *Cyberjournal for Pentecostal Charismatic Research* 2 (July 1997), available at http://www.pctii.org/cyberj/cyber2.html.

McCormick Theological Seminary provided the facilities. The theme was "The Role and Place of the Holy Spirit in the Church." Three papers were presented at this meeting. One was presented on "The Relation of the Holy Spirit to the Bible." The other two explored the role of the Holy Spirit in proclamation and the place of charismatic manifestations within the church.[4] While both groups found commonality in God's revelation of Jesus Christ as the Scripture bore witness to it, they struggled to understand the implications of ongoing revelation for faith and practice. They recognized the sovereign role of the Spirit in the bestowal of gifts upon the faith community as it seeks to address the diverse needs that arise in the church, society, and the world. Both teams began to note that they had much in common, but they took note of the fact that they differed on some important issues as well. While the number of papers they had solicited for this round of discussions was half that solicited during the first round, they concluded that they needed to solicit even fewer papers for the third round.

10. The dialogue seemed to find its rhythm when it met May 14–19, 1998, in Kappel-am-Albis, Switzerland. It provided a unique opportunity for participants to hear from Professor Walter J. Hollenweger, a former Pentecostal pastor of the Swiss Pentecostal Mission, now a minister in the Swiss Reformed Church, and to meet with the host of the dialogue, president of the cantonal Reformed Church of Zürich, the Reverend Ruedi Reich. In the absence of the Reverend Abival Pires da Silveira, the Reverend Salvatore Ricciardi acted as the Reformed co-chairperson for this session. The dialogue studied two papers on a single topic, one from each team. The topic was "The Holy Spirit and Mission in Eschatological Perspective."[5]

11. It became apparent within that context that the dialogue would be significantly aided if there were greater continuity of the members of the dialogue through the years. While those providing leadership to

4. In 1997, Wonsuk and Julie Ma collaborated on "'An Immanent Encounter with the Transcendental': Proclamation and Manifestation in Pentecostal Worship," while Jan Veenhof wrote on the subject of "Orthodoxy and Fundamentalism" with a "Short Note on Prophecy," and Cephas Omenyo addressed "The Role of the Spirit in Proclamation and Manifestations of the Charismata within the Church" on behalf of the Reformed team.

5. In 1998, Byron Klaus delivered, "The Holy Spirit and Mission in Eschatological Perspective: A Pentecostal Viewpoint," while Cephas Omenyo delivered the Reformed paper titled "The Holy Spirit and Mission in Eschatological Perspective."

the dialogue had hoped to include people for whom an international encounter would be an experience of personal growth, the lack of understanding of global Christianity by some participants continued to be a handicap to the project. Similarly, it had been hoped that the dialogue would be composed of people at a variety of educational levels from within the respective traditions. This also proved to be a handicap in the sense that the group continued to lack a common language and methodology by which to pursue their assigned tasks. At the close of this third session, then, the leaders determined to bring teams to the table that embodied greater parity.

12. From May 14–20, 1999, the dialogue discussed, "The Holy Spirit, Charisma, and the Kingdom of God" in Seoul, South Korea.[6] The Reverend David Yonggi Cho and Yoido Full Gospel Church served as the hosts of the dialogue this year. From this point on, the members of the dialogue felt that the teams that could best facilitate their common task were finally in place. Furthermore, the venue provided members of the dialogue with a first-hand opportunity to observe members from both the Reformed and Pentecostal communities where tensions were known to exist. While the primary discussion at the table focused on the topic at hand, what took place at the times of common worship, in the visits to local churches, and at other specified times proved to be significant to the hopes expressed by the exploratory committee. Local guests from both communities were invited to sit in and observe some of the discussions. At times, members of the local Christian press as well as the secular press were invited to observe particular sessions. On several occasions, members of the dialogue offered press interviews that allowed them opportunity to talk about the hopes of the dialogue and address some of the concerns that were present in the Presbyterian and Pentecostal communities in Seoul. These limited encounters proved to be highly successful in building bridges between the communities at that time.

6. In 1999, Yohan Hyun presented "The Holy Spirit, Charism and the Kingdom of God from the Reformed Perspective," while Frank D. Macchia addressed "The Struggle for the Spirit in the Church: The Gifts of the Spirit and the Kingdom of God in Pentecostal perspective." Subsequent to the 1999 meeting in Seoul, these papers were published as Yohan Hyun and Frank Macchia, *Spirit's Gifts—God's Reign*, Theology & Worship Occasional Paper 11 (Louisville: Presbyterian Church [U.S.A.], Office of Theology and Worship, 1999).

13. The first five-year round of discussions between the WARC and Pentecostals concluded in São Paulo, Brazil, May 20–24, 2000. The Independent Presbyterian Church of Brazil and the First Independent Presbyterian Church of São Paulo jointly hosted the dialogue. During this session, Milan Opočenský served as chairperson for the Reformed team. The papers that had been presented in each of the previous four years, agreed accounts from these meetings, and a working draft that was largely derived from these accounts became the materials from which members of both teams drew while preparing this report. Work was undertaken in plenary sessions, and in four groups, each working on one of the four major sections of the body of this report. Specialists were invited to work on the language of the text and to provide the introduction. One day was taken for the two traditions to meet in caucus in order to clarify their concerns. In the end, the report was submitted to the plenary for final approval.

14. This process, upon which both teams agreed, allowed for the recognition of new insights and information that could only be seen at the end of the discussion. Each year had a way of providing parts to the total discussion, but they begged for integration. The members of both teams, therefore, believe that the following statements fairly represent not only their personal concerns, but the concerns of those they sought to represent in this ongoing discussion.

I. SPIRIT AND WORD

The Spirit and the Word in the Context of the Trinity

15. Together, the members of the Pentecostal and the Reformed teams agree that we stand in communion with the Nicene-Constantinopolitan creed, in our belief that the Holy Spirit is the lord and giver of life and, together with the Father and the Son, is to be worshipped and glorified. We also believe that the Father and the Son and the Spirit send the church into the world.

16. We regard the older conception of the contrast between the Reformed and Pentecostal families as consisting of a difference in emphasis between the Word (Reformed) and the Spirit (Pentecostal) to be in need of correction. Both the Reformed and Pentecostal traditions consider Jesus Christ to be the criterion for the work of the Holy Spirit.

17. Pentecostals are aware that some have viewed the Pentecostal movement as overly concerned with the Holy Spirit. Though Pentecostals draw attention to the work of the Spirit, they do not generally detach this work from a trinitarian understanding of God's activity. Pentecostals, in general, tend to agree together that God's work and our worshipful response have a certain trinitarian structure (involving the Father through the Son in the power of the Spirit). Most Pentecostals accept a trinitarian understanding of the Godhead, although a wing of the Pentecostal movement affirms only the oneness of God.[7] If there is a center to the Pentecostal message, it is the person and work of Jesus Christ. From the beginning of the Pentecostal movement, its central message has referred to Jesus Christ as savior, sanctifier, Spirit baptizer, healer, and coming king. In fact, Pentecos-tal practice strives to conform to the biblical injunction that the yardstick of Christ must judge those things ascribed to the Holy Spirit.

18. In the context of the holy Trinity, Reformed churches have affirmed the Christological criterion for the Spirit's work but they have also paid special attention to the work of the triune God in creation. The world is a good work of the triune God who called it into existence through the Word by the Spirit and continues to sustain it. In spite of sin and rebellion, the earth remains the "theater of the glory of God." There is, as a consequence of this focus on the earth giving glory to God its creator, an openness in the Reformed tradition to the work of the Spirit in creation and culture. We must fulfill our vocation in this world, over which Jesus Christ is lord and which by the Spirit will be renewed and brought to its final consummation.

The Spirit and the Word in Creation and Culture

19. We agree that God has revealed God's self decisively in Jesus Christ, the one in whom the fullness of the Godhead dwells. God's Son is the eternal Word of God, who became flesh (cf. John 1:14, Heb 1:1–2, and Col 2:3, 9). In addition, God has revealed God's self through the Scriptures, and Scripture, as the Word of God, is not to be isolated from the agency of the Holy Spirit.

7. This dialogue has not included any representatives from this wing of the larger Pentecostal Movement. These Pentecostals are sometimes known as "Apostolics," "Oneness," or "Jesus' Name" Pentecostals. They baptize according to Acts 2:38, and tend to embrace a modalist understanding of God.

20. We agree that the Holy Spirit is present and active, not only in the Christian church, but also in human history and in various cultures. The work of the Spirit is broader than we think. Nevertheless, we believe that every culture, as well as our own churches, is in need of being reshaped by the Holy Spirit in accordance with the revelation in Jesus Christ as witnessed to in Scripture. We believe that Jesus Christ, the one in whom the fullness of God dwells, is the perfect icon of God, the decisive self-revelation to human beings (Hebrews 1).

21. With a focus on preaching and experiencing the ministry of Jesus Christ, Pentecostals have generally emphasized the work of the Spirit in culture as a preparation for the ministry of Christ through the church in the world. The corresponding emphasis has been on the sinfulness and needs of a "world without Christ." More recently, some Pentecostals have begun to reflect on the role of the Spirit in creation and culture to reveal God and to accomplish God's just and holy will, but not to the extent of believing that there is saving grace outside of the ministry of the gospel. Jesus Christ is "the way, the truth, and the life." On the other hand, without diminishing the unique role of Jesus Christ in God's saving plan, the Reformed tradition has regarded the role of the Spirit in culture more expansively and positively than solely as a preparation for the ministry of the gospel.

Spirit, Proclamation, and Spiritual Discernment

22. Together, we stress the mutual bond of the Word and the Spirit. Through the Holy Spirit, the Bible speaks the Word of God. The indispensable action of the Spirit makes the text into a living and life-giving testimony to Jesus Christ, transforming the lives of people, for the Scripture is not a dead text. This confession involves more than an articulation of a biblical truth, or an expression of doctrine. It communicates how we understand, relate to, and engage the Bible in everyday life. The Bible nourishes the people of God and enables them to discern the spirits.

23. Pentecostals and most Reformed Christians believe that Jesus Christ is "the way, the truth, and the life" and, therefore, that no one can come to the Father except through the Son (John 14:6). The Holy Spirit convinces people of sin, righteousness, and judgment (John 16:8–11), leading toward a personal response to the divine invitation to seek him and to find him (Acts 17:27). Both traditions acknowledge that

the Holy Spirit is at work among all peoples, including peoples of other faiths, preparing them to receive the proclaimed Word (Psalm 139; Acts 14:15–17). There is, therefore, a common challenge for believers from both traditions to learn together the ways in which the Spirit of God teaches the church to utilize various cultural elements in the service of God and the proclamation of the Word of God.

24. Pentecostals affirm that Christians must continue to work for Jesus Christ through the empowerment of the Holy Spirit. By proclaiming the gospel, healing the sick, and confronting demonic powers, Pentecostals seek to be involved in a vibrant proclamation of the gospel, accompanied often by manifestations of the power of God. Healing is probably the most common manifestation of God's power among Pentecostal churches worldwide. Healings (including exorcisms) manifest the presence, compassion, and power of God.

25. For Pentecostals, the anointing of the Spirit makes proclamation an event and an encounter between people and God. A Spirit-empowered proclamation of the scriptural message thus holds an important place in Pentecostal worship services. But the communication of God's will and action in Pentecostal services is not confined to the event of proclamation. There are multiple gifts of the Holy Spirit at work in Pentecostal worship to channel God's presence and to communicate God's will. The locus of discernment tends to be distributed in many Pentecostal churches among the entire congregation, so that whether gathered in worship or dispersed in society, all members are called to exercise their gifts in ministry. In various times and places, some Pentecostals have even reported that the Spirit worked so dramatically through multiple, extraordinary gifts in a particular church service, that the preached Word of God was not given as it usually is. There is a tendency in many Pentecostal congregations to decentralize the communication of God's Word and to encourage ordinary believers to speak for God alongside the preaching ministry of the ordained minister.

26. Reciprocity is established between Word, Spirit, and community so that the Spirit enlivens the Word, the Word provides a context for the Spirit's work, and the community lives out the Spirit's directions. Pentecostals place priority on the "leading of the Spirit" both individually and corporately.

27. While Pentecostals employ different methods and approaches to interpret the Bible, central to their interpretation is the conviction

that the Word of God speaks to today's world. Pentecostals strive to hear what the Word of God has to say to them and their era as they live in restored and ongoing continuity with the mighty acts of God recorded in the Bible. For Pentecostals, the Bible is a story; they read their lives into that story and that story into their lives. They stress returning to the experiences of God to which Scripture bears witness, but also moving forth into the world to witness to the deeds of God multiplied through them in new contexts. Essential to hearing the Word, therefore, is the spiritual openness and fitness of the interpreter. The gap between the Bible and the contemporary world, which is emphasized among Pentecostals, is not historical but spiritual.

28. Pentecostals generally advocate a disciplined study of the Bible that employs methods that do not alienate the reader from the text or cast doubt on the miraculous nature of God's deeds, whether in biblical times or now. For this reason, they have often been wary of historical-critical methods of interpreting the Bible. Some also follow the fundamentalist defenses of the inerrancy of Scripture and strive to enter the modernistic struggle over the proper use of historical method in interpreting the Bible. Others are trying, instead, to explore postmodern interpretations of the Bible in order to transcend the limits of historical investigation in encountering the meaning of Scripture. But Pentecostals normally emphasize that the Bible speaks and transforms lives only through the work of the Holy Spirit.

29. While Pentecostals originally came from diverse denominational backgrounds, they sought to go beyond what they had commonly experienced as "dead forms and creeds," to a "living, practical Christianity." Thus, the revelation of God through the preaching of the Bible was aided, not by conscious devotion to past denominational traditions, but to various signs and wonders of the Spirit indicating the last days, one of the important ones being prophecy. It is a Pentecostal conviction that the Spirit of God can speak through ordinary Christians in various ways that are consistent with the biblical message (1 Corinthians 12–14). Ideally, these inspired words aid the preached word in making the will of God revealed in Scripture dynamic and relevant to particular needs in the church. As the Acts of the Apostles shows, the church is to be directed today by the Spirit prophetically. "Let those who have an ear to hear, hear what the Spirit is saying to the churches (Revelation 1–3)."

30. The Bible is essential to Reformed faith and life. People entering a Reformed church normally find a Bible on the communion table or the pulpit. That the Bible is open indicates that God wants to speak. The Word of God wants to answer questions that people may carry in their hearts. The Word also wants to put a vital question to those who enter the church. Keeping an open Bible in the church is a symbolic act, which affirms that the Bible is central in Reformed experience and worship. The decisive moment in the worship service is, indeed, the reading and preaching of the Word. The entire liturgy is structured to keep preaching of the Word at the center. However, the Bible is not an end in itself, for both Scripture and preaching point to the living Word, Jesus Christ.

31. Reformed churches understand that the Word of God is addressed to the whole people of God. Thus, congregations emphasize teaching, studying, discussing, and learning the Scriptures so that the community of faith and all its members may hear the Word of God in its fullness.

32. In previous centuries, Reformed theologians usually said that all signs and wonders were confined to the apostolic age. Increasingly, theologians, pastors, and church members see that this opinion finds no ground in the Scriptures. However, a careful reading of Paul's letters leads Reformed Christians to the conviction that it would be wrong to concentrate attention on the so-called supernatural gifts, such as glossolalia and healing. In the Pauline lists of spiritual gifts, the more common gifts, such as leading, organizing, and teaching, are mentioned in juxtaposition with the more spectacular gifts. In fact, we cannot sharply differentiate "supernatural gifts" from "natural" gifts. What we see as "natural" can be seen as a miracle, whether in nature, personal experience, or the history of humankind. This is evident in the "miracles" of the growing concern for the equality of women and men, the abolition of apartheid, and the struggle for the abolition of weapons of mass destruction. In these events and efforts, we may see the Spirit working in our day for the healing of the world.

33. Reformed people acknowledge that the Word of God comes to them through the faithfulness of those who have preserved and proclaimed it, giving witness in ministry and mission throughout the centuries. The apostle Paul underscores the importance of tradition when he gives instruction concerning foundational elements of the Christian message, such as the resurrection of Jesus Christ (1 Cor 15:3) and the

Lord's Supper (1 Cor 11:23). Because the Word has reached us over a long span of time, it should be approached through any means of interpretation that will make its message intelligible. One of these means, though not the only one, is the historical-critical method. No interpretative method may take the place of the Word itself. While exegetical work helps the church discern meaning in Scriptures, it is only by the Holy Spirit that the Scriptures become the living Word of God for the church.

34. The Word of God addresses not only the church or individuals, but also the entire world, which God has deeply loved (John 3:16). This is why proclaiming the Word and living in obedience to the Word is central to the Reformed tradition, enabling the church to oppose all oppressive situations in the name of God. Such opposition is normally termed the "prophetic" task of the church, but it cannot be taken for granted that any proclamation is "prophetic." In any case, the prophetic Word is first addressed to the church and so the first task of the church is to listen to the prophets and then—faithfully and humbly—to make the meaning of God's Word clear to the present generation. The Word proclaimed by the church may become prophetic only when and where it pleases God, and it is only "after the fact" that a proclamation by a church may be considered prophetic.

35. Pentecostal and Reformed Christians conclude that the Bible is the Word of God in its witness to Jesus Christ through the work of the Holy Spirit. They tend to have different expectations concerning the role of the Spirit in culture and the significance of extraordinary gifts of the Spirit in manifesting the power of God in the proclamation of the gospel. Thus, we affirm the Bible as the Word of God, an instrument of the Spirit to proclaim the grace of Jesus Christ to all people. The Word of God inscripturated in the Bible becomes the living Word that speaks by the action of the Spirit of God, because the Spirit, who speaks through the Bible, is the same Spirit who was present in the formation of the Scriptures. This role of the Bible as an instrument of the Spirit may not be understood in an exclusive way, however, for the Spirit cannot be confined to the text of the Bible. We of the Pentecostal and the Reformed traditions may understand the prophetic task of the church somewhat differently, but we agree that the Spirit of God continues to speak in and through the church in a way consistent with the biblical message.

II. THE HOLY SPIRIT AND THE CHURCH

36. The teams of Pentecostal and Reformed theologians share the following affirmations about the Holy Spirit and the church.

- The church is the creature of the Word and Spirit.
- The church is the community of the Holy Spirit's leading.
- The church is the community of the Spirit's gifts
- The church is in but not of the world.

In each of these areas of common conviction, Reformed and Pentecostal emphases are often different. These differences are sometimes complementary, sometimes divergent. In all cases, however, ongoing dialogue helps to clarify complementarities and divergences, as well as suggest ways of deepening the ongoing conversations between us.

The Church Is the Creature of the Word and Spirit

37. Reformed and Pentecostal Christians share the firm conviction that the church is God's creation. The church is a people called by the Word and shaped by the Spirit, all to the glory of God. The gracious action of God precedes all human forms, communities, and institutions. In speaking of the church, we stress the mutual connection of Word and Spirit, and the church as creature of the Word and Spirit called upon to respond to God's grace by worship in Spirit and in truth. However, Pentecostal and Reformed Christians may use different language to express this common conviction.

38. Reformed Christians tend to use the language of "covenant" to describe the initiative of God and the formation of God's people. The covenant is the expression of God's gracious action in Christ to reconcile us to himself, and to one another. Reformed understanding of the church is based on both the promises and the commandments of God. The deepest intention of the covenant is the reconciled life, for reconciliation in Jesus Christ is the basis and motive for life according to the will of God through the power of the Spirit. The shape of the covenant is expressed in the two great commandments—love of God and love of neighbor. Reformed Christians tend to identify the faithful church as that community where the Word of God is rightly preached and heard, and where the sacraments are celebrated according to Christ's institution. Reformed Christians thus affirm that we receive the gospel of Christ

through the living community of faith, which is sustained and nurtured though the Word of God, as the Holy Spirit seals the Word in us.

39. Pentecostals tend to use the language of "the outpouring of the Spirit" to describe the initiative of God and the formation of the church as the Body of Christ. They tend to identify the faithful church as the community where Jesus Christ is lifted up, the Word of God is preached and obeyed, and where the Spirit's gifts are manifested in the lives of believers. The Spirit sovereignly bestows charisms upon the community and its members. These gifts of the Spirit manifest themselves in a variety of ways so that the role of the Word and the function of the Spirit are contextualized within the community. Each Pentecostal community, formed by the outpouring of the Spirit and shaped by the Spirit's gifts, discerns what the Spirit is saying to the church through the Word and is thereby shaped by the Spirit in conformity to the Word.

40. From the covenant, it follows that Reformed Christians nurture an awareness of living in congregations. Whereas Pentecostal Christians tend to focus more upon the life of the local assembly as it gathers together in the name of Jesus Christ in the power of the Holy Spirit.

41. The common affirmation that the church is the creature of the Word and Spirit can lead us into fruitful conversations regarding the ways the Word is given space among us and the ways the Spirit moves among us. Both Pentecostal and Reformed Christians understand worship as the church's primary response to God's grace. Furthermore, both understand that it is the Spirit who enables faithful worship by the community. Yet, the two communities of faith express the Spirit's presence and action differently. Much more conversation should occur on the concrete reality of worship. Deeper dialogue concerning the role of sacraments or ordinances, and the place of the Holy Spirit's gifts, may lead to mutual enrichment.

The Church Is the Community of the Holy Spirit's Leading

42. Both Pentecostal and Reformed Christians recognize the Spirit's leadership in the church as the church confesses its faith, gathers as a community of worship, grows in edification and fellowship, and responds to its mission in the world. In these and other ways the church is facilitated by the Spirit's guidance in the process of spiritual discernment.

43. Reformed communities affirm that the Spirit leads the church as a community in ongoing confession of Christian faith. Reformed people have always been confession-making people, exercising their God-given freedom and obligation to confess the faith in each time and place. From the earliest beginnings of the Reformation through the twentieth century, Reformed churches have formulated creeds and confessions that express the lived faith of concrete communities. The churches acknowledge the ongoing guidance of the Spirit to lead the community of faith into the truth and to make the gospel intelligible and relevant to specific places and times. This ongoing re-formulation of confessions is based on fidelity to the Scriptures—the Word of God that bears witness to the incarnate Word of God.

44. Reformed churches strive to reach consensus through mutual discernment of Word and Spirit. Yet we confess that we are imperfect hearers of the Word who may resist the Spirit's leading. As a community of redeemed sinners, we remain sinners nonetheless. "Let anyone who has an ear listen to what the Spirit is saying to the churches."

45. While some Pentecostals have enacted confessions or statements of faith written in formal propositions, frequently they manifest their beliefs through expressions of personal testimony made in daily life and worship. Pentecostals explicitly affirm that it is the Spirit who both leads and enables them to worship God. They attempt to be sensitive to the movement of the Holy Spirit because they believe that the Spirit leads them into all truth and points them towards Jesus Christ.

46. Reformed worship is the place where the gathered community confesses common faith. In creeds and confessions from the early church, the Reformation period, and contemporary settings, the worshiping assembly gives voice to the beliefs that bind individual believers together in common faith, life, and witness.

47. Ideally, spiritual discernment plays an essential role in Pentecostalism. The practice of Pentecostal spirituality collectively prepares congregations, ministries, and denominations to discern God's will in concrete situations. Functioning within many dimensions of the church as community, the discernment dynamic relies upon the Spirit's assistance and leadership for an authentication of communal prayer. This is manifested in a collective inner witness that is consistent with Scripture. Prayerful deliberations or conversations enable the local church to arrive at consensus about its response to an issue or situation. Included

in the communal discernment is the interaction between Pentecostals and society.

48. Societal changes and development sometimes awaken a Christian group to the need to wrestle with an issue. Coupled with communal discernment is personal discernment by each member. Each person participates in the discernment, ascertaining her/his judgment on the emerging or established consensus. Pivotal in personal discernment is the role of conscience. While the term is rarely used among Pentecostals, it is often implied. In the personal discernment of individual Pentecostals, the conscience is shaped, in part, by their spirituality.

49. The Pentecostal expectation is that the exercise of discernment is distributed throughout the entire congregation, so that whether gathered in worship or dispersed in society, all members are called to exercise their gifts in ministry. All individuals are accountable to the group and any individual may challenge the group as to who has "the mind of the Spirit" on an issue. Discernment, then, requires active participation by all the members of the community. They listen for the Spirit to speak through the Word communicated by preaching, teaching, testimony, and action. They are encouraged to bring their Bibles to meetings and to read them for themselves. They weigh the value of the proclamation they hear by reference to Scripture as well as "promptings" of the Spirit and prayerful reflection.

The Church Is the Community of the Spirit's Gifts

50. Although the gifts of the Spirit are often associated with Pentecostal churches, Reformed churches also acknowledge that the church is established and maintained by the gracious presence of the Spirit, who gives gifts to the people of God. Pentecostal and Reformed ways of speaking about and also receiving the gifts vary, yet both affirm that the Holy Spirit's charisms are constitutive of ecclesial life.

51. Pentecostals affirm that spiritual gifts enhance the faith of believers, deepen their fellowship with God, edify the church, and empower mission in the world. Pentecostals love and respect the Word of God, so they expect God's Spirit to reveal his power through manifestations of grace. These manifestations of spiritual gifts are signs that God is with God's people. Spiritual gifts such as healing, prophesying, casting out demons, speaking in tongues, and other charisms enrich the lives of persons and the life of the community of faith.

52. The participants in this dialogue affirm that the gifts of God to the church are real, the Holy Spirit is the giver of gifts to the church, and the gifts are given to the church to work together for the common good. Reformed as well as many Pentecostal churches acknowledge that their understanding of the Spirit's gifts is broader than the classic list of spiritual gifts in 1 Corinthians 12:8–10. Furthermore, consideration of the Spirit's gifts is shaped by the overarching theme found in 1 Corinthians 12:4–7, "Now there are varieties of gifts, but the same Spirit, and there are varieties of service, but the same Lord; and there are varieties of activities, but it is the same God who activates all of them in everyone. To each is given a manifestation of the Spirit for the common good."

53. Reformed Christians affirm that the Spirit's gifts are experienced in the congregational life of Reformed churches. Every congregation can point to numerous instances where, in official and unofficial ways, words and acts have led congregations in faithfulness. Wherever in the church acts of reconciliation are initiated, words of the good news of Christ are proclaimed, gestures of consolation are shared, injustices addressed, or prayers for healing and wholeness are uttered, the Holy Spirit is at work among the people of God. Yet, representatives of Reformed churches confess that their churches are sometimes too casual in seeking and receiving the Spirit's gifts. Reformed Christians must proclaim forcefully that it is God who gives the gifts, and not we ourselves.

54. As we, the Reformed and Pentecostal participants in this dialogue, have reflected on the biblical texts and the life of the church, we have been convinced that no single gift or set of gifts is normative for every believer, every congregation or every church in every time, or place. We share the conviction that gifts are not permanent possessions of believers or congregations, for the Spirit gives various gifts at different places as those gifts are needed.

55. We also agree that no biblical listing of gifts is a template to be laid over the entire church. On the one hand, we recognize that many Pentecostals limit the gifts of the Holy Spirit to those mentioned in 1 Corinthians 12:8–10. They do not value the charismatic nature of those mentioned elsewhere in the Bible (cf. 1 Cor 12:27–30; Rom 12:3–8; Eph 4:11; 1 Peter 4:10–11). On the other hand, many Re-formed Christians recognize the theoretical possibility that the gifts mentioned in 1 Corinthians 12:8–10 might somewhere be appropriately exercised, but normally they do not encourage or even sanction them to be exercised

in their own services. In addition, there are those in both traditions who value one gift over the contribution of another, or who seem to limit the Holy Spirit's sovereign distribution of gifts.

56. These things being said, it is important to note that most Pentecostals affirm the fact that the gift of tongues is not expected to be given to all Christians. Many of them do argue, however, that the ability for Christians to speak in tongues enjoys a privileged position. They contend that the Pentecostal experience enjoyed by the 120 in Acts 2, an experience in which they spoke in other tongues as the Spirit gave them utterance, is ultimately available to all who believe (Acts 2:38–39). In this sense, many Pentecostals distinguish between speaking in tongues as a gift of the Holy Spirit (not available to all) and speaking in tongues as sign or evidence (potentially available to all) that one has been baptized with the Holy Spirit (Acts 1:8, 2:1–4).

57. It is our mutual conclusion that these positions are ultimately no less than concessions to the reality of our separated existence as Chris-tian churches. We believe that those who embrace these positions, or elevate their status by giving voice to them in doctrinal or political statements, must be challenged to recognize their limitations. They need to be asked to broaden their understanding of the gifts, which the Holy Spirit desires to give to the church. Only in so doing can they enter fully into the life of the church as the body of Christ. Only in so doing can they participate in what it means to be a priesthood of all believers. Only in so doing can they experience the fullness of what Joel prophesied, and Peter proclaimed on the day of Pentecost, that God's Spirit would be poured out on all flesh, thereby equipping them to participate in God's work in the world.

58. Reformed Christians affirm that God calls men and women and endows them with different gifts to exercise various forms of ministry in order to equip the whole people of God for mission in the world. Reformed churches express this conviction by affirming that all are commissioned to ministry by their baptism. The classic understanding of "priesthood of all believers" leads Reformed churches to encourage all Christians to participate fully in the life and ministry of the church. Some Reformed churches embody the ministry of the whole people of God by not confining ordained office to the ministry of Word and sacrament. These churches ordain persons as elders and deacons to be full partners with ministers in the service of the church. Other churches

commission members to such ministries of the church as caring for the poor and the marginalized, teaching Sunday school, leading youth ministries, furthering women's ministries, and more. Thus, the gifts given to individual members are recognized and encouraged.

The Church Is in but Not of the World

59. Both teams in this dialogue affirm the fact that, since the church is meant to be an instrument for the transformation of the world, "it is in the world, but not of the world." The church as the community of believers should be a "model," making evident—even in an inadequate way—what the future kingdom will be. Just as unity in the faith is manifested on the local level through the reciprocal love of the members of the congregation, similarly the unity of the Spirit already granted to us by God is manifested in the relations between congregations, groups, churches, and denominations on the regional, national, and global level.

60. The church works in fidelity with the Word and Spirit to live out the message and will of God. The members of the community offer themselves up as the eyes, ears, mouths, and hands, which allow the Spirit and the Word to address needs that arise in the church or the world.

61. From time to time, Reformed churches have been involved in prophetic acts for altering oppressive situations in society. Sometimes, Reformed churches have been part of oppressive structures. Thus, the church's life must be informed by the sustained study and application of Scripture to various situations and social systems, and also by active engagement in the various aspects of society as the church bears witness to the reign of God.

62. Pentecostals focus more on individuals than on structures, viewing persons as individuals. When a person is in need, Pentecostals will often attend to the immediate need, without always analyzing the systemic issues that might give rise to the situation. As they probe more deeply, they uncover systemic issues that produce or aggravate the pastoral issue being addressed. Some Pentecostals, then, confront systemic issues out of strong pastoral concerns about an individual or a group of people. While Pentecostals have frequently been stereotypically portrayed as passive and "other-worldly," programs of personal renewal at grassroots levels have had far-reaching implications for social transformation.

III. THE HOLY SPIRIT AND MISSION

63. The relation between the Holy Spirit and mission clarifies the issue of who determines mission and how mission is best carried out in each context. Is mission primarily the work of the church, or does the church participate in the mission initiated by God?

Holy Spirit and Missio Dei

64. When we say we are involved in *missio Dei*, it is a correction of the earlier notion that the mission, in which Christians are involved, is only the mission of the church. The church is a sign of the reign of God that has been inaugurated by Jesus Christ. While it has been called into this privilege, it does not claim to limit God's reign and sovereignty in all God's creation. We see that mission has its source and authority in the triune God. The biblical foundation points to the imperative for us to witness to all people in word and deed (Matt 28:18–20; Luke 24:46–47; John 20:21–23; Acts 1:8).

65. We affirm that the Holy Spirit empowers women and men for mission in God's world. In the Reformed community, it is not usual to define this empowerment as the baptism with the Holy Spirit. The empowerment as a gift is implied in the grace given to the members of the communities. In recent times, however, it has been recognized that bestowal of grace has a goal: that Christians may become coworkers of God in Jesus Christ (1 Cor 3:9). Therefore, some have proposed the concept of "vocation" as an element with specific significance beside justification and sanctification.

66. In the experience of Acts 2, Pentecostals are convinced that they have a mandate for mission before the return of the Lord. They see that mandate as rooted in the eschatological significance of the prophecy in Joel 2:28–30. Most Pentecostals believe that baptism in the Holy Spirit is for the empowerment of believers to be effective witnesses of the gospel to the ends of the earth (Acts 1:8). This empowerment includes divine calling, equipping, commissioning, and the continuing presence of the Holy Spirit throughout mission.

67. Together, we affirm that *missio Dei* has implications for the ways we view culture and religions. We believe that the sovereign God is present in all societies and cultures. We believe that the Spirit of Christ

goes ahead of the church to prepare the ground for the reception of the gospel.

The Holy Spirit and Culture

68. Pentecostals and Reformed believers are both challenged to learn together the ways in which the Spirit of God teaches the church to utilize various cultural elements, and how these elements can be put into the service of God in accordance with the biblical revelation.

69. The Holy Spirit is present and active in human history and culture as a whole as well as in the Christian church. However, every culture has to be transformed and reshaped by the Holy Spirit, in accordance with the revelation of Jesus Christ as witnessed to in Scripture.

70. Pentecostals emphasize the work of the Spirit in support of the missionary outreach of the church in the world. Their conviction is that human culture stands in alienation from God and God's truth. The ministry of the gospel is meant to liberate people from captivity to that which is godless in culture. They further believe that godlessness in culture degrades human dignity and occasions social oppression. The ministry of the gospel implies first the salvation of humanity, but also the enhancement of human dignity and liberation.

71. Pentecostals and Reformed people believe that cultures are elements within God's creation and so embody many positive elements despite the existence of sin. The relationship between the gospel and culture is dialogical; no one operates in a cultural vacuum. Therefore, witness to the gospel should be embodied in culture. Our mission efforts demonstrate that we have not always paid due attention to issues of culture.

72. Whether there are salvific elements in other religions, however, is an issue that is currently being debated by individual theologians within the Reformed family. While Pentecostals and many Reformed find it impossible to accept the idea that salvation might be found outside Jesus Christ, some Reformed agree with the ecumenical observation made at the World Conference on Mission and Evangelism at San Antonio, Texas, U.S.A. in 1989, that "We cannot point to any other way of salvation than Jesus Christ, at the same time, we cannot set limits to the saving power of God" (cf. Acts 17:28).[8]

8. See the "Reports of the Sections: Section I: Turning to the Living God," Heading IV. "Witness Among People of other Living Faiths," paragraph 26, in the *International*

73. On the whole, Pentecostals do not acknowledge the presence of salvific elements in non-Christian religions, because they view this as contrary to the teaching of the Bible. The church is called to discern the spirits through the charism of the Holy Spirit informed by the Word of God (1 Cor 12:10, 14:29; cf. 1 Thess 5:19–21; 1 John 4:2–3). Pentecostals, like many of the early Christians, are sensitive to the elements in other religions that oppose biblical teaching. They are, therefore, encouraged to received the guidance of the Holy Spirit.

The Multifaceted Mission

74. Within an eschatological perspective, the mission of the church is to witness to the truth that the kingdom of God, which yet awaits full consummation in the future, has already broken into the present age in Jesus Christ. The ministry of Jesus Christ, therefore, continues in the world by the power of the Spirit working through the eschatological people of God. The integrity of mission is bound up in a commitment to multi-dimensional mission. Those dimensions include, but are not limited to proclamation of the gospel (Matt 28:19–20, Acts 1:8), fellowship (2 Cor 5:17–20), service to the world (Matt 25:34–36), worship, and justice (Acts 2:42–47).

Service to the World

75. The grace of the Holy Spirit, given to us by Jesus Christ through the proclamation of the reign of God, prompts us to serve and participate in the mission of God in the world. This mission includes both proclamation and social engagement, which cannot be separated. Mission is concerned with the righteousness of our horizontal relationship with our neighbors and nature, as well as the vertical relationship with God.

76. We recognize that the understanding of mission varies with the social location of the given situation. The Holy Spirit empowers and leads us to work for the structural transformation of society as well as the individual transformation of ourselves, without committing the church to a specific political ideology. This transformation is an ongoing process and realization of the prayer for the coming of the kingdom of God.

Review of Mission 78, nos. 311–12 (July/October 1989) 351.

IV. SPIRIT AND KINGDOM

Definition of the Kingdom

77. The kingdom of God is apocalyptic and prophetic, both present gift and future hope. The kingdom of God is the broad theological term that represents God's sovereign, gracious, and transformative reign of righteousness and truth in the face of, but also beyond the forces of evil and sin. The kingdom cannot be identified strictly with earthly rule, although God reigns and acts in history. Neither can the kingdom be identified strictly with the church, although the church and all creation exist in the eschatological hope of the fulfillment of the kingdom.

Spirit, Kingdom, and Eschatology

78. Eschatology has often been confined to a theology of the last things, related to the consummation of the kingdom of God. For Reformed and Pentecostal churches, eschatology is not only a theology of the last things as the concluding part of our doctrinal system, but also an overall perspective of our theology and life. Although the kingdom of God has already come in Jesus Christ through the power of the Spirit, it is yet to be fulfilled in the future with the return of Christ. Until then, God rules in the world in the power of the Spirit, who grants a foretaste of the fulfilled kingdom (2 Cor 1:22; 5:5; Eph 1:7–14). God calls us to proclaim and participate in the kingdom of God.

79. Reformed and Pentecostal churches agree that the church is birthed by the Spirit and serves as an instrument of the kingdom that Jesus Christ proclaimed and inaugurated. The church is called to serve the kingdom rather than be self-serving or an end in itself. The Spirit's role in ushering in the kingdom relates to its presence in the church

80. Both Reformed and Pentecostals also agree that the gospel that is at the heart of the church's mission, therefore, is not only directed to individual life in the Spirit and to hope for life after death, but is also future oriented and directed to the resurrection of the dead, and the new heavens, and the new earth. Christian hope is not just individual and heaven-bound, but is social and cosmic (Romans 8), and directed toward the kingdom-to-come at Christ's return.

81. Thus, for Pentecostal and Reformed Christians, to hold eschatology as a context for understanding mission means that the ultimate demands of God's eternal kingdom continue to confront Christians and

the churches with the challenge of obedience. Our experience of God's Spirit as an experience of "eternity" in time must be viewed in relation to the horizon of God's ultimate future for humanity and all of creation, which is yet to be fulfilled. The victory of Christ over sin and death, and the presence of God's Holy Spirit, urge us toward courage and hope in our obedience to God's missionary call. But since the kingdom of God has not yet come in fullness, we confront trials and weakness with patience. We experience the dynamic tension between the "now" and the "not yet" of the fulfillment of God's kingdom in the world by engaging in patient action and active patience. Our actions and our prayers yearn patiently but fervently for God's will to be done on earth as it is in heaven.

82. Reformed churches affirm the second coming of Christ. Yet we are aware that God's time is different from ours. Thus, every form of prediction of the end time is excluded. The final victory of Christ gives ultimate significance to life in this world as God's time breaks into our time. Life in Christ is eschatological life.

83. The Reformed community knows that Christ will come as judge, but stresses that the judge is none other than the savior. Judgment is not confined to the future, for judgment of sin and death happens in our time as well. The motive and attitude of our mission should always be love and compassion, reflecting the grace of the Lord Jesus Christ, the love of God, and the communion of the Holy Spirit.

84. Pentecostalism was born in a milieu of growing disillusionment with 19th century theological optimism concerning the coming of the millennial reign of Christ. This post-millennial theology, in Britain and America at least, was being displaced in some circles by a premillennial eschatology, which focused on the return of Jesus to rapture the church. It was the personal return of Christ to bring the kingdom rather than the return of Christ to receive the kingdom, which was already to have been established on earth. This eschatology has shaped Pentecostal missions since that time. It implies a focus on mission as evangelism.

85. Pentecostals believe that Christians move relentlessly toward that ultimate fulfillment of God's kingdom through prayer and battle against the forces of evil. Meanwhile, this tension between the "now" and the "not yet" of Christian hope grows ever more intense, as the Spirit of God is poured out in ever-greater abundance in the direction of final fulfillment at Christ's return.

86. From their inception, Pentecostals have held to a firm belief that the return of Christ was close at hand. Early Pentecostals zealously proclaimed the message of the gospel to the whole world, in light of the return of Christ. Scripture passages, such as John 16:12–16, Matt 25:31–46, 1 Thess 4:13–17, and 2 Pet 3:8–9, continue to fuel the missionary zeal of Pentecostals. The Holy Spirit's work in inspiring Pentecostals to missionary activity, service, and giving is in anticipation of the kingdom of God. The eschatological urgency that Pentecostals feel, therefore, should not be thought of only as the hope for the return of Christ, but a firm realization that there remains a responsibility to humanity of providing for the needs of people, such as shelter, education, food, and medical concerns.

87. Generally, Pentecostal mission cares for the total person. Indeed, prayer for healing and ministry to the personal needs of people, such as food and education, have always been present in Pentecostal missions. It does suggest, however, that Pentecostal missions have not always challenged social or structural issues prophetically. There are at least two reasons for this. The first is that the social location of Pentecostals was, on the whole, marginal to society, and Pentecostals had limited access to the power centers of the social establishment. Second, those structures were viewed as the part of the system, which Jesus' coming would replace by the righteous reign of God.

Spirit, Kingdom, Creation

88. The relationship of creation to the Spirit and the kingdom is a pivotal eschatological theme for many churches, both Reformed and Pentecostal. The topic challenges restricting the signs of God's reign to human history. Creation as a topic within Spirit and kingdom introduces the cosmos as an object of God's engagement.

89. For Reformed and Pentecostal churches, the Holy Spirit is integrally involved in creation. Both recognize the Spirit's role at the beginning of creation as well as acknowledge the Spirit's role in the sustaining and renewing of creation. For Reformed churches and some Pentecostal churches, the expectation of the kingdom includes the restoration and renewal of the cosmos.

90. In Pentecostal worship, sighs too deep for words are given expression. These are often understood as speaking in tongues (Rom 8:26), offered in anticipation of the kingdom of God yet to come in fullness.

Such a yearning for the kingdom implies a desire for the salvation of the lost and the redemption of the entire creation. Examples of their concern for creation are demonstrated through Pentecostals' prayer for rain, especially during droughts, or their prayer for a bounteous harvest. All creation benefits from this concern, and they believe that without God's blessing, creation itself will not be sustained.

91. For the Reformed churches, the expectation of the coming of our savior does not exclude, but includes the expectation of the kingdom. The fulfilled kingdom is not just the collection of all believers but the shalom for the totality of creation. It represents the restoration and renewal of the cosmos. Churches of the Reformed tradition strive to be faithful to the creation because God remains faithful to it. Human beings are part of the cosmos, and so together with the whole creation are invited to participate in the celebration of life.

Spirit, Kingdom, World

92. The location of the world within the topic of Spirit and kingdom is central to identifying the boundaries of the arena in which the Spirit and kingdom intersect in history. Key questions are: Is the work of the Spirit confined to the church? Does the kingdom engage the world? Is the world an arena of the Spirit or the kingdom?

93. Reformed churches acknowledge that all Christians, as stewards of the rich gifts of God, are called to act in responsible faith towards all creation. Therefore, we are called to proclaim, both in word and deed, the will of God concerning personal and social injustices, economic exploitation, and ecological destruction. Moreover, Reformed churches affirm that the Holy Spirit guides the faithful to work for both personal and structural transformation of society, thus participating in the ongoing process and realization of the prayer for the coming of the kingdom of God.

94. Pentecostals differ on how they view the role of the Holy Spirit in sustaining, reforming, or transforming human society. Some Pentecostals interpret reality dualistically. They understand that a state of warfare exists between the people of God and "the world." They believe that the Holy Spirit is the one who will triumph over the "principalities and powers and spiritual wickedness in high places." How that warfare is defined varies from those who interpret the warfare in moral terms to those who employ the term "spiritual warfare" in describing

the battle between the godly and ungodly powers. Pentecostals, who employ moral terms, identify the role of the Spirit as one who restrains evil in the world. Others identify the role of the Spirit as one who invites Christians to engage in the reforming and transforming of society. This perspective also recognizes the role of the Holy Spirit in reproving the human society in terms of righteousness.

95. Some Pentecostals around the world engage the political arena from the underside. Many are in countries where there is no political space for them to engage the political order directly. Their social locations shape their understanding of the Holy Spirit. However, among these are those who respond differently from the majority. They create alternative societies modeling resolutions to societal issues within their ecclesial structures. The issues they address include, but are not limited to such evils as racism, classism, materialism, and sexism.

CONCLUSIONS

96. Several clear benefits have emerged as a direct result of this dialogue. One of the obvious fruits enjoyed so far has been the friendships that have been established across denominational lines and the lines of our various traditions. These friendships have expanded beyond the realm of everyday life into the recesses of our common spiritualities and our ecclesial experiences. Genuine ecumenism begins when Christians find each other and learn to enter into the lives of one another.

97. A second obvious benefit of the dialogue to date has been the individual studies that have been offered in the form of papers presented. Some of these have found their way into publication, thereby challenging those who cannot participate at the limited space a dialogue table allows. In addition, press reports from the meeting have been published in a number of papers and journals, expanding the awareness of this dialogue in a number of ecclesial and scholarly communities. They have found their way into classrooms and are contributing to the ecumenical formation of the next generation of pastors and teachers in both communities.

98. Thirdly, the dialogue has been able to give and to receive from Christians in each of the regions in which it has convened its meetings. It has delved into the lives of Christians, who live sometimes in difficult situations, whether they be members of a minority community in the Italian Alps, an African-American community in the U.S.A., an afflu-

ent Reformed community in Switzerland, a Pente-costal congregation separated from family members in Korea by an artificial boundary, or a Reformed community in a large Brazilian city, teeming both with hope and despair.

99. Finally, the dialogue had helped its participants realize the critical necessity for ongoing contact between these two vital Christian traditions. With the completion of this report, the participants in this dialogue wish to encourage others in their respective communities to join in this mutual exploration.

Part 3

Pentecostal Reflections on *The Nature and Mission of the Church*

12

The Nature and Purpose of the Church: Theological and Ecumenical Reflections from Pentecostal and Free Church Perspectives

Veli-Matti Kärkkäinen

INTRODUCTION

The subtitle for the Faith and Order document *The Nature and Purpose of the Church* (hereafter, NPC) is illustrative of its purpose: "A Stage on the Way to a Common Statement."[1] This document marks a significant milestone in the ecumenical and theological reflection on the church. Yet, as its subtitle also indicates, it is a working paper, a document in the making, with a modest purpose: one stage in the long process of formulating a common understanding of what the church is and what is its purpose.

The format of NPC follows that of *Baptism, Eucharist, and Ministry* (BEM): It is an exercise in a convergence text. It states the minimum that the churches behind it are able to say in common. It explicates the various divergences, yet does not attempt to solve them, but leaves them for further discussion.

1. "The Nature and Purpose of the Church," Faith and Order Paper 181 (Geneva: WCC Publications, 1998). The present essay was first published as "'The Nature and Purpose of the Church.' Theological and Ecumenical Reflections from Pentecostal/Free Church Perspectives," *Ecumenical Trends* 33.7 (2004) 1–7. It is reprinted here with kind permission.

The format chosen for the document sets limits for the work: as a typical ecumenical text, it needs to be generic enough in trying to include the major traditions' views and—by definition—be subject to more than one specific interpretation. Depending on the perspective and background, what is said, for example, about sacraments, can be read in more than one way. This is the challenge and the beauty (!) of convergence texts. The BEM document is a wonderful example of this, and during the years its reception has proved that the convergence method is workable, especially in the beginning stages of ecumenical reflections on major topics.

In this paper, I will first take a brief look at the structure and contents of "The Nature and Purpose of the Church." Second, I will offer a critical analysis of the key themes that I see emerging from Pentecostal and Free Church perspectives. Rather than trying to survey the whole document evenly, I will be selective and take the liberty of focusing on critical issues as I see them. The first chapter, dealing with the question of ecclesiality, receives the most attention in my reflection. I will take into consideration, where appropriate, the amendments or changes present in the new draft, especially regarding ways they may shed light on the developments the Commission on Faith and Order wants to introduce to the process. Third, I will engage in a critical assessment of the document as a whole: its main weaknesses and challenges. I will also try to point to tasks for the future. I undertake this as a friendly, appreciative critic of the process. Certainly, I could add a section on the praises the document deserves; all of us are certainly indebted to this significant document and especially to the continuing process. I am confident my analysis and even critique makes it clear how much I value the text.

PRELIMINARY COMMENTS ON THE STRUCTURE AND CONTENTS

A few preliminary comments on the structure and contents are in order. First of all, NPC follows the current ecumenical consensus in anchoring the church in the life of the triune God. It is a sincere attempt to build a trinitarian ecclesiology.

Second, communion ecclesiology has been adopted as the main theological framework. In Faith and Order, communion ecclesiology has become the dominant approach at least since Santiago de Compostela; in ecumenical ecclesiology, following the lead first of the Eastern Orthodox and then Roman Catholic theologies, the church as *koinonia* has become a received tradition, even if a more precise understanding of what communion ecclesiology means is still under reflection (e.g., what is its relation to "visible" unity or "how much" communion does there need to be in order to have "unity"?).

Third, the theme of mission and service is appropriately dealt with in the document. Indeed, as we will notice in what follows, NPC follows yet another development in contemporary ecumenical ecclesiology, the idea of the missional church: the church does not primarily *have* mission as a task but *is* missionary by nature (as, for example, Vatican II's *Ad gentes*, no. 2, succinctly states).

Fourth, the theme that is not as explicitly evident—surprisingly enough—is the main question behind not only this document but the whole work of Faith and Order, namely: (visible) unity. Do not misunderstand me here. I am not saying that the document does not speak of the church's unity: it does. Rather, I contend that when speaking of the *nature* and *purpose* of the church, the question of its unity is such a critical theme that it deserves a more visible place in the document. One could argue that the chapter on communion ecclesiology sufficiently address that theme. That chapter does speak to key issues of unity and, in a way, that is the central section on the conditions of unity. Nevertheless, I have to admit that, when first reading the document, I kept asking myself, why not a more explicit, more powerful section on the unity of the church, perhaps a final chapter in which all the various threads would be pulled together in terms of what they have to say about the church's unity?

A CRITICAL ANALYSIS OF KEY THEMES

Chapter I. The Church of the Triune God

NPC anchors the church in the life of the triune God (I. A), following Vatican II's *Lumen gentium* (especially nos. 1–4) and the current ecumenical consensus.

However, the way no. 9 expresses the trinitarian foundation is quite weak: "The Church belongs to God. It is the creation of God's Word and Holy Spirit. It cannot exist by and for itself." Hardly anybody has reason to deny a generic statement like this. It does not say much indeed. The new draft adds a little bit here but does not make a significant contribution by mentioning that the "church is called into being by the Father" who "sent the Holy Spirit to lead these believers into all truth . . ." More helpful is the way *Lumen gentium* (no. 1) puts it, as well as the remarkable document, *Perspectives on Koinonia*, between Roman Catholics and Pentecostals (no. 29): "Both Pentecostals and Roman Catholics believe that the *koinonia* between Christians is rooted in the life of the Father, Son, and Holy Spirit. Furthermore, they believe that this trinitarian life is the highest expression of the unity to which we together aspire."[2]

NPC highlights the trinitarian foundation of the church with the idea of the church as the *creatura Verbi et creatura Spiritus*—a typically Protestant idea. It is not that this expression is wrong—it is biblically grounded—but I wonder: why this binitarian formula? Why not, first of all, maintain the trinitarian language? And secondly, when speaking of the Word and Spirit specifically, speak of the christological and pneumatological foundation of the church?[3] The christological foundation of the church can not be limited to the role of the "Word" alone. The church is also the body of the Christ. Helpful is the way no. 11 speaks of the mutuality of christology and pneumatology in that Christ is both the receiver and the giver of the Spirit. One need not go as far as the well-known account of Catholic theologian, Heribert Mühlen, who speaks of the church as the continuation of the anointing of Christ with the Spirit at his baptism, in order to highlight the mutual condition of Christ and the Spirit as the dual foundation of the church.[4] The new draft makes a significant contribution when, in speaking of biblical images of the church (people of God, body of Christ, temple of the Holy Spirit), it adds reference to Pentecost (no. 22 [no. 23 in the 1998 version]). It is impossible to talk about the role of the Spirit in ecclesiology in the New Testament without reference to Pentecost.

No. 10, which speaks of the church as the "communion of those who live in a *personal* relationship with God" (my emphasis), is to be

2. See the full text in chapter 9 of this collection.

3. As does, for example, the Orthodox John Zizioulas, *Being as Communion: Studies in the Personhood and the Church* (Crestwood, NY: St. Vladimir's Seminary Press, 1985) 132, 136, 140; and the Lutheran Wolfhart Pannenberg, *Systematic Theology*, vol. 3 (Grand Rapids: Eerdmans, 1998) 16–17.

4. Heribert Mühlen, *Una Mystica Persona: Die Kirche als das Mysterium der Identität des Heiligen Geistes in Christus und den Christen: Eine Person in vielen Personen*, 2nd ed. (Paderborn: Schöning, 1967). See Wolfgang Vondey, *Heribert Mühlen: His Theology and Praxis: A New Profile of the Church* (Lanham, MD: University Press of America, 2004) 115–32.

welcomed as long as we do not confuse "personal" with "individualistic," as often happens in Pentecostal and Free Church ecclesiologies.

No. 12 gives a tentative discussion of the "marks" of the church. I like the way "oneness" is connected here to eschatology: "It [the church] is one because the God who binds it to himself by Word and Spirit is the one creator and redeemer making the Church a foretaste and instrument for redemption of all created reality." This loaded statement not only helpfully highlights the truly trinitarian nature of the church, but also connects the purpose of the church to the eschatological redemption of the whole creation. Furthermore—again in line with *Lumen gentium* (no. 1)—it speaks of the church as an "instrument" of God's purposes. This is a helpful way of connecting the church to the purposes of the triune God in bringing about the new creation.

Wisely enough, NPC does not dare to speak of the church as "sacrament," the *Lumen gentium* idea, which is being widely criticized by the Protestants. In my mind, to speak of the church as sacrament is not so much wrong as it is confusing and less than helpful. While sacramentality, or the sacramental principle, is wider than any single sacramental act, if the church as a whole is called the sacrament, the contours of the term get fuzzy.[5]

Going back to the marks of the church (oneness, holiness, catholicity, apostolicity), for me it would be more helpful to pull together the various sections that speak of the marks rather than having them distributed throughout the paper. When the marks are mentioned in no. 12, it only speaks of them as the "gift" of God; only later (nos. 38–41) does the document also speak of them as "tasks" given to us. In other words, the holiness of the church, for example, is not only a quality of the church deriving from the holiness of God but also a task to be pursued. Having pulled these sections together would have presented a more coherent theology.

Concerning the mark of apostolicity, I have a comment and a concern. Apostolicity is defined here as living in the "succession of the apostolic truth" (no. 12), obviously the Word and ecclesial tradition. Now, for a Protestant, this sounds good, better than the Roman Catholic view that—especially in the past—has tended to stress the semi-technical episcopal succession. Yet, even with my wholehearted "Amen" to con-

5. No. 23 of NPC contains a helpful note on the various interpretations of the idea of the church as sacrament.

necting apostolicity to the Word, I wonder if this is still a limited understanding. We need to ask of ourselves, what is the original intention of defining the church as apostolic? It obviously is to connect the church to the life of the apostolic church, that is, the New Testament church, the church of the apostles. Aside from the discussion concerning the *means* of determining apostolicity (i.e., whether through the succession of the apostles or otherwise), it is a current ecumenical consensus that apostolicity means life in line with the life of the apostolic church. It is more than adherence to Scripture. It has to do with Pentecost, the pouring out of the Spirit, the mission,[6] and the expansion of the church, social, and other concerns (e.g., the sharing of goods among the apostolic church).[7] From a Pentecostal perspective, it is significant that the very first Pentecostal church back at Azusa Street named itself the *Apostolic Faith Mission*: charismatic gifts such as healing and preaching of the "Full Gospel" and resisting the fragmentation of the divided society were seen to be "marks" of apostolicity according to the Acts of the Apostles.[8]

As already mentioned, the way NPC relates mission to the nature and purpose of the church is very helpful. While it would be better to say, "the church is missionary by nature" (*Ad gentes* no. 2), the acknowledgment of the fact that "mission belongs to the very being of the church" (no. 27) reflects the contemporary idea of the church as mission. Even though the document does not use the current mantra, *missio Dei*, materially it expresses the idea of God's mission in one of its theologically most pregnant statements, found in no. 28, speaking of the church as mission: "Thus the church, embodying in its own life the mystery of salvation and the transfiguration of humanity, participates in the mission of Christ to reconcile all things to God and to one another through Christ." Pentecostals will applaud the declaration that "Christians are called to proclaim the Gospel in word and deed," even though the document does not explicate what the deeds might be. They will likewise endorse the note that the church is called to address with the gospel both non-Christians and nominal ones (no. 27).

6. Indeed, the new draft (no. 36 [27 in the 1998 version]) connects apostolicity and mission in a very helpful way: "Mission thus belongs to the very being of the Church. This is a central implication of affirming the apostolicity of the Church."

7. See further my "The Apostolicity of Free Churches: A Contradiction in Terms of an Ecumenical Breakthrough?" *Pro Ecclesia* 10.4 (2001) 389–400.

8. See Veli-Matti Kärkkäinen, "Pentecostalism and the Claim for Apostolicity," *Evangelical Review of Theology* 25.4 (2001) 323–36.

Chapter II. The Church in History

No. 35 states helpfully that the church is both an eschatological reality and a historical reality, "exposed to the ambiguity of all human history," thus reminding us of the fact the Church is still *in via*, the idea that prompted *Lumen gentium* to speak of the church as a pilgrimage people in line with Old Testament imagery.

In subsection B of chapter II, titled "Sign and Instrument of God's Design," the document picks up the idea expressed earlier of the church as "instrument" and sign, and it even connects it to the biblical idea (Ephesians 3) of *mysterion* (no. 43). All in all, this is a more helpful way to relate the purpose of the church to the life of the Trinity than to speak of the church as sacrament. Yet, the way the document speaks of the church as sign continues to have a sacramental ring to it: ". . . the church is the instrument through which God wants to bring about what is signified by it," namely, salvation of the world and renewal of the human community. In other words, the church—paralleling sacraments—is a sign that effects what it signifies; thus it is "more" than a mere sign. While many Pentecostals may regard this language as too "strong," I don't see anything for us to be concerned about. This is a wonderful way of speaking of the church *in via* as a sacramental sign of the triune God through which he fulfills the eternal purposes.

Chapter III. The Church as Koinonia (Communion)

This section presents an outline of communion ecclesiology as understood in contemporary ecumenical thinking. It contains very few surprises. It traces in detail the biblical idea of *koinonia* and relates it to the purposes of the triune God to bring about a new humanity and new creation. It also reflects in a helpful way the prominent ecumenical idea of "unity-in-diversity." Practically speaking, this is also the only place where NPC speaks specifically of the local church, especially the way local churches form a communion among themselves. Nonetheless, while the idea of unity appears here, as already mentioned, the text does not adequately deal with the implications of communion ecclesiology for the question of the church's visible unity.

Chapter IV. Life in Communion

Having presented the basic biblical and theological orientations to contemporary communion ecclesiology, NPC devotes considerable space to ecumenical guidelines on how to live out the life of communion in the church, both in terms of sacraments and ministry, including ecclesiastical leadership.

Theologically, it is good choice to relate the talk about sacraments (baptism and Eucharist) to the context of communion, since that is the primary setting for sacraments—ironically, as they often signify the lack of communion among the churches! Theologically, it is also a helpful choice to preface the discussion of sacraments with the extended note on "Apostolic Faith," that is, the teaching of the Word. The way no. 73 speaks of the "apostolic faith" as something that "does not refer to one fixed formula or to a specific phase in Christian history" is very insightful. The document rightly asserts that "apostolic faith is confessed in worship, in life and service—in the living tradition of the Church." I believe it is time for Pentecostals to learn this lesson—and to help fellow Protestants to grasp it, too—that tradition is not something related only to the past, but is a living, dynamic Spirit-event!

No. 72 would have provided a grand opportunity for the drafters of the document to expand on what "apostolic life" is. Indeed, it speaks of the "apostolic tradition" in helpful ways, mentioning witness, proclamation, celebration of sacraments, prayer, lover, joy, even social service. Yet, it fails to mention aspects, such as healings and other charismatic gifts (even though the last sentence mentions the word *gifts,* but in terms of local churches sharing gifts) that obviously were an integral part of the apostolic life, and thus apostolic tradition.

Section D of chapter III, on "ministry," picks up some key ideas of BEM but does it so briefly that it does not offer any genuine contributions. The last two quite extensive sections deal with hierarchy and episcopacy. Here, again, the need to stay within the confines of a convergence document makes the text quite generic. How can you, for example, talk about primacy (section F) in any specific way without opening deep ecumenical wounds and causing an ecumenical impasse?

Chapter V. Service in and for the World

The last chapter is a kind of extended epilogue that picks up the idea expressed several times in the document concerning the purpose of the church, not as an end in itself but as an "instrument" and sign through which God carries out his eternal purposes. This chapter opens up the question of ethics and morality in relation to the purpose of the church, but hardly begins to draw implications.

TAKING STOCK: TASKS FOR THE FUTURE

The fact that I feel compelled to raise a number of critical questions and point to a few quite serious weaknesses of the document are not meant to imply that I would undermine the significance of the document in any way. Rather, my intention is to facilitate further discussion and to pool resources for this joint ecumenical enterprise.

Perhaps, the most critical observation relates to the document's total lack of reflection on the dramatic changes happening in the mosaic of the Christian church in our own times. Just take a look at the growing body of literature recording the phenomenal changes in the make up of the church as a result of Christianity's moving from the global North to the southern hemisphere.[9] Add to the picture the phenomenal growth of Pentecostalism and Free Churches as well as all kinds of independent churches, and you live in a very different world from the era of Christendom. Yet, as unbelievable as it sounds, the document under discussion is written from the perspective of that bygone era. No mention is made of these historic changes that have utterly transformed global Christianity—not even in the most recent draft.

The terminology used and the issues addressed in the document represent ecclesiologies of traditional churches in the West. The questions raised by the majority world (!) are safely dismissed, as if Christendom still existed and ecumenical reflection on the church could dismiss what happens in the (global) real world. African and Asian Christians find no mention of exorcism or the role of exorcists or prophets or healers in the ministry section. The text offers a sad testimony to the failed attempts of the ecumenical movement, in general, and of Faith and Order, in particular, to extend itself beyond the established Western and male-dominated church structures.

9. For starters, see Philip Jenkins, *The Next Christendom: The Coming of Global Christianity* (Oxford: Oxford University Press, 2001). You don't have to agree with everything Jenkins presents to still be awakened from the theological and ecumenical slumber plaguing so much of academic theology and official ecumenism.

In the ranks of the WCC in the past few years, there has been a sincere desire to connect with both non-western theologies and spiritualities. After Harare, the WCC established a five- to seven-year consultation between Pentecostals and its member churches with the hope of learning more about Pentecostal churches, their ecclesiologies, ministry patterns, and so on. The missions desk has arranged several consultations, in preparation for the Athens 2005 World Conference, with non-Western Christians in Africa, Latin America, and elsewhere and invited a large number of Pentecostals and charismatic Christians to talk about healing, exorcism, prophecy, and other topics usually dismissed in the wider discussion on the church and its mission.

Questions raised by Pentecostal-Charismatic churches such as the role of charisms—from prophecy to speaking in tongues, healing, visions, and exorcism—are completely missing in NPC. There are a few references to "gifts," but in each case it is difficult to determine what is meant by the term.

The complete dismissal of the topic of healing—be it less spectacular such as that practiced in many mainline churches from Roman Catholic to Anglicans and to various Protestant churches, or the more "miraculous" as in Pentecostal and Charismatic assemblies—is hard to explain when speaking of the ministry of the church. There would have been ample opportunity at least to mention healing, such as in no. 30, which speaks of various facets of what "Christ's mission encompassed." How can one talk about Christ's mission, even with references to the Gospels, and fail to mention healing and exorcisms?

Since NPC represents mainly the mindset of established churches of the Christendom era (a reality which indeed no longer exists!), there is very little if any talk about the need for constant renewal of the church, including its structures. One of the reasons for that is also the lack of discussion of the charismatic structure of the church. There are references to the Holy Spirit, as I have indicated above, but one wonders if a thoroughly pneumatological, and thus charismatic, ecclesiology is represented here. By saying this, I am not diverting from a healthy trinitarian approach. Rather, I make the obvious observation that ecclesiologies in the West have been one-sidedly built on christological foundations. That charge is of course not new; Eastern Orthodox theologians have reminded us of that for decades. So, I am not saying anything new nor very profound. My challenge here to the process is that, when it comes to a genuinely pneumatological ecclesiology, the key are not the mere number of references but whether pneumatology is acknowledged as an essential part of the church and its structure.[10]

An ecclesiology that reflects the status quo does not easily lend itself to constant, dynamic expansion, reaching out to new areas and people groups, a feature so evident in apostolic church of the New Testament. One of the side effects of this neglect is that the role of the whole people of God—the laity—does not receive due attention even though BEM already moved in that direction.[11]

Let me finish my challenges to the continuing process of theological and ecumenical reflection on the church, its nature and purpose, by saying something that may sound quite out of context. Having discussed the various theological resources, NPC brings to the task of constructing a convergence text on ecumenical ecclesiology, I submit for your consideration the thesis that, in the midst of all this work, there is still surprisingly little said specifically on the *ecclesiality* of the church! What do I mean by this? The question of ecclesiality relates to the very essence of the theology of the church, namely, to the conditions for the being of the church; in other words: what makes the church the church.[12]

It is true that NPC talks about the relationship between the Trinity and the church, it talks about biblical images of and perspectives on the church, it talks about the church as communion, and so on. But it does not raise the all-important question of the minimum conditions, if you will, of being a church. That is, of course, a highly disputed question. To illustrate it, we need only to think of the different understandings of the ecclesiality among the episcopal churches (Roman Catholic and Eastern Orthodox Churches, which make the office of the bishop a condition for the being of the church) and Free Churches (which do not). The way

10. See further my "Spirit, Church, and Christ: An Ecumenical Inquiry into a Pneumatological Ecclesiology," *One in Christ* 4 (2000) 338–53; and "Church as Charismatic Fellowship: Ecclesiological Reflections from the Pentecostal–Roman Catholic Dialogue," *Journal of Pentecostal Theology* 18 (2001) 101–22.

11. See further my "The Calling of the Whole People of God into Ministry: The Spirit, Church, and Laity," *Studia Theologia: Scandinavian Journal of Theology* 54.2 (2000) 144–62.

12. A great recent introduction to the topic is offered by Miroslav Volf in his critical dialogue between Free Church ecclesiologies and Roman Catholic (C. Ratzinger) and Eastern Orthodox (J. Zizioulas): *After Our Likeness: The Church as the Image of the Trinity* (Grand Rapids: Eerdmans, 1998).

NPC talks of the sacraments, especially the Eucharist, as well as of the office of the bishop, seems to be quite unaware of the urgency of this question. For episcopal churches, as we all know, the office of the bishop is not just a conventional way of leading the church, but a key condition for the church's ecclesiality. The same applies to the celebration of the Eucharist. It is not only a commemoration of the death of Christ on the cross but—in line with the eucharistic ecclesiology of both Catholic churches—an event that "makes the church." These two—episcopacy and Eucharist—are thus interrelated events, since it takes a bishop who stands in apostolic succession to preside over the Eucharist.

Why am I insisting on this issue, especially now that I have already mentioned that many of the questions dealt with in the document do not seem to be very relevant to most nontraditional churches or even traditional churches outside the West? The reason is simple: new churches—at least Christian communities that regard themselves as churches—are mushrooming everywhere in the world. Can the concept of ecclesiality—the true being of the church—simply be ignored by the "official ecumenical apparatus" represented by the traditional churches of the West? The assessment that it is indeed ignored seems to be a realistic ecumenical observation. In the significant document under discussion, one would expect help to deal with this foundational issue, but the text does not offer much help. Maybe a study process should be initiated to begin to tackle this thorny issue: how do we come to some kind of minimum understanding of the conditions for ecclesiality that can be embraced by traditional and non-traditional churches? I am not naive about that task, but unless it is adopted as one of the key issues, the dismissal of the major portion of our Christian communities will continue into the future.

13

The Nature and Purpose of the Church: A Pentecostal Reflection on Unity and *Koinonia*

Frank D. Macchia

The 1998 Faith and Order document, *The Nature and Purpose of the Church* (NPC), is symbolic of a growing emphasis in ecumenical conversations on ecclesiology.[1] The fifth world conference on Faith and Order in Santiago de Compostela, in 1993, occasioned the document by calling for a study on the nature and purpose of the church. The NPC serves as a text that seeks to summarize former insights as a provocation for further discussion and revision. The document is a work in progress. To contribute to this conversation, I wish to explore from a Pentecostal perspective the issues of unity, *koinonia*, and the church as both divine and human reality.

WHAT MAKES THE CHURCH ONE?

The document begins with the goal of visible unity based in the *koinonia* (communion) of God as Trinity in which the church participates both as a community and as individuals.[2] "The path to unity is to make that

1. This essay was originally published as "The Nature and Purpose of the Church: A Pentecostal Response," *Ecumenical Trends* 34.7 (2005) 1–6 and is printed here in revised form with kind permission.

2. *The Nature and Purpose of the Church,* Faith and Order Paper 181.13 (Geneva: WCC Publications, 1998). The changes made in the revised version of NPC, published as *The Nature and Mission of the Church,* Faith and Order Paper 198 (Geneva: WCC Publications, 2005), are not reflected in this essay.

communion ever more visible" (no. 60). The NPC notes that as long as there are different understandings of what constitutes visible unity, *koinonia* cannot be fully realized visibly (no. 60). The expression of *koinonia* in the unity of the church is indeed both a gift and calling, but there are different understandings as to the precise nature of this unity.

Veli-Matti Kärkkänen noted rightly that the NPC does not tackle the issue of the ecclesiality of the church, the question of what makes the church the church.[3] The issues of whether or not the office of the Bishop and the Eucharist are necessary to the being of the church are not discussed. I do think that the NPC implicitly recognizes the problem of ecclesiality by noting that there are different understandings as to what constitutes unity, a problem that will hinder its visible realization (no. 60). But there is no specificity offered as to what these understandings may be and what is necessary to its fulfillment. Since the NPC's stated goal in the introduction is to take seriously the path to visible unity, the lack of specificity about different conceptions of that unity, or what is necessary to its realization, is unfortunate. From a Pentecostal perspective, I would like to offer a few observations.

First, Pentecostals will find themselves at home in the NPC's statements about unity, due to the focus on the proclamation of Jesus Christ as that which determines the essence and purpose of the church. Allow me to explain. The NPC understands the christological contribution to the creation of the church in the context of the proclamation of Jesus Christ through "preaching, sacraments, and service" (no. 10). Pentecostals understand the christological contribution to the founding of the church similarly in the proclamation of Jesus Christ (in word and deed), except they would focus on charismatic (and not sacramental) "signs following." For example, the Pentecostals noted in the final report of the international dialogue with the World Alliance of Reformed Churches (WARC): "By proclaiming the gospel, healing the sick, and confronting demonic powers, Pentecostals seek to be involved in a vibrant proclamation of the gospel, accompanied often by manifestations of the power of God" (no. 24).[4]

But this difference between the NPC and the Pentecostals is relatively minor considering the lack of specific attention on the Eucharist and church office in the Faith and Order document. Both the NPC and

3. See the essay by Kärkkäinen in chapter 12 of this collection

4. See the text of the document in chapter 11 of this collection.

most Pentecostals locate the significance of the sacraments in their role in furthering the proclamation of the Word. Interestingly, the NPC does not consider specifically locating the christological contribution to what constitutes the church in the office of the bishop or the Eucharist. The lack of focus on the Eucharist is especially puzzling in the light of the document's emphasis on *koinonia* as the essence of the church. The NPC could have presented Pentecostals with a greater challenge, had it placed more specific focus on the implications of the Eucharist for the unity of the church.

Second, the NPC does place a specific focus on faith and baptism as the means of entry into the mystery of Christ's redemptive work: "By faith and baptism, persons participate in the mystery of Christ's death, burial, and resurrection" (no. 55). Most significantly, the NPC states, "Baptism is the gift of the Holy Spirit and the way of incorporation into the body of Christ" (no. 76). Most Pentecostals would sharply distinguish between water baptism and Spirit baptism. Though Oneness Pentecostals would make water baptism integral to Christian initiation, most trinitarian Pentecostals would not. Yet, Pentecostals are beginning to reconsider the significance of water baptism for Christian initiation and the gift of the Spirit. In the final report of the international Roman Catholic-Pentecostal dialogue, 1985–1989, the Pentecostals noted, "all Pentecostals would consider baptism to be an integral part of the whole experience of becoming Christian . . . Pentecostals do feel the need to investigate further the relationship between baptism and salvation in light of specific passages which appear to make a direct link between baptism and salvation (e.g., John 3:5; Mark 16:16; Acts 22:16; 1 Pet 3:21)" (nos. 50–51).[5] On the other hand, this statement is followed by one that has most Pentecostals regard water baptism more as a witness to a personal identification with Christ than the decisive act of that identification (no. 52). The consequences are noted in a following statement, "Pentecostals do not see the unity between Christians as being based in a common water baptism, mainly because they believe that the New Testament does not base it in baptism. Instead, the foundation of unity is a common faith and experience of Jesus Christ as lord and savior through the Holy Spirit" (no. 55).

Pentecostals emphasize that the unity of the church is based in the divine action and not an ecclesiastical form. The Pentecostals have noted

5. See the text of the document in Chapter 9 of this collection.

in concert with the WARC in the final report of their first international dialogue: "The church is a people called by the Word and shaped by the Spirit, all to the glory of God. The gracious action of God precedes all human forms, communities, and institutions" (no. 37). Pentecostals will always place their emphasis on the action of God through Christ and the Spirit in determining that, which brings us into the *koinonia* of God and helps us to realize that *koinonia* more visibly in unity and service. The specific role of water baptism in Christian initiation, the reception of the Spirit, and the unity of the church is an issue, however, that is yet to be fully explored among Pentecostals.

Particularly thorny in such a discussion will be the issue of the baptismal formula, since Oneness Pentecostals insist on baptism in Jesus' name only. All Pentecostals, on the other hand, would find agreement with the NPC that water baptism has to do with the vocation and "ordination" of all Christians to service (no. 76). The document exhibits a strong emphasis on mission and service as essential to the church (nos. 27–32) and to the giftedness of all members of the church (no. 82). Though I agree with Kärkkänen, that the NPC lacks specificity as to the charismatic structure of the church, I do think this structure is implicitly affirmed, not only in the statements about the universal giftings of all Christians, but also in the insistence that "the church is a communion of co-responsible persons" (no. 94). The emphasis of the NPC on baptism as the ordination of all Christians confirms this idea.

It is important at this point to explore what the NPC states about *koinonia*, especially since this approach to ecclesiology is so near to the substance of how Pentecostals understand the nature and purpose of the church, and yet so foreign to Pentecostal language.

KOINONIA AND PNEUMATOLOGY

As the NPC notes in the introduction, the formation of the document was originally inspired by the report of the assembly of the World Council of Churches (WCC) in Canberra, "The Church as *Koinonia*: Gift or Calling?" The title of this report reflects a tension between *koinonia* as a divine (eschatological) gift and as a calling toward unity in the context of human (historical) reality caught up in ambiguity, sin, and divisions.

The NPC's focus on *koinonia* is due to the fact that this concept has emerged in a number of ecumenical statements, conciliar and bilateral, as key to understanding the nature of the church and its unity. Though the NPC is aware of the danger of its overuse, it accurately summarizes the attention given to the theme in past ecumenical conversations, especially with regard to the potential of this concept for an ecumenical convergence on the nature and purpose of the church and with regard to the church's struggle to actualize its unity. Consistent with this trend, the NPC acknowledges that *koinonia* is the "foundation and way of living together in visible unity" (no. 1). As a gift of God, *koinonia* comforts Christians striving for visible unity with the assurance that separated Christians share already "a profound degree of unity" (no. 60). In other words, our divisions, though scandalous, do not reach to heaven! For those who may not recognize the scandal of divisions, *koinonia* is a call to recognize that "the path to unity is to make that communion ever more visible" (no. 60). *Koinonia* is both a gift and a calling.

In *koinonia*, the church is not defined in an overly juridical way in service to a kind of clericalism. For the NPC, *koinonia* as a gift of God governs the ministries and gifts of the church: "The church is a communion of co-responsible persons: no function, no gift, no charisma is exercised outside or above this communion" (no. 94). On the other hand, neither is the church merely a volunteer association of individual believers but rather a communion that participates together in God: "The church is not the sum of individual believers in communion with God. It is not primarily a communion of believers with each other. It is a common partaking together in God's own life whose innermost being is communion" (no. 13). *Koinonia* describes the essential "depth, closeness, and quality of relationship implicit in the various models of the church offered in Scripture" (no. 49).

Koinonia helps us understand why the church is vital to God's redemptive plan: "Communion is the gift of God whereby God draws humanity into the orbit of the generous, divine, self-giving love which flows between the persons of the Trinity" (no. 54). It connects the church with humanity and creation itself, for there is a "natural bond between human beings and between humanity and creation which the new life of communion builds upon and transforms but never wholly replaces" (no. 60). *Koinonia* is also an eschatological hope: "The final destiny of the church is to be caught up in the intimate relation of Father, Son, and Holy Spirit to praise and to enjoy God forever" (no. 59).

By way of response, Pentecostals would not typically formulate their ecclesiology through a concept of trinitarian *koinonia*. That is, trinitarian *koinonia* is not generally a concept used in their teaching or preaching. As Miroslav Volf has noted more generally, "The idea of correspondence between church and Trinity has remained largely alien to the Free Church tradition."[6] Though *koinonia* is a New Testament concept, it is naturally not explicitly used in the biblical text as a description of the inner life of God or of the church's participation in it. Though the Gospel of John implies a correspondence between our fellowship with Christ and Christ's fellowship with the Father (14:11, 20), the elaborate analogy (or participatory relationship) between the trinitarian life of God and the fellowship of the church is a theological insight drawn from later trinitarian theology. This fact is not necessarily problematic in itself, though it serves to explain why Pentecostals, who tend to be biblicistic in orientation, would not have come to emphasize it. The formulation is not without its problems, however. Some have questioned the assumption that the transcendent mystery of the inner life of God can be used to explain the *koinonia* of the church.[7] I think the concept is useful, but I wonder if there is not a tendency to discuss it in ecumenical contexts as an abstract concept rather than as a reality discovered from the bottom up within the diverse field of the Spirit's presence.

After all, *koinonia* is implicitly a *pneumatological* concept in Scripture. The church, after receiving the Spirit at Pentecost, enjoyed *koinonia* (Acts 2:42). Pentecostals would not start with a notion of God's inner fellowship but rather, as the third article of the Apostles' Creed does, with the church as the realm of the Spirit (the forgiveness of sins and faith for life everlasting, as well as, we should add, multiple gifts of the Spirit). The Pentecostals thus noted concerning the nature of the church, in "Perspectives on *Koininia*," that the Catholics "stress the God-givenness of the *koinonia* and its trinitarian character" (no. 31), while Pentecostals "stress that the Holy Spirit convicts people of sin, bringing them through repentance and personal faith into fellowship with Christ and one another" (no. 32).

Nevertheless, *koinonia* can be a useful concept for Pentecostal ecclesiology. Thus, "Perspectives on *Koinonia*" concludes that "Pentecostals have been reminded of the importance of the communitarian dimension of the New Testament understanding of *koinonia*" (no. 33). Since

6. Miroslav Volf, *After Our Likeness: The Church as the Image of the Trinity* (Grand Rapids: Eerdmans, 1998) 195.

7. Volf, *After Our Likeness*, 198–99.

koinonia can be said to occur "in the Spirit" as the bond of love (both within God, between God and humanity, and within creation), the accent of the NPC is not necessarily in tension with Pentecostal worship. As Volf has noted, *koinonia* can enrich a Free Church ecclesiology by deepening its understanding of ecclesial communion.[8] The church is not just an association of individual believers but a participation together *in the Spirit* in the loving communion enjoyed within God's triune life. Again, as the NPC notes, "The church is not the sum of individual believers in communion with God. It is not primarily a communion of believers with each other. It is a common partaking together in God's own life whose innermost being is communion" (no. 13).

One way forward for Pentecostals in response to the NPC would be to follow the advice of Walter Kasper to strive for "[a]n ecclesiology devised under the influence of pneumatology according to the archetype of the Trinity . . ."[9] The challenge here more broadly is in how to construe this archetype with regard to the issue of the *filioque*. The challenge for Pentecostals, of course, is in how Kasper's suggestion will relate trinitarian Pentecostals with Oneness Pentecostals, who reject an ontological Trinity. Helpful here is the fact that the NPC begins its discussion of the trinitarian foundation for the church with the economic Trinity. The church signifies what "God will bring about through Christ by the power of the Spirit" (no. 18). The church is the creation of Word and Spirit, which are inseparable (nos. 9–12). As the Spirit is active in Christ from Christ's conception to his resurrection, so in the life of the church the Spirit forms Christ in all members and in their community (no. 11). Particularly challenging to Pentecostals is the NPC's insistence that *koinonia* participates in Christ crucified causing the church to share in the sufferings of humanity (no. 55). Though Pentecostals have a notion of "groaning" with the suffering creation for the liberty of the Spirit (Rom 8:26), they tend to be triumphalistic in their understanding of the life of faith. All Pentecostals can appreciate together from such insights the *koinonia* that God the Father initiates with humanity through the Son and in the Spirit.

So, what is really to be the dominant theological category for the nature and purpose of the church: trinitarian *koinonia* or pneumatol-

8. Ibid., 196–98.

9. Walter Kasper, "Present Day Problems in Ecumenical Theology," *Reflections* 6 (Spring 2003) 78–80, here 80.

ogy? Do we start with a general notion of *koinonia* and then seek to develop from within that logic what the roles of the Son and the Spirit are? If we do this, we run the risk of a discussion that will tend to be abstract and doctrinally determined. Or, do we begin with the polyphonic and diverse presence of the Holy Spirit and the Spirit's witness to Christ to the glory of the Father, so that the experience of the Spirit testified of in Scripture and elaborately experienced in the churches can have a chance to nourish and challenge our doctrinal formulations? This is the route favored implicit among most Pentecostals.[10] Pentecostals always like to ask, "What is God doing in our midst?" The implications of this question for an ecumenical ecclesiology as proposed by NPC have yet to be explored.

CHURCH AS DIVINE GIFT AND HISTORICAL REALITY

Implicit throughout the NPC is the idea that the church is both a divine and a human reality. It is fitting to explore this issue as our final concern. The document starts with the church as the creation of the triune God. Highlighted is the mutual working of Word and Spirit (nos. 9–11). As noted above, "in Christ the Spirit is active from conception to resurrection, so in the life of the church the Spirit forms Christ in all believers and in their community" (no. 11). However, except for a few remarks in no. 17, not much is said of the Father as the one who sends the Son and the Spirit. This lack is unfortunate, since the Father as the ultimate source of all life and light is a powerful symbol of our unavoidable unity as both gift and challenge, for it is from the Father of our Lord Jesus Christ that the "whole family in heaven and on earth is named" (Eph 3:14–15). Not much else is said in the NPC about the role of the economic Trinity in birthing the church, which seems to be a gap in the document, causing the discussion on *koinonia* as the essence of the church to appear abstract and disconnected from the actual mutual working of Word and Spirit in the Christ event, and after Pentecost in the birthing and growth of the church.

The NPC defines *koinonia* first as a divine reality in which the church participates (no. 13). The marks of the church are defined solely as divine gifts (no. 12). The models of the church chosen for discussion follow a trinitarian pattern: people of God (Father), body of Christ (Son),

10. See Shane Clifton, "Pentecostal Ecclesiology: A Methodological Proposal for a Diverse Movement," *Journal of Pentecostal Theology* 15.2 (2007) 213–32.

and temple of the Holy Spirit (Spirit) (see nos. 17–25). This section on the models of the church requires expansion in order to explain more richly the various concrete dynamics of the church's existence in history. For example, the model of the church as the bride of Christ is briefly dismissed as merely a sign of the church's intimate but subordinate relation to Christ (no. 25). In the book of Revelation, and in many Free Churches, however, the bride of Christ model is powerfully symbolic of the church's obligation to be faithful, while waiting for the return of Christ the groom, and offers an alternative to the more organic model of "body of Christ," where the relationship with Christ is implied as granted in sacramental initiation. A richer description of various models of the church can thus tease out the many tensions among communions as to the nature of the church. As a result, the NPC's conclusion, that *koinonia* explains the relational richness at the heart of the various models of the church, would seem less generic and more open to a variety of interpretations.

At any rate, the message in the opening section of the NPC is clear: The church is defined as a creation of God's grace *extra nos* (apart from anything we can do to create it). This beginning with the church as a divine creation is not meant to exclude the essential role of the church's mission in the world. A subsection on "God's Purpose of the Church" immediately follows in which the church's role in mission, witness, and social reconciliation is briefly discussed (see nos. 27–32). Lest the purpose of the church be separated in any way from its nature as a creation of God, the NPC notes that "mission belongs to the very being of the church" (no. 27). This fact implies that the creation of the church *extra nos* includes an essential *in nobis* (in us) as well.

But does not the idea of the church *in nobis* imply that the church is also in some real sense a human reality as well? One has to answer in the affirmative, if the church is not to be reduced to a platonic idea detached from reality. The Reformation wrestled already with this problem and attempted to solve it through a distinction between the *ecclesia visibilis* (visible church) and the *ecclesia invisibilis* (invisible church). The visible church was subject to all of the limitations of the finite world, implying the ancient notion of the church as a *corpus per mixtum*. The real church determined through divine election and responsive to the Word of God was not visible, because it was not simply identifiable with the visible, institutional church. This distinction stirs up questions about the historicity of the church.

One of the major problems facing ecclesiological reflection, since the dawn of critical historical consciousness in the era of the Enlightenment, has been the dialectic of spirituality and historicity in judging the nature of the church. Since the Enlightenment, the church has been forced to consider the problems of its own historicity with unprecedented realism and intensity. The question that was implied in such critical self-reflection was how the church could be both a historical reality, with all of the ambiguities involved in such finitude, and yet a fellowship of the Spirit of God for the mission and the kingdom of God in the world. As Peter Hodgson and Robert King noted, "The question is how the church can be both a divine gift and a human institution, both a spiritual and a historical reality, without confusing the dimensions of its being and without separating them."[11] To face this challenge, the NPC follows the section, "The Church of the Triune God," with a section on "The Church in History." In this next section, the realm of history is defined as the realm of human ambiguity, change, sin, and divisions (see nos. 35–37). The marks of the church are discussed again, but this time from the vantage point of our participation in them within the fallen conditions of historical existence (see nos. 38–41).

One wonders if there is not an inherent tension in the NPC between a tendency to sharply distinguish the church's eschatological existence from its historical existence, on the one hand, and its expressed wish to include mission and service as part of the church's very essence, on the other (see nos. 27 and 111). If mission and service are at the essence of the church, would not a more integrated discussion of the marks of the church as both eschatological gift and historical purpose be called for than currently exists in the separated discussions of no. 12 and nos.38–41?

The NPC utilizes the distinction between the church as eschatological reality and historical reality because the former is understood as the gift of participation in the inner life of God's *koinonia* (nos. 13 and 35). In defining the church's historical existence, the NPC wants to leave open the question as to whether or not the church in its essence can be said to "sin." However, if historical existence is ambiguous and conditioned by sin, and the "mission" and "service" at the essence of the church integrally involve the church's actual witness in history, there is no way of escaping

11. Peter C. Hodgson and Robert C. Williams, "The Church" in *Christian Theology*, eds. P. C. Hodgson and R. H. King (Minneapolis: Fortress, 1982) 262.

the fact that the church sins. After all, the church's living mission and service in history involves human weakness and falleness.

This entire discussion, inspired by the NPC, represents a significant challenge to Pentecostal ecclesiology. Pentecostals need to think about the general issue of the eschatological and historical realities of the church's existence, since restorationism and primitivism make them vulnerable to an idealistic and implicitly timeless understanding of existence in the Spirit (contrary to their tendency to focus on the Spirit's concrete work in the world). Pentecostals tend to view themselves as striving toward the restoration of the ideal church of Pentecost. Their description of this ideal implies, at times, a reality removed from the falleness and vicissitudes of historical existence: God's Spirit comes in revival to lift us from the realm of human frailty and sin, and to grant us something of the triumphant ideal once more. A more realistic understanding of the primitive churches in all of their tensions and limitations might help Pentecostals view the living witness of the church less triumphalistically, as would a deeper understanding of the connection of the eschatological Spirit with the Word incarnate in the crucified Christ. It might help them to recognize the voice of the Spirit more profoundly within the history of the church's witness and, today, among the many different Christian communions. The unity of the church will not be viewed as a gift that merely comes "suddenly from heaven" but rather through a dialectical historical process involving humble and open ecumenical exchanges and courageous forms of common witness.

In general, I regard it important to avoid any implication of a dualism of the church's essence and its visible, historical form. It is possible to include both within an integrated discussion rather than separate them in two distinct sections. For example, Paul Tillich noted that the marks of the church have been actualized only paradoxically and ambiguously as a sign of the church's historicity, subject to all of the finite limitations of any social institution. Tillich locates the relationship of eschatology and history in the paradox of human essence and existence, in which we *are* what we are as the church by God's grace *in spite of* what we are in the ambiguities and contradictions of actual existence. The essence of the church, for Tillich, does not leave us unchallenged in our existence but is our inner *telos*, effective in us in a struggle against our ambiguities.[12]

12. Paul Tillich, *Systematic Theology*, vol. 3, *Life and the Spirit: History and the Kingdom of God* (Chicago: University of Chicago Press, 1963) 107–10, 138–40, 149–61, and 162–82.

In another effort to avoid this dualism, Reformed theologian, Jan Milic Lochman, noted that the notion of the *ecclesia invisibilis* can lead easily to an avoidance of the historical, institutional church in favor of a platonic idea. He proposes that the *ecclesia invisibilis* be the faith, hope, and love of the community of the faithful that is inspired continuously by the Spirit of God, in the midst of the concrete witness of ambiguous and historically conditioned visible churches. According to Lochman, the Spirit of God is referred to as the "*great ecclesiological dialectician*" with the result that "the struggle for the true church takes place in its earthly, concrete congregation—but in constant protest of its actualized form in the direction of hope and change."[13] The contrast here is not between timeless essence and historical existence but rather between historical existence eschatologically free and open to a new and liberating future, and historical existence, bound to sin and death. There are other ways of framing the issue as well, since the relationship between eschatology and history is a complex issue. The point here is that, from a Pentecostal perspective, the divine *koinonia* at the essence of the church is not abstract from history but within history accessible in the realm of the Holy Spirit.

CONCLUSION

In general, I regard the NPC to be a significant summary of ecumenical discussions thus far on the church as gift and calling. The NPC thus challenges Pentecostals to consider more carefully the significance of participation in the *koinonia* of God as both an individual and communal dynamic. It also encourages a careful consideration of the role of baptism in Christian initiation and vocation, as well as the significance of the crucified Christ in the living out of *koinonia* in response to a suffering world. Lastly, it challenges us to consider the scandal of our visible divisions and the need to face the quest for visible unity as a historical reality more directly as the needed and logical consequence of our spiritual life together.

On the other hand, Pentecostals can pose questions in response to the NPC with regard to the Spirit as the field of our experience of Christ, especially from the charismatic structure of the church, as the

13. J. M. Lochman, in F. Buri, H. Ott, and J. M. Lochman, *Dogmatik im Dialog*, vol. 5, 1 (Gütersloh: Gütersloher, 1973) 135.

point of departure for understanding the precise nature of communion. Pentecostals can ask for a more integrated understanding of the divine and human nature of the church that avoids any hint of a platonic dualism of ideal form and imperfect manifestations. Both the NPC and Pentecostals can consider more carefully the role of the Eucharist in the nature and purpose of the church. The NPC is a work in progress, so there is much work yet to be done in our journey together as the people of God who attempt to understand the nature and purpose of the church. But, then again, this is true of everything we do for the glory of God.

14

Pentecostal Contributions to *The Nature and Mission of the Church*

Wolfgang Vondey

The Faith and Order document, *The Nature and Mission of the Church* (NMC), has solicited a wide response from the Christian community since its inception in 1998, then entitled *The Nature and Purpose of the Church.*[1] The process of study on this document that has taken place in the ecumenical studies group of the Society for Pentecostal Studies is no exception. NMC is the first major ecumenical consensus statement with the promise of containing significant contributions from the Pentecostal community.[2] It demands and deserves careful scrutiny and feedback. Although no formal response to the document exists from Pentecostal churches, the ecumenical studies group has produced

1. A shorter version of this essay was first published as "A Pentecostal Perspective on The Nature and Mission of the Church." *Ecumenical Trends* 35.8 (2006) 1–5 and is used here with kind permission. See also Wolfgang Vondey, "Pentecostal Perspectives on *The Nature and Mission of the Church*: Challenges and Opportunities for Ecumenical Transformation," in "*The Nature and Mission of the Church*": *Ecclesial Reality and Ecumenical Horizons for the Twenty-First Century*, eds., Paul M. Collins and Michael A. Fahey, Ecclesiological Investigations 1 (New York: Continuum, 2008) 55–68, and Wolfgang Vondey, "Point de vue pentecôstiste (Dossier à propos du document Nature et Mission de L'Église)," *Unité des Chrétiens* 149 (January 2008) 23–26.

2. World Council of Churches, ed., *The Nature and Mission of the Church. A Stage on the Way to a Common Statement*, Faith and Order Paper 198 (Geneva: World Council of Churches, 2005), and its predecessor, *The Nature and Purpose of the Church: A Stage on the Way to a Common Statement*, Faith and Order Paper 181 (Geneva: WCC Publications, 1998).

a number of statements on earlier drafts of the ecumenical text.[3] These attempts reveal not only the increasing ecumenical commitment among Pentecostals; they also reflect a maturing ecclesiology among the ethnically, culturally, and theologically diverse Pentecostal community.

On the following pages, I will address Pentecostal perspectives on NMC with particular emphasis on the fact that the emphasis was changed from the nature and *purpose* of the church to the nature and *mission* of the church. In the first part, I will outline the four major approaches Pentecostals have taken to the ecumenical document during the study process. The second part of this paper focuses on the implications of the change in terminology from "purpose" to "mission" in light of the four Pentecostal approaches. Rather than offering a selective view of the key themes of the document, I will conclude with a Pentecostal assessment of the church's mission and its relationship to the church's nature and purpose.

PENTECOSTAL APPROACHES TO *THE NATURE AND MISSION OF THE CHURCH*

Pentecostals have taken the first steps away from remaining anonymous ecumenists toward full "solicited" participation in the ecumenical movement.[4] Interaction with NMC at this early stage of Pentecostal engagement in ecumenical dialogue reveals that the heart of this ecumenical endeavor is formed largely by a concern for a genuine Pentecostal ecclesiology. Four approaches to the ecumenical document can be identified at this stage:

3. See Veli-Matti Kärkkäinen, "'The Nature and Purpose of the Church.' Theological and Ecumenical Reflections from Pentecostal/Free Church Perspectives," *Ecumenical Trends* 33.7 (2004) 1–7; Jeff Gros, "Pentecostal Response to *The Nature and Purpose of the Church*," *Ecumenical Trends* 33. 7 (2004) 1; Thomas P. Rausch, "A Response to Veli-Matti Kärkkäinen on 'The Nature and Purpose of the Church," *Ecumenical Trends* 33.7 (2004) 8–11; Frank D. Macchia, "*The Nature and Purpose of the Church*: A Pentecostal Response," *Ecumenical Trends* 34.7 (2005) 1-6; Edmund Rybarczyk, "A Response to Dr. Frank Macchia," *Ecumenical Trends* 34.7 (2004) 7–10; Caleb Oladipo, "A Response to Dr. Frank Macchia," *Ecumenical Trends* 34.7 (2004) 10–12.

4. Cf. Veli-Matti Kärkkäinen, "'Anonymous Ecumenists'? Pentecostals and the Struggle for Christian Identity," *Journal of Ecumenical Studies* 37.1 (2000) 13–27.

Pentecostal Perspectives on the Nature of the Text and Its Function as an Ecumenical Document

Pentecostal scholars have situated earlier drafts of NMC in the context of larger ecumenical efforts in the second half of the twentieth century to produce broad consensus statements on individual issues of doctrine and praxis. Particular references can be established to the publication of the convergence document "Baptism, Eucharist, and Ministry" (BEM) of 1982.[5] Critique of that text, particularly from the Roman Catholic and Eastern Orthodox perspectives, went clearly beyond the agreements reported in BEM and pointed to issues of visible separation that require further and deeper attention to the questions of ecclesiology.[6] The Eastern Orthodox evaluation of BEM anticipates much of the Pentecostal attitude toward the nature of NMC, "Differences stated in the document show the reality of the divisions among churches rather than the weakness of the text."[7] Nevertheless, similar to the Catholic perspectives, Pentecostals point to "a somewhat underdeveloped ecclesiology"[8] and the further need to resolve some of the remaining problematic differences in contemporary theologies of the church. Much "depends on the churches and their desire and ability to structure their life and to fulfill their ministry in such a way as to implement creatively the principles"[9] upheld by the consensus statement. The lessons learned from BEM could serve well in the refining of NMC as a global ecumenical text.

Pentecostal Perspectives on the Structure and Central Themes of the Document

Pentecostals generally situate the formation of NMC within the formative influence of the official Pentecostal-Roman Catholic dialogue and its documents, "Perspectives on Koinonia" (1989) and "Evangelization,

5. See Kärkkäinen, "The Nature and Purpose of the Church," 1–2.

6. See Michael A. Fahey, ed., *Catholic Perspectives on Baptism, Eucharist, and Ministry. A Study Commissioned by the Catholic Theological Society of America* (Lanham, MD: University Press of America, 1986) 9–24; Gennadios Limouris and Nomikos Michael Vaporis, eds., *Orthodox Perspectives on Baptism, Eucharist, and Ministry* (Brookline, NY: Holy Cross Orthodox Press, 1985).

7. Limouris and Vaporis, *Orthodox Perspectives*, 95.

8. See this observation of the Catholic response to BEM in Fahey, *Catholic Perspectives*, 24.

9. Limouris and Vaporis, *Orthodox Perspectives*, 95.

Proselytism and Common Witness" (1997). Agreement is found largely on the basis of an ecclesiology that portrays the church as *koinonia* or trinitarian communion, although the basis for this theology is perceived less as an abstract and speculative concept than an experiential, doxological reality.[10] Frank Macchia points out, "Since *koinonia* can be said to occur 'in the Spirit' as the bond of love (both within God, between God and humanity, and within creation), the accent of . . . [NPC] is not necessarily in tension with Pentecostal worship."[11] In general, Pentecostals would likely reconsider the formal structure of the document before offering any critique of its central themes. Concerns among Pentecostals about the content of the text focus on the historical reality of the church, the relationship of church and trinity, the (minimal) conditions of ecclesiality, as well as the ministry of the church and its relationship to spiritual gifts, healing and worship.[12] As Macchia points out, "Pentecostals always like to ask, 'What is God doing in our midst?'"[13]

Pentecostal Perspectives on the Potential Ecumenical Ramifications of the Document

Pentecostals view the development of the document, at the least, as a summary of ecumenical discussions on the church and a work in progress. From an ecclesiological perspective, the text challenges Pentecostals to consider more carefully the role of baptism, the Eucharist, and social justice as part of Christian initiation, vocation, and ministry. The notion of *koinonia* challenges the sometimes triumphalistic attitude of Pentecostals toward the life of faith.[14] On the other hand, Pentecostals lament that the text does not address the unity of the church more explicitly and extensively as part of a global ecumenical ecclesiology.[15] The prominent place the document gives to Jesus' prayer for unity in John 17 reflects the ecumenical convictions of early twentieth century North American Pentecostalism, which saw itself as a movement of the Holy

10. See Macchia, "The Nature and Purpose of the Church," 3–4.

11. Ibid., 4.

12. See Kärkkäinen, "The Nature and Purpose of the Church," 6.

13. Macchia, "The Nature and Purpose of the Church," 4.

14. Ibid.

15. Ibid., 1–2.

Spirit at the beginning of the global fulfillment of Jesus' prayer.[16] NMC, on the other hand, is based almost exclusively on ecclesiologies of traditional churches in the West and ignores, for example, the changes in faith and praxis in the southern hemisphere, not only among Pentecostals. As a result, the charismatic, doxological, and evangelistic elements of the Christian life are not integrated in a vision of worldwide Christian unity. Pentecostals see potential ramifications of NMC as strongest in the area of ecclesiology proper (e.g., faith, baptism, Eucharist, ministry, church government) and as weakest in the actualization of Christian unity in the culturally, ethnically and linguistically diverse churches of global Christianity.

Pentecostal Perspectives on the Development of an Ecumenical Ecclesiology

This perspective reveals the analytical-critical position of Pentecostals to NMC and the Pentecostal evaluation of the promises and opportunities the document entails with regard to the future development of an ecumenical ecclesiology in general. Pentecostals are critical of the ecclesiological task as it relates to a global ecumenical perspective of faith and praxis as long as this task is carried out within the confines of the hypothesis that there exists a singular, universal ecclesiology. Instead, many Pentecostals suggest that there exists a plurality of ecclesial self-understandings and nuances that are theologically complementary and desirable, since they are often born from and determined by a community's experience and praxis of faith rather than a division of doctrine.[17]

16. Cf. Cecil M. Robeck Jr., "Taking Stock of Pentecostalism: The Personal Reflections of a Retiring Editor," *Pneuma: The Journal of the Society for Pentecostal Studies* 15.3 (1993) 37. See Charles F. Parham, *A Voice Crying in the Wilderness*, 3rd ed. (Baxter Springs, KS: Apostolic Faith Bible College, 1902, 1910; 3rd ed., n.d.) 61–67; W. F. Carothers, *The Baptism with the Holy Ghost and Speaking in Tongues* (Houston: Carothers, 1906–7) 25; W. J. Seymour, "Christ's Messages to the Church," *The Apostolic Faith* 1.11 (October 1907–January 1908) 3; W. J. Seymour, "The Baptism of the Holy Ghost," *The Apostolic Faith* 2.13 (May 1908) 3.

17. See Amos Yong, *The Spirit Poured Out on All Flesh: Pentecostalism and the Possibility of Global Theology* (Grand Rapids: Baker Academic, 2005) 121–202; Simon Chan, "Mother Church: Toward a Pentecostal Ecclesiology," *Pneuma: The Journal of the Society for Pentecostal Studies* 22.2 (Fall 2000) 177–208; Miroslav Volf, "The Nature of the Church," *Evangelical Review of Theology* 1.26 (2002) 68–75; Veli-Matti Kärkkäinen, *An Introduction to Ecclesiology: Ecumenical, Historical & Global Perspectives* (Downers Grove, IL: InterVarsity, 2002) 167–233.

Consequently, the immediate task of ecclesiology is seen as much in the formal "declaration" of convergence as it is found in the "actualization" and "application" of an ecumenical praxis in the Christian ecclesial communities.

The recent initiative to rename the Faith and Order document, and to replace the term "purpose" with the term "mission," has not yet been addressed by the Pentecostal community. In what follows, I will deal with the implications of this change in light of the four Pentecostal approaches outlined above: the nature of the text and its function as an ecumenical document, the structure and central themes of the document, the potential ecumenical ramifications of the text, and the development of an ecumenical ecclesiology.

PENTECOSTAL PERSPECTIVES ON THE PURPOSE AND MISSION OF THE CHURCH

The change in terms from "purpose" to "mission," in the title of the document, is a fortuitous one. It reflects the ecumenical insight that the God-given intention for the church is realized in history and actualized in the world only when the church pursues its purpose with a sense of unity, integrity, urgency, and mission. At the same time, the divine "purpose" of the church is an essential part of the church *as mystery* and cannot be fully explained in any document, while the focus on "mission" speaks of the divine purpose primarily as it is revealed to the church *in history*. To this end, NMC speaks with particular frequency about the church's mission in terms of "proclamation" and "concrete actions" in the world.

The title of the document implies that the mission *of* the church is intrinsically connected with its nature *as* the church. Indeed, the text acknowledges that "mission . . . belongs to the very being of the Church" (no. 35) and speaks of this task primarily in terms of worship, service, and proclamation (no. 36) in relation "both to the nature of God's being and the practical demands of authentic mission" (no. 35). "The mission of the church is to serve the purpose of God" and, hence, "the church cannot be true to itself without . . . preaching the Word, bearing witness to the great deeds of God and inviting everyone to repentance . . . , baptism . . . and the fuller life" of Christian discipleship (no. 37). This task is cast primarily in the image of the proclamation of the gospel "in word and deed" (nos. 35 and 110) which entails advocacy and care for the poor and marginalized, the exposure and transformation of unjust structures, works of compassion and mercy, and the healing and reconciliation of relationships between creation and humanity (no. 40). The heart and integrity of the church's mission is formed by "witness through *proclamation*, and *concrete actions* in union with all people of goodwill" (no. 47). The following illustration offers a broad synthesis of NMC's ecclesiology of mission.

NMC ecclesiology

church = nature + mission [proclamation + concrete action]

The meaning of the church's mission has been an important part of the Pentecostal dialogue with the Roman Catholic Church and a major theme during its fourth phase 1990–1997. The Pentecostals in this dialogue bound the meaning of mission not to proclamation and concrete actions but more intimately to the church's call to *evangelize* and identified its mission explicitly as a response to Christ's commission in the Scriptures, and as the task to proclaim the same Christ as Lord and Savior in the world today, in light of the hope of Christ's imminent return in judgment and the hope of a new creation.[18] Simply put, for Pentecostals, mission *is* evangelization. However, this emphasis should not be perceived as a reduction of the missionary task of the church to the articulation of the gospel but instead as a preference in theological focus and positioning of the ecclesial self-understanding of Pentecostals in the ecumenical landscape. NMC highlights that "evangelization is . . . the foremost task of the church" (no. 110), but the absence of any further definition of this task reveals the underlying assumption that evangelization is largely synonymous with the ministry of service and proclamation advocated throughout NMC.[19] Put differently, no distinction is made between evangelization and service, on a missiological level, and between evangelization and mission, on the ecclesiological level.[20]

18. See chapter 12 in this collection. See also Veli-Matti Kärkkäinen, "Evangelization, Proselytism, and Common Witness: Roman Catholic-Pentecostal Dialogue on Mission, 1990–1997," *International Bulletin of Missionary Research* 25.1 (2001) 16–18, 20–22; Veli-Matti Kärkkäinen, *Ad Ultimum Terrae: Evangelization, Proselytism and Common Witness in the Roman Catholic Pentecostal Dialogue, 1990–1997*, Studies in the Intercultural History of Christianity 117 (Frankfurt: Lang, 1999).

19. Cf. Neville Callam, "The Mission of the Church in the World Council of Churches' Text on the Nature and Purpose of the Church," *International Review of Mission* 90.358 (2001) 239.

20. Cf. Wolfgang Vondey, *People of Bread: Rediscovering Ecclesiology* (New York: Paulist, 2008) 105–40.

This neglect is particularly surprising in light of the recent emphasis on new evangelization in many churches.[21] In light of the four Pentecostal approaches outlined above, this aspect points to a number of critical issues.

The Nature of the Text and Its Function as an Ecumenical Document

Despite Pentecostal participation in the drafting process of NMC, the document reflects very little Pentecostal language. As a consensus statement that combines the views of various ecclesial traditions, this cannot be expected. Even so, from a global ecumenical perspective, the language of the document should reflect and invite the participation of all churches in casting a common vision of the nature and mission of the church. The question is, therefore, can Pentecostal observers find their theological position reflected in the document? The ethnic, economic, and socio-cultural diversity among Pentecostals accentuates this question and shifts the attention geographically and ecclesiologically away from the West and toward the southern hemisphere to include greater theological emphasis on liberation, exorcism, healing, the transformation of cultures, dialogue among religions, and the reconciliation of nations. In order to function as an ecumenical consensus text in the twenty-first century, Pentecostals call for a more consistent integration of non-western Christians, who experience the nature and mission of the church in ways often radically different from the established European and North American mindset.[22] The successful functioning of NMC as a global consensus statement will depend largely on the preservation and accentuation of the languages and stories of the various ecclesial traditions in the final document.

21. Cf. Wolfgang Vondey, "New Evangelization and Liturgical Praxis in the Roman Catholic Church," *Studia Liturgica: An International Ecumenical Review for Liturgical Research and Renewal* 36.2 (2006) 231–52; World Council of Churches, ed., "Mission and Evangelism: An Ecumenical Affirmation," *International Review of Missions* 71 (1982) 427–51.

22. See Amos Yong, *The Spirit Poured Out on All Flesh*, 167–202; Allan Anderson, *An Introduction to Pentecostalism: Global Charismatic Christianity* (Cambridge: Cambridge University Press, 2004) 187–286; David Martin, *Pentecostalism: The World Their Parish* (Oxford: Blackwell, 2002); Manuel Quintero, *Jubileo, La Fiesta del Espiritu: Identidad y Misión del Pentecostalismo Latinamericano* (Maracaibo, Venezuela: Comisión Evangélica Pentecostal Latinamericana, 1999).

The Structure and Central Themes of the Document

A successful revision of the nature and function of the document will depend largely on the structure of the text and its themes. At this time, many Pentecostals would be hard-pressed to find their emphasis on mission as evangelization reflected in the text of the ecumenical document. The Pentecostal concerns focus essentially on the document's definition of the church's mission in terms of proclamation and concrete actions and may be summarized as follows.

First, mission *as* evangelization places emphasis on "proclamation" only insofar as the act of proclamation encompasses not only the content of the message of salvation but also the whole life of the Christian and the community. Proclamation is therefore always a witness to the gospel in worship and holiness, a task that Pentecostals find accomplished primarily through the work of the Holy Spirit.[23] NMC speaks of proclamation primarily as a verbal process and situates it in the communication of the gospel through words and a fleeting comment on "the love of its members for one another, the quality of its service to those in need, a just and disciplined life and a fair exercise of power and authority" (no. 88).[24]

Second, mission as evangelization places emphasis on "concrete actions" only insofar as these actualize the substance and manner of what is proclaimed in a person's witness to the world. NMC neglects to point out not only what kind of concrete actions belong to the nature and mission of the church and thus form "the practical demands of authentic mission," but also how these actions are made possible and these demands can be met in the tangible reality of the churches. The Pentecostal community views the "baptism in the Holy Spirit" as essential for every believer to receive empowerment for Christian witness. NMC acknowl-

23. Cf. Carmelo E. Álvarez, "Mission as Liberating Spirit: Disciples and Pentecostals in Venezuela," *Discipliana* 62.4 (2002) 116–28; J. A. B. Jongeneel, 'Ecumenical, Evangelical and Pentecostal/Charismatic Views on Mission as a Movement of the Holy Spirit', in *Pentecost, Mission and Ecumenism: Essays on Intellectual Theology: Festschrift in Honour of Professor Walter J. Hollenweger*, ed. J. A. B. Jongeneel (Frankfurt: Lang, 1992) 231–46; Veli-Matti Kärkkäinen, "Mission, Spirit and Eschatology: An Outline of a Pentecostal–Charismatic Theology of Mission," *Mission Studies* 16.1 (1999) 73–94; Andrew M. Lord, "Mission Eschatology: A Framework for Mission in the Spirit," *Journal of Pentecostal Theology* 11 (December 1997) 111–23; John Christopher Thomas, "The Spirit, Healing of Mission: An Overview of the Biblical Canon," *International Review of Mission* 93.370 (2004) 421–42.

24. Cf. Callam, "The Mission of the Church in the World Council of Churches," 239.

edges the gifts of the Holy Spirit as necessary for the fulfillment of the church's mission (no. 83), yet it speaks of them primarily in terms of obligations, responsibility, and accountability without first referring to the Spirit's empowerment for evangelization through words of wisdom, knowledge, prophecy, spiritual discernment, sanctification, healing, or the working of miracles.

The notion of "mission as evangelization" reflects the emphasis Pentecostals place on the doxological, eschatological, and charismatic aspects of the life of the church that form the heart of the church's mission.[25] NMC says surprisingly little about the role of praise, worship, or spiritual warfare in mission. Absent from the church's proclamation and concrete actions is any sense of urgency. The church is "open to the free activity of the Holy Spirit" while being exposed to change, individual, cultural and historical conditioning and the power of sin (no. 50), yet nothing is said about the concrete individual, cultural and historical forms this work of God's Spirit takes in the church and in the world. In other words, NMC runs the risk of disconnecting eschatology and pneumatology from ecclesiology. The resulting image portrays the church as a heavenly city, in a constant stage of missionary pilgrimage, without any social, political, cultural, or moral impact on the world here and now, as it presents the possibility of opening to the full realization of the kingdom of God at any time and any place. This concern reflects not only the centrality of eschatology in Pentecostal ecclesiology but also a different way of telling the story of the church to a global audience.

The Potential Ecumenical Ramifications of the Text

The Faith and Order document holds a number of promises for the Pentecostal community, as an ecumenical consensus on the nature and mission of the church begins to emerge. The chief benefit is the mere exposure to the ecumenical consensus already achieved, which is a reality still unknown to many Pentecostals. The value Pentecostals place on pneumatology, eschatology, and doxology for an understanding of the church could be complemented by the emphasis NMC places on trinitarian theology, history, and service in the world. Pentecostals could learn about the unity and agreement already existing among the visibly

25. Cf. Vondey, "Pentecostal Perspectives," 4; Wolfgang Vondey, "Presuppositions for Pentecostal Engagement in Ecumenical Dialogue," *Exchange: Journal for Missiological and Ecumenical Research* 30.4 (2001) 344–58.

divided churches and the significance of preserving and nourishing that unity for the fulfillment of the church's eschatological mission. In praxis, this means that Pentecostals, among others, are called to consider the implications of an emerging theological convergence on the nature and mission of the church and the concrete steps that can be taken toward mutual recognition in the faith and praxis of the churches. NMC proposes to be a work in progress.[26] The success of this endeavor depends not only on what is being said in the document, but also on how it is being said, and whether it ever reaches those who should listen.

In the second half of the twentieth century, the ecumenical movement produced a number of significant consensus statements. From a Pentecostal perspective, the ecumenical ramifications of the global consensus process depend only secondarily on the challenge to accept the implications of these common affirmations into the life of the churches. The primary challenge that remains to this day is to introduce the agreed statements first of all to the various communities that participated in its production.[27] This is a particular challenge among the numerous Pentecostal communities, which still lack the structures, institutional support, public recognition, and promotion of the ecumenical agenda. The task of incorporating an ecumenical sensitivity in the life of its communities rest only partly on the shoulders of Pentecostals; it is fundamentally a task that has to be supported by the whole ecumenical community.

The Development of an Ecumenical Ecclesiology

The successful distribution of the final document in the churches and communities of the Pentecostal traditions could speak to the importance of the ecclesial life in communion, and call Pentecostals to consider the significance of baptism, Eucharist, and ministry in a way that has not been achieved by previous ecumenical documents. Despite well-known concerns about the predominance of sacramental categories in the ecclesiology of NMC, the development of an ecumenical ecclesiology is likely not hindered by distinctions of ecclesial praxis but challenged

26. The subtitle of NMC calls it "a stage on the way to a common statement." On the process see also Alan D. Falconer, "The Church: God's Gift to the World – On the Nature and Purpose of the Church," *International Review of Mission* 90.359 (2001) 396–97.

27. Cf. Vondey, "Presuppositions for Pentecostal Engagement," 356–358; Wolfgang Vondey, "Appeal for a Pentecostal Council for Ecumenical Dialogue," *Mid-Stream* 40. 3 (2001) 45–56.

more immediately by ecumenical prejudices, assumptions, and generalizations.[28] The most important among those is the presumed antithesis of Pentecostalism and ecumenism.

In essence, there is no contradistinction between an ecumenical ecclesiology and a Pentecostal ecclesiology. Pentecostal theology is ecumenical by virtue of the origin in and emergence of Pentecostals from virtually all forms and branches of the visibly divided churches. Rather than perceiving Pentecostals as distinct from the established theological and religious traditions from which they emerged, the ecclesiality of worldwide Pentecostalism can be perceived only in continuing awareness of other confessions not as an alternative to but as a root and source of Pentecostal life and praxis.[29] A more ecumenical way of expressing the Pentecostal contribution to an ecumenical ecclesiology would be to say that Pentecostals are no longer pursuing the ecclesial life from which they emerged although they remain ecclesiologically bound to their experience of that life.[30] As a result, there exists a variety of "experiences" among Pentecostals, depending on the negative or positive influence of particular forms and elements of ecclesial faith and praxis on a person's life. For example, some may have found the celebration of the Eucharist life-transforming, while others have lost all sense for its significance in the daily ritual of the ecclesial life in which they were raised.

Pentecostals would reserve room for such experiences and migrations within and among ecclesial communities as part of the nature and mission of the church which, not only for Pentecostals, is always being renewed. In many ways, therefore, the ecclesial experience of Pentecostals finds the mission of the church starting not outside of its boundaries but within.[31] From there, the church's mission extends into the world only to return again to itself. Worship, service, and proclamation are acts of the churches that originate *within* the churches and are directed *toward* the

28. Cf. Rybarczyk, "A Response to Dr. Frank Macchia's Paper," 9.

29. See chapter 5 of Wolfgang Vondey, *Beyond Pentecostalism: The Crisis of Global Christianity and the Renewal of the Theological Agenda*, Pentecostal Manifestos 3 (Grand Rapids: Eerdmans, 2010), forthcoming.

30. Cf. Wolfgang Vondey, "Pentecostalism and the Possibility of Global Theology: Implications of the Theology of Amos Yong," *Pneuma: Journal of the Society for Pentecostal Studies* 28.2 (2006) 289–312.

31. See the emphasis on change and conversion within the Church in Groupes des Dombes, *Pour la conversion des églises: Identité et changement dans la dynamique de la communion* (Paris: Centurion, 1991).

churches in order to affirm the unity, holiness, catholicity, and apostolicity of the one church *beyond* the churches and into the world. This continuous dynamism is what moves the whole church along the way and confronts it with the kingdom of God. In contrast to the ecclesiology of NMC, Pentecostal ecclesiology can be illustrated as follows.

Pentecostal Ecclesiology

church = mission = evangelization [inside the church > toward world > toward kingdom of God]

Such an ecclesiological concept stands in sharp contrast to the theology of NMC, which speaks of the church as a combination of its nature and mission and defines the latter in terms of proclamation and concrete action. For Pentecostals, church is a reflective, discerning reality that finds consensus about its nature and mission not only in formal statements but in an often painful process of repentance, forgiveness, conversion, and renewal in and among the churches *while* the church proclaims the gospel to the world. I suggest that this form of evangelistic, contextual, critical, non-triumphant, and pragmatic Pentecostal ecclesiology has much to say to what often appears as an idealistic, romantic, and authoritarian ecclesiology in the text of NMC. In light of these insights, the next stages in the development of an ecumenical consensus on the nature and mission of the church will likely prove to become a catalyst in the development of a genuine ecclesiology in the Pentecostal traditions which, surprisingly, still have not produced a comprehensive theology of mission. The path that leads Pentecostals to a full formulation of their own ecclesiology is surprisingly ecumenical. It follows from a core lesson that Pentecostals have learned from their history and that they share with the ecumenical community: The nature, mission, and unity of the church is found neither in ourselves nor in others alone but in the relationships in which we engage one another.

Contributors

Carmelo E. Álvarez (Th.D., Free University Amsterdam) is Affiliate Professor of Church History and Theology, Christian Theological Seminary, Indianapolis, Indiana.

Harold D. Hunter (Ph.D., Fuller Theological Seminary) is Director of the International Pentecostal Holiness Church Archives and Research Center, Oklahoma City, Oklahoma.

Douglas Jacobsen (Ph.D., University of Chicago) is Distinguished Professor of Church History and Theology at Messiah College, Grantham, Pennsylvania.

Veli-Matti Kärkkäinen (D. Theol., University of Helsinki) is Professor of Systematic Theology at Fuller Theological Seminary, Pasadena, California.

Frank D. Macchia (D. Theol., University of Basel) is Professor of Theology at Vanguard University of Southern California, Costa Mesa, California.

Raymond R. Pfister (Th.D., Université Marc Bloch) is Principal of Birmingham Christian College, Birmingham, England.

Cecil M. Robeck Jr. (Ph.D., Fuller Theological Seminary) is Professor of Church History and Ecumenics at Fuller Theological Seminary, Pasadena, California.

Paul van der Laan (Ph.D., University of Birmingham) is Professor of Theology at Southeastern University, Lakeland, Florida.

Wolfgang Vondey (Ph.D., Marquette University) is Associate Professor of Systematic Theology at Regent University School of Divinity, Virginia Beach, Virginia.

Index of Names

Index of Subjects

Made in the USA
Coppell, TX
19 July 2021